UNDERSTANDING PASCAL
A Problem Solving Approach

UNDERSTANDING PASCAL
A Problem Solving Approach

STEVEN L. MANDELL • COLLEEN J. MANDELL

WEST'S
Computer Education Series

WEST PUBLISHING COMPANY • St. Paul   New York   Los Angeles   San Francisco

COPYEDITING: Editing, Design, and Production
TEXT DESIGN: Adapted by Lucy Lesiak Design
COVER DESIGN: Editing, Design, and Production
COMPOSITION: The Clarinda Company

TRS-80 is a trademark of the Radio Shack Division of Tandy Corporation. Apple is the registered trademark of Apple Computer, Inc. Commodore 64 is a trademark of Commodore Business Machines. IBM PC is a trademark of International Business Machines Corporation.

COPYRIGHT © 1985   By WEST PUBLISHING COMPANY
50 West Kellogg Boulevard
P.O. Box 64526
St. Paul, MN   55164-0526

Printed in the United States of America

Library of Congress Cataloging in Publication Data

Mandell, Steven L.
   Understanding PASCAL.

   Includes index.
   1. PASCAL (Computer program language)   I. Mandell, Colleen J.   II. Title.
QA76.73.P2M33 1985   001.64'24   85-3353
ISBN 0-314-89691-0

PHOTO CREDITS

1,3 Courtesy of International Business Machines Corporation; **4** Courtesy of Apple Computer, Inc.; **6** top left: Courtesy of BASF Systems Corporation; top right and bottom: Courtesy of Commodore Electronics Limited; **7** Fairchild Camera and Instrument Corporation; **8** Courtesy of Amdek Corporation; **13** Courtesy of Sperry Corporation; **29** Courtesy of Evans & Sutherland and Mechanical Dynamics, Inc.; **49** Courtesy of International Business Machines Corporation; **69** Courtesy of RCA; **95** Courtesy of International Business Machines Corporation; **117** Courtesy of COMSAT; **143** Courtesy of International Business Machines Corporation; **161** Courtesy of Baxter Travenol Laboratories, Inc.; **181** Courtesy of Sperry Corporation; **195** Courtesy of Evans & Sutherland Computer Corporation; **217** Courtesy of Sperry Corporation; **237** Courtesy of International Business Machines Corporation; **253** Courtesy of Westinghouse Electric Corporation; **259** Courtesy of Animation Graphics, Inc.

UNDERSTANDING PASCAL
A Problem Solving Approach

AUTHORS

Colleen J. Mandell, B.S., M.S., Ed. D.; Educator; Software Developer, Psychometrist; Associate Professor, College of Education, Bowling Green State University

Steven L. Mandell, B.A., B.S. Ch.E., M.B.A., D.B.A., J.D.; Computer Book Author; Software Developer; Computer Lawyer; Associate Professor of Computer Systems, Bowling Green State University

EDUCATIONAL CONSULTANT

Julie G. Fiscus, B.A., M.A.; Computer Educator

CONTENT SPECIALISTS

Susan K. Bauman, B.S.; Computer Educator; Computer Programmer
Robert A. Szymanski, B.A., M.B.A.; Computer Educator; Computer Programmer
Russ Thompson, B.S., M.B.A., Computer Educator; Programmer/Analyst
Dieter J. Zirkler, B.A., M.A.; Computer Educator; Mathematician; Psychologist

CRITICAL EVALUATORS FOR WEST'S COMPUTER EDUCATION SERIES

Bruce Don Bowen, Crestview Elementary School, Layton, Utah; **Charles M. Bueler,** Assistant Superintendent for Instruction, Hannibal Public Schools, Hannibal, Missouri; **Dr. Tom Burnett,** Assistant to Superintendent for Computer Technology, Lincoln Public Schools, Lincoln, Nebraska; **Sharon Burrowes,** Wooster City Schools, Wooster, Ohio; **Bruce B. Burt,** West Chester School District, West Chester, Pennsylvania; **Vincent Cirello,** East Meadow High School, Curriculum

Center, East Meadow, New York; **Don M. Cochran,** Bartlesville High School, Bartlesville, Oklahoma; **Dr. George E. Cooke,** Indiana Area School District, Indiana, Pennsylvania; **Carolyn Cox,** Virginia Beach City Public Schools, Office of Curriculum and Staff Development, Virginia Beach, Virginia; **Joseph Crupie,** North Hills High School, Pittsburgh, Pennsylvania; **Charles R. Deupree,** Ionia Public Schools, Ionia, Michigan; **Dr. Helen Ditzchazy,** Assistant Superintendent, Jackson Public Schools, Jackson, Michigan; **Dr. John H. Emhuff,** Assistant Superintendent, Instruction, Mt. Vernon, Indiana; **Ms. Carol Haynes,** Prospect School Learning Center Director, Hinsdale, Illinois; **Ken Hendrickson,** Oak Park Elementary School, Newbury Park, California; **Dr. Sandra Howe,** Kalamazoo Public Schools, Kalamazoo, Michigan; **Monica Ilas,** Madison Elementary School, Lakewood, Ohio; **Doris Kassera,** Media Specialist, Eau Claire Elementary Schools, Eau Claire, Wisconsin; **Colvin Kindschi,** Oak Park Elementary School, Newbury Park, California; **Douglas Krugger,** Computer Operations Center, School District of the City of Erie, Erie, Pennsylvania; **Mary E. Larnard,** Newburyport High School, Newburyport, Massachusetts; **Wally Leech,** The Media Center, Greater Johnstown School District, Johnstown, Pennsylvania; **Letitia Martin,** Indian Hills Elementary School, North Little Rock, Arkansas; **Marilyn Mathis,** Murfreesboro City Schools, Murfreesboro, Tennessee; **Dr. Judith K. Meyers,** Lakewood City Schools, Coordinator Media Services, Lakewood, Ohio; **Mark A. Mitrovich,** Principal, Clarkston High School, Clarkston, Washington; **Willis Parks,** Coordinator of Computer Education, North Canton City Schools, North Canton, Ohio; **Bette Pereira,** Harrison High School, Harrison, Ohio; **Bruce Raskin,** Mathematics-Microcomputer Department Chairman, Miami Springs Junior High School, Pembroke Pines, Florida; **Gary R. Reichelt,** Clackamas Community College, Portland, Oregon; **Lynda M. Reynen,** Computer Science Director, Ft. Pierce Central High School, Ft. Pierce, Florida; **Leon Roland,** Computer Coordinator, Billings Public Schools, Billings, Montana; **Richard Sheets,** Computer Specialist, Mesa Public School District #4, Mesa, Arizona; **Charlotte Shepperd,** Seguin High School, Seguin, Texas; **W. Richard Smith,** Clovis West High School, Fresno, California; **John R. Speckien,** Director of Curriculum Development, Boulder Valley School District, Boulder, Colorado; **Raymond J. Tombari,** Braintree High School, Braintree, Massachusetts; **Joanne Troutner,** Computer Coordinator, Tippecanoe School District, Lafayette, Indiana; **Jan Van Dam,** Computer Curriculum Coordinator, Rochester Community Schools, Rochester, Michigan; **A. Thomas Vincent,** Coordinator of Vocational Education, Gallup McKinley County Public Schools, Gallup, New Mexico; **Richard Weisenhoff,** Howard County Public Schools, Elliott City, Maryland.

REVIEWERS FOR *Understanding Pascal: A Problem Solving Approach*

Don M. Cochran
Bartlesville High School
Bartlesville, Oklahoma

Mary E. Larnard
Newburyport High School
Newburyport, Massachusetts

Gary Reichelt
Clackamas Community College
Portland, Oregon

Charlotte Shepperd
Seguin High School
Seguin, Texas

W. Richard Smith
Clovis West High School
Fresno, California

John R. Speckien
Director of Curriculum
    Development
Boulder Valley School District
Boulder, Colorado

Jan Van Dam
Computer Curriculum
    Coordinator
Rochester Community Schools
Rochester, Michigan

A NOTE ON THE READING LEVEL

The reading level of **Understanding Pascal: A Problem Solving Approach** has been checked and verified to fall within the tenth through twelfth grade span. Nine samples of approximately 100-150 words were checked. The following indexes were used: Estimated Dale, Fog Index, Flesch Grade Level, Smog Index, and the Frye.

Edward D. Fiscus, Ph.D.
Associate Professor and Chair
Department of Special Education
College of Education
Bowling Green State University
Bowling Green, Ohio

Preface

TO THE TEACHER

The computer revolution has excited the education profession more than any other technological advancement. It is clear that students must be able to master computer skills if they are to survive in a technology-based world. The goal of West's Computer Education Series is to provide the necessary learning packages to support the classroom teacher in accomplishing the objectives of the computer curriculum.

Before embarking on West's Computer Education Series, great care was taken to plan the overall concept of a fully integrated series as well as to assess the particular requirements for each individual text. An extensive survey of computer educators was done across the country in the very early stages of development. After the basic plans for the series were established, many teachers and computer coordinators were asked to comment on the general scope of the series and the specific content for each of the texts. The manuscripts were read and evaluated by many computer educators, and student and teacher feedback was obtained through field testing. Computer professionals were then assigned the task of technically verifying all of the material. Many changes and refinements were incorporated throughout the development of each text, and great care was taken to maintain the integrity of the series each step along the way. The result of this very careful development and review process is a product the authors and the publisher are proud and confident to present to the educational community.

Three additional factors were given top priority during this project: Reading level, pedagogical design and teacher materials. Students must be presented material at the appropriate reading level if educational objectives are to be accomplished. Grade spans have been kept to a maximum of three years, thus enabling a close targeting of both level and relevancy of examples. The pedagogical design of each book was carefully developed based upon grade level and subject matter. Additionally, the series was developed with an overall pedagogical plan, making it very easy for the teacher and the students to move from one text to the next. We have employed outlines, learning objectives, vocabulary lists, learning checks, summary points, tests, glossaries and other devices appropriate to specific titles to enhance the educational process for the student.

The teachers' manuals that accompany each text in West's Computer Education Series are complete, thorough and easy to use for teachers at any level of computer expertise. The manuals offer an extensive package of materials to assist the teacher in reinforcing the concepts introduced in the texts.

ABOUT THIS TEXT

Pascal recently has become widely accepted as an effective language for teaching structured problem-solving and programming skills. The increasing implementation of UCSD-based Pascal systems on microcomputers has been a driving force behind its success. This book presents structured problem solving through UCSD Pascal. All problems have been run through both Apple and IBM machine implementations: Apple II Pascal and UCSD p-System.

Each chapter contains standard pedagogical devices: A chapter outline, learning objectives, and introduction provide a framework for permitting the student to focus on the current material. Numerous sample computer programs are included to help the student make a smooth transition from the abstraction of language rules to the concrete design of program instructions. Learning Checks with inverted answers are included as a means of self-testing before proceeding to the next section. Summary points and a vocabulary list are used to reinforce the most important concepts presented in the chapter. Finally, a chapter test and programming problems allow the teacher and students to evaluate the level of mastery of the material.

The teacher's manual to support this book is divided into three parts: Classroom Administration, Test Bank, and Additional Teacher Materials. In the administration section a standard format is used for each chapter to assist the teacher: Summary, Objectives, Vocabulary, Outline, Learning Activities, Answers to Chapter Test, Solutions to Programming Problems in Text, and Additional Programming Problems with Solutions. The test bank section includes by chapter over 600 true/false and multiple choice questions with the associated answer key. The final section of the teacher's manual includes blackline masters for transparencies, tests, and student study sheets as well as a resource list and expanded glossary.

TO THE STUDENT

In writing and editing **Understanding Pascal: A Problem Solving Approach** the authors and editors had one goal in mind: To help you learn the Pascal language and the problem solving skills needed to use that knowledge. In developing this text a number of features were included to help you recognize important ideas and to make remembering the material easier.

Chapter Outline

Each chapter begins with an outline that gives you an overall picture of what is covered in the chapter and prepares you to read more effectively.

Learning Objectives

This list which follows the chapter outline tells you specifically what you will achieve by studying and understanding the chapter.

Learning Checks

A list of questions and their answers follows each section within the chapter. You will be able to check your progress if you stop to answer the questions as you study. If you are able to answer the Learning Check questions correctly, you are ready to go on to the next section.

Sample Computer Program

The many sample computer programs will help you understand the chapter and learn how to write your own programs.

Summary Points

A point-by-point summary at the end of each chapter restates the important ideas covered to make studying and remembering easier.

Vocabulary List

A list of the important new terms and concepts with their definitions is included at the end of each chapter as another study aid. A complete book glossary appears at the end of the book.

Chapter Test

End of chapter tests with vocabulary and word problems will let you check how much of the chapter material you remember and understand.

Programming Problems

Programming problems for each chapter will help you build programming skills.

ACKNOWLEDGMENTS

Many individuals have been involved in the development of the material for West's Computer Education Series. These professionals have provided invaluable assistance for the completion of a series of this magnitude: Greg Allzani, Kim Girnus, John Gregor, Steve Hoffman, Craig Howarth, Rhonda Raifsnider, and Jeff Sanborn on student material; Mike Costarello, Margaret Gallito, Sara Hosler, Gloria Pfeif, and Jennifer Urbank on instructor material; Norma Morris and Donna Pulschen on manuscript development; Shannan Benschoter, Linda Cupp, Charles Drake, Lisa Evans, Janet Lowery, Sally Oates, Valerie Pocock, Brian Sooy, Candace Streeter, Nancy Thompson, and Michelle Westlund on manuscript production; and Meredith Glynn and Kathy Whitacre on photographs.

The production management of all of the books in the series is a tribute to the many talents of Marta Fahrenz. The educational surveys and teacher communications were designed and maintained by editor Carole Grumney, a very special person. Debora Wohlford, sales manager for elementary/high school texts, has been extremely important in market research and in helping to shape the scope of the series. One final acknowledgment goes to our publisher and valued friend, Clyde Perlee, Jr., without whose support the project would never even have been attempted.

Contents

CHAPTER 9   FUNCTIONS AND PROCEDURES   161

CHAPTER 10   PREDEFINED FUNCTIONS AND USER-DEFINED DATA TYPES   181

APPENDIX A IDENTIFIERS 277

APPENDIX B SYNTAX DIAGRAMS 278

APPENDIX C PASCAL RESERVED WORDS 283

APPENDIX D PASCAL STANDARD IDENTIFIERS 284

APPENDIX E PASCAL OPERATORS 285

APPENDIX F FILER AND EDITOR BASICS 286

GLOSSARY 291

INDEX 295

UNDERSTANDING PASCAL
A Problem Solving Approach

CHAPTER 1

Introduction to Computer Programming and Pascal

OUTLINE

LEARNING OBJECTIVES

After studying this chapter, you should be able to:

1. Define the following terms:
   computer program
   programming language
   programmer
   acronym
   machine language
   input
   output
   hard copy
2. Give a brief history of the Pascal language.
3. Explain what a computer system is and list its three basic components.
4. List the three parts of the central processing unit and explain what each part does.
5. Describe various input and output devices and their specific purposes.
6. Explain what is meant by compiling and executing a program.

INTRODUCTION

A computer is a machine. It has many different parts that work together to do a specific job. Like any machine, the computer will only do what it is told to do. The list of instructions that tells the computer what to do is called a **program.** These instructions are written to solve a specific problem.

Programs must be written in a language that the computer can understand. Such languages are called **programming languages.** A person who writes a computer program is called a **computer programmer** (or a **programmer** for short). This book will teach the reader to become a programmer. Programmers have a great deal of power. A programmer can make a computer do all kinds of interesting things, but the computer must be told what to do in the correct way. Since the computer cannot think for itself, an exact program must be written. If a single step is left out of a program, the results from the computer may be completely different from what is expected. If the right words and punctuation aren't used, the computer won't understand the instructions.

In this book, the rules of the programming language Pascal will be explained. The reader will also learn how to write programs in a clear, logical way.

BACKGROUND ON PASCAL

Pascal is considered to be one of the best general-purpose computer programming languages. A general-purpose language is one that can be used to write many different types of programs.

Pascal is a fairly new programming language. It was designed by Professor Niklaus Wirth of Switzerland in 1969 and 1970. Professor Wirth named the language after Blaise Pascal, a 17th century mathematician and philosopher. Pascal was only 19 when he invented a mechanical adding machine. He invented the adding machine to help his father, who was a tax collector and had to do a lot of arithmetic by hand. A picture of the adding machine is shown in Figure 1-1.

The programming language Pascal has a capital letter only at the beginning of the word. Some programming language names are written in all capital letters. This is because these names are **acronyms.** An acronym is a word whose letters each stand for another word. For example, BASIC stands for *B*eginner's *A*ll-*P*urpose *S*ymbolic *I*nstruction *C*ode. Since Pascal is named after a person and is not an acronym, only the first letter of the word is capitalized.

WHAT CAN COMPUTERS DO?

Computers like the one shown in Figure 1-2 can be very useful. Basically, though, computers can do only a few things. They can do arith-

Figure 1-1 PASCAL'S ADDING MACHINE

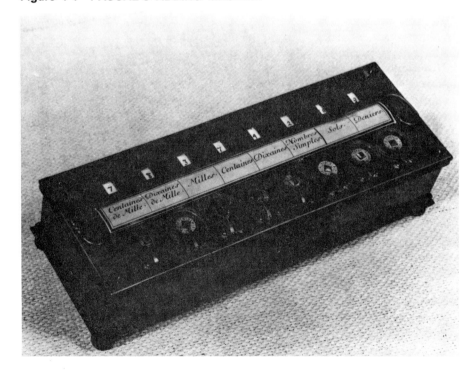

Figure 1-2 APPLE IIe MICROCOMPUTER

metic, and they can make comparisons. For example, a computer can determine that the letter A comes before the letter B and that 197 is greater than 10. Since there are so few things a computer can actually do, what is it that makes it so useful? Computers are useful for three basic reasons:

1. They are fast.
2. They are accurate.
3. They can store information.

With care, a person can add 100 numbers together and find the correct result. But the chances of making an error somewhere along the way are considerable. Also, it is a boring job. This is the kind of task that is ideal for the computer. The computer can do the work very quickly. It will not get bored or add four and four and get seven. Also, it can store the information away to be used again.

LEARNING CHECK 1-1

1. What is a computer program?
2. Why is only the first letter of the programming language Pascal capitalized?
3. List two things computers can do.

Answers:
1. A computer program is a list of instructions that a computer can use to solve a problem. 2. Only the first letter is capitalized because Pascal is named after a person and is not an acronym. 3. They can do arithmetic; they can make comparisons.

PARTS OF A COMPUTER SYSTEM

Microcomputers are small computers that are meant to be used by one person at a time. Sometimes they are called **personal computers.** The parts of a computer system are basically the same, whether it is a microcomputer or a very large computer such as those used in big corporations. The basic parts of a computer system are:

1. Input devices.
2. Central processing unit.
3. Output devices.

The parts of a computer system are shown in Figure 1-3.

Input Devices

Input is the **data** that are put into the computer so that the computer can process them. The data are the facts that the computer processes to obtain the needed results. The **input devices** most commonly used with a microcomputer are:

1. The keyboard.
2. The disk drive or cassette recorder.

The user can enter data into the computer by typing them to the keyboard or by having the computer read them from a diskette or cassette tape. Sometimes a diskette is called a floppy disk because it is made of soft plastic that is pliable. Figure 1-4 shows a disk drive and a floppy disk.

Central Processing Unit

The **central processing unit (CPU)** is the heart of the computer. In a microcomputer, the CPU is contained on a single silicon chip. This silicon chip is called the **microprocessor.** A microprocessor is shown in Figure 1-5. The CPU of a computer is made up of three main parts:

Figure 1-3 PARTS OF A COMPUTER SYSTEM

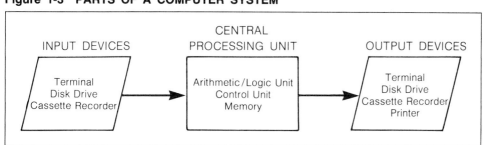

5

**Figure 1-4   ABOVE: FLOPPY DISKETTE WITH DISK DRIVE
BELOW: CASSETTE RECORDER**

1. Control unit.
2. Arithmetic/logic unit.
3. Main memory.

Control Unit

As its name implies, the **control unit** is in control of the activities in the CPU. The control unit does not process or store any data, but directs the operations of the other parts of the computer. Instructions given to the computer by the user are interpreted by the control unit, which sends out signals to circuits to execute the instructions. The appropriate input devices are directed to send the necessary data to the computer. The control unit also keeps track of which parts of the program have already been executed and which ones remain. Finally, it controls the execution of specific instructions, collects the output, and sends it to the designated output device, for example a display screen.

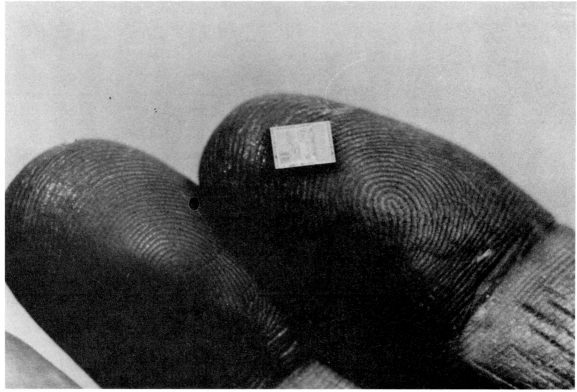

Figure 1-5 MICROPROCESSOR
Steady progress in complexity and power marks the history of the microprocessor.
The silicon chip shown here is Bell Laboratories' newest.

Arithmetic/Logic Unit

The **arithmetic/logic unit (ALU)** is the computer's own personal mathematician. It performs arithmetic computations and logical operations. A logic statement makes a comparison and then takes action based on the result. For example, consider the instruction, "If today is Friday, then pick up your paycheck and go to the bank; if not, don't." This is not exactly the type of logic statement a computer would work with, but the idea is the same. The computer would work with a logic statement more like this: "If this is the end of the input data, then make the calculations and print the results; if not, read the rest of the input data." Arithmetic and logic statements are the only type of instructions that the ALU can execute.

Main Memory

Main memory is the storage area where the computer keeps information that is given to it. This storage area holds instructions, data, and the intermediate and final results of processing. Main memory is made up of a large number of storage locations, each of which can hold a small amount of information. These storage locations may be thought of as mailboxes lined up in a row.

7

Output Devices

Output is the result that comes from the computer after it has finished processing the input. The **output devices** that are commonly used with a microcomputer are:

1. The monitor.
2. The disk drive or cassette recorder.
3. The printer.

Printing output to the monitor gives the user the program results in a quick, readable way. Output that is printed to the monitor is called **soft-copy** output. Having the results printed on paper, on the other hand, gives the user a way of keeping the results so that they can be referred to easily. This is called **hard-copy** output. A printer is shown in Figure 1-6. Putting information on a floppy disk or a cassette allows it to be used by the computer again. Each of these methods has its own advantages, depending on the circumstances.

COMPILING AND EXECUTING A PROGRAM

When a program is entered to the computer, it must be translated into a language the computer can understand before it can yield results. This language is called **machine language.** The program that is entered to the computer is called the **source program.** It has this name because this program is the source for the computer's translation.

The translation is accomplished by either an **interpreter** or a **compiler.** The difference between an interpreter and a compiler is that the compiler creates an **object program** that contains the entire source program in machine language. Once this object program is loaded into the computer's memory, the computer is able to execute

Figure 1-6 DAISY WHEEL PRINTER

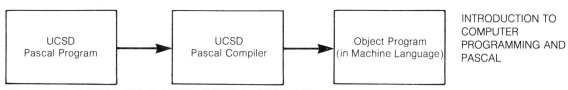

Figure 1-7 COMPILING A UCSD PASCAL PROGRAM

the program. An interpreter, on the other hand, translates the source program statements into machine language one statement at a time. This saves space in the computer's memory. It can also be very inefficient, however. Program statements that are used more than one time must be translated each time they are executed.

This book will study the University of California at San Diego Pascal Compiler (**UCSD Pascal Compiler**). In UCSD Pascal, the compiler program is on a disk. When a program needs to be compiled, the UCSD Pascal Compiler must first be loaded into the computer's memory. Figure 1-7 illustrates how a UCSD Pascal program is compiled. The UCSD Pascal Compiler is the Pascal compiler that is most widely used for microcomputers.

Once a program is compiled the computer is able to **execute** it. When a program is executed, the computer reads the object program from the beginning to the end and does what the program statements tell it to do.

LEARNING CHECK 1-2

1. What is meant by compiling a program?
2. What is meant by executing a program?
3. List some input and output devices commonly used with a microcomputer.

Answers:

1. Compiling a program means the computer creates an object program that contains instructions for the computer in machine language. 2. Executing a program means the computer reads the object program from beginning to end and does what the program statements tell it to do. 3. input: keyboard, disk drive, and cassette recorder output: monitor, disk drive, cassette recorder, and printer.

SUMMARY POINTS

- This chapter has discussed some basic facts about computers. Computers need to be told what to do. The instructions for computers must be written in a programming language. In this book, the programming language Pascal will be explained. Pascal was developed by Professor Niklaus Wirth in 1969 and 1970.

- The things that computers can actually do are limited. Computers can do arithmetic and they can make comparisons. What makes them so useful is that they are very fast and accurate and have memories where information can be stored and used again.
- A computer must compile a program before it can execute it. When a program is compiled, an object program is created. The object program is in machine language so the computer can understand the program.
- Computer systems have three basic parts:

  1. Input devices.
  2. Central processing unit.
  3. Output devices.

VOCABULARY LIST

Arithmetic/logic unit (ALU) The part of the CPU that performs arithmetic and does logical operations.

Acronym A word whose letters each stand for another word.

Central processing unit (CPU) The part of a computer that does the work. The CPU also directs the order in which operations are done and has a memory.

Compiler A program that translates an entire source program into machine language. The resulting program is the object program.

Computer programmer A person who writes instructions for the computer to solve a problem.

Control unit The part of the CPU that determines the order in which computer operations will be performed.

Data Facts that the computer uses as input.

Execute To read and carry out the instructions in a program.

Hard copy Output that is printed on paper.

Input Data that are put into a computer to be processed.

Input devices Equipment such as a keyboard, disk drive, or cassette recorder, used to enter data into a computer.

Interpreter A program that translates a source program into machine language a line at a time.

Machine language The language a program must be in for a computer to be able to execute it.

Main memory Storage area where the computer keeps information.

Microcomputer A small digital computer with most of the capabilities of larger computers; the center of the computer is the microprocessor.

Microprocessor A single silicon chip in a microcomputer, on which the CPU is located.

Object program The program that results when a compiler translates a source program into machine language.

Output Results the computer obtains after processing input.

Output devices Equipment such as a monitor, disk drive, cassette recorder, or printer used to store or print out information.

Personal computer See **microcomputer**.

Program A list of instructions for a computer to use to solve a specific problem.

Programming languages Languages that can be used to give instructions to a computer.

Programmer See **computer programmer**.

Soft copy Output that is temporarily displayed on the monitor.

Source program A program that must be translated into machine code before it can be executed.

UCSD Pascal Compiler The compiler most widely used for Pascal on microcomputers.

CHAPTER TEST

VOCABULARY

Match a term from the numbered column with the description from the lettered column that best fits the term.

1. Hard copy

   a. Equipment such as a monitor, disk drive, or printer used to store or print information.

2. Main memory

   b. Output that is printed on paper.

3. Central processing unit

   c. Data that are put into a computer to be processed.

4. Machine language

   d. A person who writes instructions for the computer to solve a problem.

5. Output devices

   e. Storage area where the computer keeps information.

6. Soft copy

   f. Equipment such as a keyboard, disk drive, or cassette recorder used to enter data into a computer.

7. Microprocessor

   g. The compiler most widely used for Pascal on microcomputers.

8. Input

   h. A small computer with most of the capabilities of larger computers; the center of the computer is the microprocessor.

9. UCSD Pascal Compiler

   i. The part of a computer that does the work.

10. Input devices

    j. A word whose letters each stand for another word.

11. Computer programmer

    k. A language that can be used to give instructions to a computer.

12. Programming language

    l. Results the computer obtains after processing the input.

13. Acronym

    m. The language a program must be in for a computer to be able to execute the program.

14. Output

    n. A single silicon chip in a microcomputer in which the CPU is located.

15. Microcomputer

    o. Output that is temporarily printed to the monitor.

QUESTIONS

1. Who invented the programming language Pascal? Who was Blaise Pascal?
2. What are the three parts of a computer system?

3. What are the three parts of the central processing unit?
4. What does each part of the central processing unit do?
5. Study the computer system you will be using. What are the input and output devices this system uses?
6. Why are computers so useful to people? Give three reasons.
7. What is the difference between a compiler and an interpreter?
8. Give an advantage of an interpreter. Give an advantage of a compiler.

CHAPTER 2

The Programming Process

OUTLINE

LEARNING OBJECTIVES

INTRODUCTION

STEPS IN PROBLEM SOLVING
Understanding the Problem • Developing a Solution • Sample
Problem

> **LEARNING CHECK 2–1**

TOP-DOWN PROGRAMMING

FLOWCHARTING

PSEUDOCODING

> **LEARNING CHECK 2–2**

SUMMARY POINTS

VOCABULARY LIST

CHAPTER TEST
Vocabulary • Questions

LEARNING OBJECTIVES

After studying this chapter, you should be able to:

1. List the six steps in developing a program.
2. Explain what is meant by understanding a problem.
3. Develop algorithms for simple problems.
4. Define top-down programming.
5. Give two characteristics of structured programming.
6. List four advantages of top-down programming.
7. Draw flowcharts for simple problems.
8. Explain the differences between a single-alternative decision step and a double-alternative decision step.
9. Pseudocode simple programs.
10. Explain what is meant by a loop.

INTRODUCTION

People who are good programmers are also good problem solvers. Writing a program is a way of solving a problem by using a computer. This chapter will examine problem solving in a systematic way. The steps in reaching a solution to a problem will be explained. Flowcharting and pseudocoding will also be introduced in this chapter as two ways of representing a solution to a programming problem.

STEPS IN PROBLEM SOLVING

People solve problems every day. Most problems have a number of solutions. There is often more than one way to arrive at the correct answer to a problem. Figure 2-1 shows a maze. There are many ways of getting from the start to the finish in this maze, but one way is shorter than the others. By stopping for a minute and looking ahead, the most direct route can easily be found. Programming problems generally are not this easy to solve, but a little time spent studying them can save considerable time and trouble later. There are some basic steps that can help the programmer develop a program in an efficient way. These steps are listed below.

1. Understand the problem.
2. Develop a solution to the problem.
3. Write the program.
4. Type the program into the computer and run it.
5. Correct any errors in the program.
6. Test the program.

In this chapter, the first two steps will be discussed in detail.

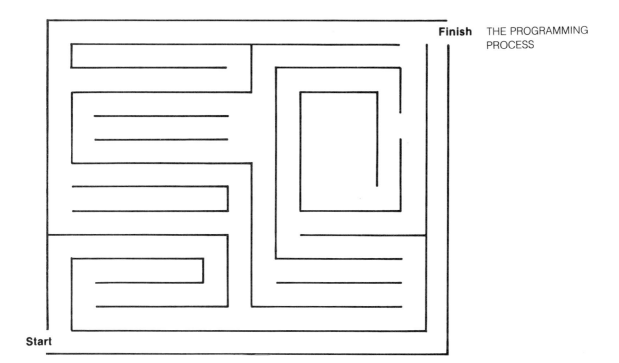

Figure 2–1 A MAZE

Understanding the Problem

It is impossible to get somewhere if it is not clear where you are
going. To write a program it is necessary to know what results are
needed. This means the programmer must have a clear idea of what
the output should be. When the programmer decides what kinds of
results are desired, then it can be determined what information will
be needed to obtain those results. This means deciding what kind of
input is necessary in order to obtain the correct output.

If a program is needed to convert inches into yards, the output
will be given in yards. The input will be the number of inches to be
changed into yards and also the number of inches there are in one
yard. The programmer now has all of the information necessary to
solve the problem.

Developing a Solution

Once the necessary input and output are determined, it is time to
write down the steps needed to obtain the correct results from the
input. The sequence of steps needed to solve a problem is called an
algorithm. The algorithm must list every step necessary to obtain the
correct results from the input. Remember that the computer cannot
tell if a step is left out. It depends on the programmer to tell it everything.

15

Sample Problem

Solving programming problems is like many jobs people do every day. Making a pizza is a good example. The desired output is a pizza that tastes good. First, the exact type of pizza must be determined. In this example, the desired output will be a pepperoni and cheese pizza. Once the type of pizza has been decided, it will be apparent what ingredients are needed. For a pepperoni pizza the input would look something like this:

Dough	*Toppings*
flour	sauce
water	cheese
yeast	pepperoni
salt	

The needed input and output are shown in Figure 2-2.

Next, the steps in making the pizza must be listed. The major steps could look like this:

1. Preheat oven.
2. Prepare dough.
3. Put sauce and toppings on pizza.
4. Cook the pizza.

These steps are a basic algorithm for solving the problem of how to make a pizza. This algorithm will be further refined by breaking each of these steps into many smaller steps. For example, step 2 could be broken down this way:

1. Read the dough recipe.
2. Get the ingredients ready.
3. Measure each ingredient.
4. Mix the ingredients.
5. Let the dough rise.
6. Grease the pan.
7. Spread the dough in the pan.

Figure 2-2 INPUT AND OUTPUT FOR MAKING A PIZZA

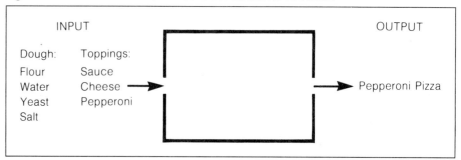

Even some of these steps could be broken down further. Step 3 could contain many substeps. Figure 2-3 shows how making a pizza could be broken into many smaller jobs. In Figure 2-3 only step 2, preparing the dough, has been broken down further. Of course, this could be done for each of the steps.

LEARNING CHECK 2-1

1. What are the six steps necessary in developing a program?
2. What is meant by understanding the problem?
3. What is meant by an algorithm?
4. Write an algorithm for a task you have done, such as making a bed, building a shop project, or cleaning your bedroom.

Answers:

1. Understand the problem.
   Develop a solution to the problem.
   Write the program.
   Type the program into the computer and run it.
   Correct any errors in the program.
   Test the program.   2. The programmer must know exactly what results the program is expected to yield. From that information, the programmer can determine the needed input.   3. The sequence of steps needed to solve a problem.

TOP-DOWN PROGRAMMING

In many ways, writing a program is similar to making a pizza. A small program can probably be written all at once. A large program is much easier to write if it has been broken down into many **subprograms**

Figure 2–3   STEPS IN MAKING A PIZZA

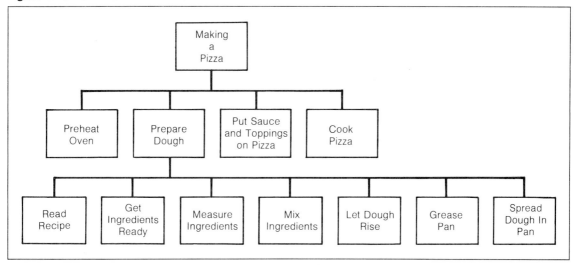

or **modules**. Pascal is a **structured programming language.** Structured programming languages have two basic characteristics:

1. They allow a large program to be broken down into subprograms.
2. They allow the programmer to control the order in which statements will be executed in a clear, efficient way.

It is this first characteristic of structured programming that will be discussed here.

Developing a solution to a large problem can be very difficult because of the large amount of detail. This is where **top-down programming** becomes very helpful. Top-down programming refers to the process of breaking a large program into smaller and smaller subprograms. Another way of putting it is that the programmer is going from a generalized algorithm to the specific algorithm. This allows the programmer to deal with the major problems first and worry about the specific details later. For example, in making the pizza, the first thing dealt with was not how much flour needed to be used in the dough. This would not be dealt with until the subtask of making the dough was actually undertaken.

Top-down programming helps the programmer keep in mind an overall view of the problem. It also increases the chance of the programmer realizing early in the programming process whether or not a particular solution will work. This approach can save time. This style of program development helps the programmer to write a program that is efficient and logical.

FLOWCHARTING

One of the ways of visually representing the steps in a program is to use a **flowchart**. Flowcharts have symbols that have specific meanings.

Figure 2–4 FLOWCHARTING SYMBOLS

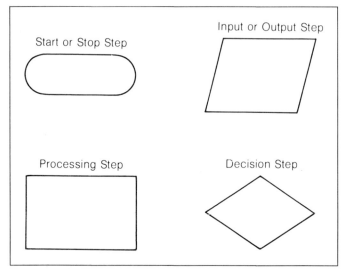

Figure 2-4 shows some of the symbols used in a flowchart. The flow-chart for a program adding three numbers together is illustrated in Figure 2-5. Arrows are drawn between the symbols to show in which direction the program is going. The first symbol represents the beginning of the program. The second symbol is an input step: the three numbers are read to the computer. Next is the processing step. Processing steps are where the work of the program is actually done. In this case, the three numbers are added together. The last symbol is a stop step, showing where the program ends. In a flowchart, a **deci-sion step** is represented by the diamond-shaped symbol. A decision step is used when the computer is making a comparison. What would happen if a program was to read a letter and only print the letter if it was a consonant? The steps in solving this problem would look like this:

1. Read letter.
2. Compare letter to list of consonants.
3. If letter is a consonant, print it.

Figure 2–5 FLOWCHART FOR FINDING SUM

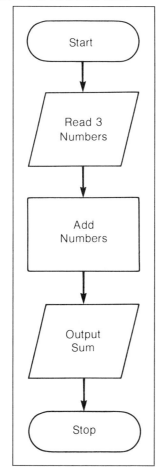

The flowchart for this program is shown in Figure 2-6. The comparison here is a **single-alternative decision step**. Something is done only if the letter is a consonant. If the letter is a vowel, nothing will be done.

A **double-alternative decision step** is one where something is done if the step is true and something different is done if the step is false. An example would be a program that reads in two letters and then prints out the one that comes last alphabetically. The algorithm would look like this:

1. Read two letters.
2. Compare the two letters.
3. If first comes alphabetically after second, then print first.
4. If first is not alphabetically after second, then print second.

The flowchart for this program is shown in Figure 2-7. In this flowchart, the "Yes" route is taken if the first letter is larger than the second. Otherwise the "No" route is taken.

Loops can also be represented by using flowcharts. A loop allows a particular part of a program to be repeated as many times as needed. Suppose a program needed to be written that would

1. Read 20 numbers.
2. Add the numbers together.
3. Print the total.

Figure 2–6 FLOWCHART SHOWING SINGLE-ALTERNATIVE DECISION STEP

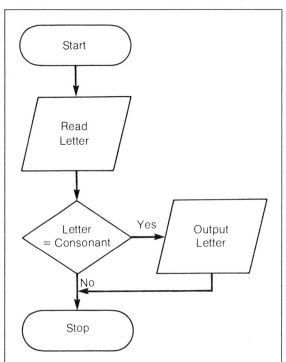

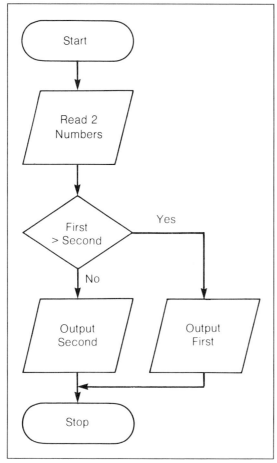

Figure 2–7 FLOWCHART SHOWING DOUBLE-ALTERNATIVE DECISION STEPS

This could easily be written with a loop. The flowchart for this program is shown in Figure 2–8. The name "Count" is used to keep track of the number of times the loop has been executed. When the loop has been executed 20 times, "Total" will be printed. Notice that before the loop is entered "Total" is set to zero. This is done so the first number read can be added to "Total."

Flowcharting makes the logic of a program easy to follow. It helps the programmer to visualize how a program will be written.

PSEUDOCODING

Pseudocode is a narrative description of a program's logic. While a flowchart only presents the logic of a program, pseudocode often resembles an actual program. Pseudocode uses English statements to express a program's actions. Pseudocoding is often more useful than flowcharting in developing a program, because pseudocode is more similar to an actual computer program than a flowchart.

Pseudocode can be used to represent simple and complex Pascal

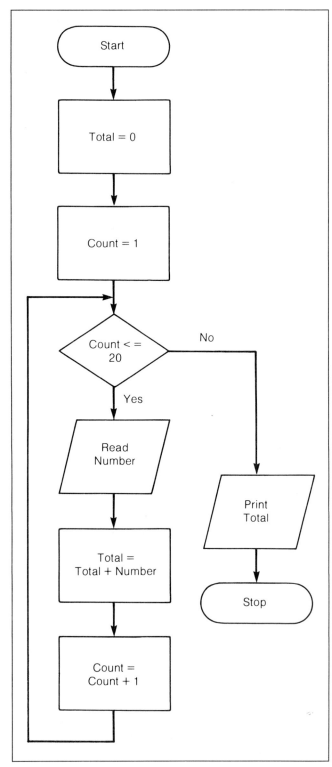

Figure 2–8 FLOWCHART DEMONSTRATING USE OF A LOOP

programs. Remember how a flowchart was used to represent a program that read three numbers, added them together, and printed the
sum? The pseudocode below represents the same program.

Start

    Read X, Y, Z
    Add X, Y, and Z
    Sum = X + Y + Z
    Print SUM

Stop

The single-alternative decision step requires the program to ask one
question. In pseudocode, the question looks like this:

    If (an expression is true) then
      statement(s)

The action or actions directly under the "If" are only executed if the
expression is true. People often use this type of logic to make decisions. For example, if you like pizza and go to a restaurant, you might
decide:

    If (this restaurant has pizza) then
      order pizza

The double-alternative decision step considers the actions to be executed whether an expression is true or false. The pseudocode of a
double-alternative decision step is illustrated below.

    If (an expression is true) then
      statement(s)
    Else
      statement(s)

The action or actions directly below the "Else" are only executed if
the expression is false. The pseudocode below describes a program
that reads two numbers and prints the larger of the two. Compare this
program to the flowchart in Figure 2–7.

Start

    Read X and Y
    If X > Y then
      print X
    Else
      print Y

Stop

Loops can also be represented in pseudocode. Look at the general
form of this loop in pseudocode:

> While (an expression is true) do
>   statement(s)
> End

This loop will be executed as long as the expression following the "While" is true. Notice that the word "End" marks the point where the loop stops. Here is the pseudocode for the program that is flow-charted in Figure 2-8:

> Start
>
>   TOTAL = 0
>   COUNT = 1
>   While COUNT < = 20 do
>   Read NUMBER
>   TOTAL = TOTAL + NUMBER
>   COUNT = COUNT + 1
>   End
>   Print TOTAL
>
> Stop

Pseudocoding a program allows you to clearly see the logic of a program. Pseudocode lets the programmer concentrate on a program's logic rather than the syntax, or grammatical rules, of a programming language. Try to pseudocode programs before actually writing the Pascal version. You can often avoid many painful hours of fixing programs by first constructing and checking pseudocode versions.

◤LEARNING CHECK 2-2

1. Think of a job you have done. Break it down into smaller jobs, following the example in Figure 2–3.
2. Write down every step needed to solve this equation:

$$\frac{14 + 8 - 12}{2} + \frac{6}{3}$$

3. What is pseudocoding?
4. Give two characteristics of structured programming.

Answers:

1. Run dishwasher. a. Load dishes. b. Put in soap. c. Start dishwasher. d. After dishwasher is done, unload dishwasher. 2. a. 14 + 8 = 22 b. 22 − 12 = 10 c. 10/2 = 5 d. 6/3 = 2 e. 5+2 = 10/ 3. Pseudocoding is a narrative description of a program's logic. 4. a. It allows large programs to be broken down into smaller subprograms. b. It allows the programmer to determine the order in which statements will be executed in a clear, logical way.

SUMMARY POINTS

- This chapter has discussed ways of developing programs. It is important to develop a program in a logical way. This will make writing a program progress quickly and there will be less chance of errors. Before a program can be written, it is important to understand its purpose. Then the needed input and output can be determined. The steps needed to solve the problem should be written down. The list of steps is called an algorithm.
- Large programs can be broken down into more manageable subprograms. This approach is termed top-down programming. Since Pascal is a structured programming language, the programmer can write subprograms that work together to solve a large problem.
- Flowcharting is a way of visually representing a program. Each symbol represents a step in solving the problem.
- Pseudocoding is a method of writing a program out in English. Using this method, the program can then easily be translated into a programming language.

VOCABULARY LIST

Algorithm   A sequence of steps used to solve a problem.

Decision step   A step in solving a problem where a comparison is made. The action that will be taken next depends on the results of that comparison.

Double-alternative decision step   A decision step in which a subsequent step is done only if the comparison in the decision step is true. A different subsequent step is done if the comparison is false.

Flowchart   A method of visually representing the steps in solving a problem.

Loop   A structure that allows a section of a program to be repeated as many times as is needed.

Modules   See **subprogram**.

Pseudocode   Program statements written briefly in English, not in a programming language: a narrative description of the programming logic.

Single-alternative decision step   A decision step in which a subsequent step is done only if the comparison made in the decision step is true. If the comparison is false, nothing is done.

Structured programming language   A programming language that allows a large problem to be broken down methodically into smaller units. It also allows the programmer to control the order in which a program will be executed in a simple, efficient way. This approach leads to programs that are logical and easy to understand.

Subprogram   A part of a larger program that performs a specific job.

Top-down programming   A method of writing computer programs in which a large problem is broken down into smaller and smaller problems that are easier to solve than one large problem.

CHAPTER TEST

VOCABULARY

Match a term from the numbered column with the description from the lettered column that best fits the term.

1. Pseudocode

    a. A decision step in which a subsequent step is executed only if the comparison made in the decision step is true. A different subsequent step is taken if the comparison is false.

2. Data

    b. A narrative description of a program's logic.

3. Flowchart

    c. A programming language that allows a large problem to be broken down methodically into smaller units. It also allows the programmer to control the order in which a program will be executed. This leads to programs that are logical and easy to understand.

4. Top-down programming

    d. To read and carry out the instructions in a program.

5. Subprogram

    e. A part of a larger program that performs a specific task.

6. Algorithm

    f. The facts the computer uses to get results.

7. Double-alternative decision step

    g. A sequence of steps used to solve a problem.

8. Program

    h. A method of writing computer programs where a large problem is broken down into smaller and easier to solve problems.

9. Execute

    i. A decision step in which a subsequent step is taken only if the comparison made in the decision step is true. If the comparison is false, nothing is done.

10. Single-alternative decision step

    j. A method of visually representing the steps in solving a problem.

11. Structured programming language

    k. A list of instructions used by a computer to use to solve a specific problem.

QUESTIONS

THE PROGRAMMING
PROCESS

1. Think of a job you have done. What was the input needed to do the job? What was the result? What were the steps necessary to get the job done? Be as specific as possible.
2. Write an algorithm to solve the problem below. George has $10.00. He wants to go to the movies. It costs $3.00 to get into the show. Popcorn will cost him 80¢. After the movie, he would like to go to the bookstore and buy some paperbacks. If he buys two paperbacks at $1.75 each, how much money will he have left? There will be a 5% sales tax on the books.
3. List the four flowcharting symbols mentioned in this chapter and tell what each represents.
4. Write a flowchart for a program that will read in two names and print the name that comes first alphabetically. Write the pseudocode for this program.
5. Write the pseudocode for a program that will read the scores on ten tests. Use a loop to do this. The grades will be assigned by the following scale:
   a. A—90 points or better
   b. B—82 points or better
   c. C—74 points or better
   d. D—60 points or better
   e. F—less than 60 points
   Print the correct grade for each score.

CHAPTER 3

Data Types and Parts of a Pascal Program

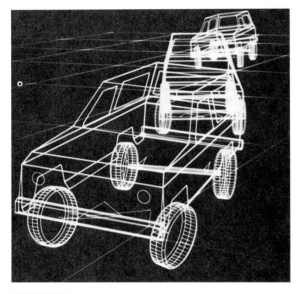

OUTLINE

LEARNING OBJECTIVES

After studying this chapter, you should be able to:

1. Write valid Pascal identifiers.
2. Describe the difference between a program variable and a program constant.
3. Write Pascal variable declaration statements.
4. Write Pascal constant declaration statements.
5. Identify the six types of data discussed in this chapter and describe the characteristics of each.
6. Identify the basic parts of a Pascal program.
7. Use the semicolon in a simple Pascal program.

INTRODUCTION

Pascal is a structured programming language. The rules for writing programs in Pascal are very specific. This chapter will cover some of the rules for giving names to values stored in the computer and for using different types of data in a program. The basic parts of a Pascal program will be explained. At the end of the chapter this material will be used to write a simple Pascal program.

DATA

Computer programs use data. Data are the facts given to the computer so that it can obtain the desired results. To write a Pascal program converting feet to miles, the computer needs to know two things before it could find the answer. First, the computer needs to know how many feet there are in a mile. Second, the computer needs to know the number of feet to be changed to miles. At that point, the computer will have all the data needed to find the answer. Here is the pseudo-code for this program:

```
Start
      Read FEET
      MILES = FEET / FEET-IN-A-MILE
      Print MILES
Stop
```

The flowchart is shown in Figure 3-1.

VARIABLES

When the CPU stores programs, data, and output, it does not do so randomly. It uses a systematic method to assign a location to each data

Figure 3-1 FLOWCHART FOR PROGRAM TO CONVERT FEET INTO MILES

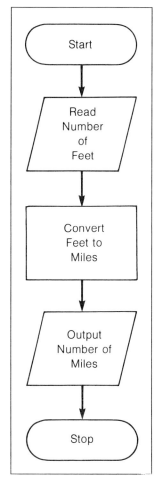

item and instruction. These are called **storage locations:** collectively, they make up the computer's memory. Each storage location has an address so that the CPU can find the item's location in memory when it needs to use that item. In order to process data, the CPU needs to first locate each instruction and piece of data.

As previously discussed, computer storage can be compared with a large row of mailboxes. Each mailbox is a specific location with its own address. Each can hold one item of information. Since each storage location has a unique address, program instructions can reference particular items by giving their addresses. One of the most important things about Pascal is that the programmer may assign names to these locations. Then it is not necessary to know where the computer is storing these values. These names are called **variable names** (or **variables** for short). These variables are stored values that may change while a program is being run. It is a good idea to choose a variable name that describes what each variable represents. These are called **descriptive variable names.** In the example above, two variable names would be needed. FEET would be a good choice to stand for the number of feet to be changed to miles. This is an example of an **input variable.** This value is put into the computer to get the needed results. The result could be given the variable name MILES. This is called an **output variable.** It is the result the computer gives. The result MILES will change depending on the value of the input variable FEET.

CONSTANTS

One more data value is needed in the example above. It is the number of feet in a mile. This is called a **constant.** The value of a constant remains the same throughout the program. The number of feet in a mile is a value that will not change. To stand for 5280 (the number of feet in a mile), the constant name FEET__MILE could be used. Figure 3-2 is a data table. It shows the variables and constants used by this program.

IDENTIFIERS

There are some rules in Pascal for constructing variable names. All variables must be **valid** Pascal **identifiers.** An identifier must always start with a letter of the alphabet. The rest of the identifier can be made up of any combination of letters and numbers. Identifiers are valid if they meet these rules. Here are some examples of valid Pascal identifiers:

```
GRADE_POINT
NUM1346
MONTH10
```

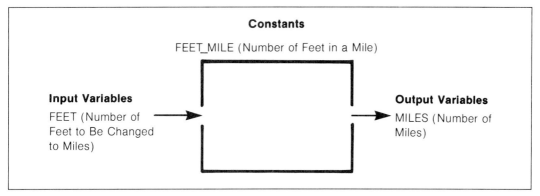

Figure 3-2 DATA TABLE FOR PROGRAM TO CONVERT FEET INTO MILES

Note the use of the underline character in the first example. It is the only character that can be used other than a letter or a number. It can be used to separate words to make them more readable. The UCSD Pascal compiler ignores the underline character. It is used to make identifiers easier to read. Another way of making easy-to-read identifiers is to use a combination of small and capital letters:

NumItems

InchesLong

SalesTax

The UCSD Pascal compiler treats capital and small letters as if they were the same. Because of this, the compiler would treat the four variable names below as if they were all exactly alike:

YEARSOLD   YearsOld   yearsold   YEARS_OLD

Which one is the easiest to read? The easier the variables are to understand, the easier it will be for other people to follow your program. Why are the variable names listed below invalid?

1_MILE	(begins with a number)
YEARS OLD	(has a blank space)
SALES#	(has a character that is not allowed)

In addition to variables, identifiers must be used to represent constants and other routines such as procedures and functions, which will be discussed later. These names can be as long as the programmer desires. But the UCSD Pascal compiler will only look at the first eight characters in the identifier. The following two variables are both valid:

MONTH_NUM   MONTH_NUM11

33

They will be treated by the compiler as if they were identical, however, since the first eight characters in each are the same.

RESERVED WORDS

In Pascal there are certain **reserved words.** These reserved words have a specific meaning to the compiler. They cannot be used as variable or constant names. The following is a list of some common reserved words:

AND	ELSE	IF	RECORD
ARRAY	END	NOT	THEN
BEGIN	FILE	OF	TO
CONST	FOR	OR	TYPE
DO	FUNCTION	PROCEDURE	VAR
DOWNTO	GOTO	PROGRAM	WHILE

Predefined or **standard identifiers,** like reserved words, have a specific meaning to the compiler. They should not be redefined by the programmer. The documentation for your UCSD Pascal compiler contains a complete listing of reserved words and standard identifiers for your compiler.

DATA TYPES

All variables in a Pascal program must be assigned a data type. The data type assigned to a particular variable depends on what kind of values that variable will contain. In the following sections the data types INTEGER, REAL, CHAR, STRING, BOOLEAN, and LONG INTEGER will be defined. Pascal also allows the programmer to make new data types. These are called user-defined data types and will be covered in Chapter 10.

INTEGER

An **integer** is a whole number and its opposite. It never has a decimal point. An integer can be either positive or negative. If there is no sign in front of the number, it is assumed that the number is positive. Here are some examples:

$$-2532 \quad +48 \quad 7 \quad -10 \quad 0$$

What is wrong with these examples?

25.48	(decimal point)
+4,687	(comma)
387*	(character other than a digit)

Notice that a comma cannot be used to separate large numbers. The data type INTEGER is used to store integers.

DATA TYPES AND
PARTS OF A PASCAL
PROGRAM

Notice that a comma cannot be used to separate large numbers. The data type INTEGER is used to store integers.

REAL

The data type REAL is for storing real numbers. Any number with a decimal point is real. For example:

$$2567.0 \qquad 0.6 \qquad -385.0 \qquad +467.1121$$

All real numbers must have at least one digit on either side of the decimal point. As in type INTEGER the plus sign may or may not be included. What is incorrect in these examples?

$-.65$	(no digit on left side of decimal point)
100	(no decimal point)
$+487.$	(no digit on right side of decimal point)

CHAR

Data type CHAR is any single character on the keyboard. The character must be enclosed in single quotation marks. Some examples are as follow:

'*'   'B'   '2'   '%'   'Y'

What is wrong with these examples?

'0	(missing right quotation mark)
'22'	(more than one character inside quotation marks)
%	(quotation marks missing)

STRING

STRING is a data type that can store character strings. Any characters on the keyboard may be used. The entire string is enclosed in single quotation marks:

'12448 Cloverdale Rd.'
'What are you doing today?'
'   '
'578-42-8856'

Below are two incorrect examples.

'Uriah Heep	(missing right quotation mark)
"Double Cheese"	(double quotation marks used)

What if a string looked like this:

'DON'T SIT UNDER THE APPLE TREE.'

The compiler would see the single quotation mark in DON'T as the end of the string. This can be fixed by using two single quotation marks together.

'DON''T SIT UNDER THE APPLE TREE.'

When this line is printed, only one single quotation mark will appear in DON'T.

BOOLEAN

The data type BOOLEAN is probably the most difficult for the beginner to understand. A BOOLEAN variable can be true or false. These are the only two choices. For example, if the variable CORRECT is a BOOLEAN variable, it must be equal to either true or false. It may help to think of a BOOLEAN variable as a switch. The switch is either turned on or off.

LONG INTEGER

In UCSD Pascal, a variable of data type INTEGER may not be greater than 32767 or less than -32767. If it is possible that the value of an integer variable may be larger or smaller than these numbers, the variable should be declared as data type LONG INTEGER. Data type LONG INTEGER may contain any integer up to 36 digits in length.

◤LEARNING CHECK 3-1

1. Which of the following are valid variable names?
   a. TOP20
   b. AMOUNT$
   c. GameScore
   d. GRATEFUL_DEAD
   e. BEGIN
   f. 1st
   g. Look Out
   h. SALES%
   i. outer
   j. CHEVY1957
2. How many different ways can the variable name "top__10" be written? Name five. Will the compiler see all of these names as being the same?
3. Which data type is each of the following?
   a. FALSE
   b. -1.28
   c. 4678
   d. '$'
   e. 'STOP THAT CAR'
   f. 0.689
   g. '379-50-5466'
   h. 'Marvin K. Mooney'

i. TRUE   **k.** 0

j. '4'   **l.** '45,122'

4. Are these integers valid or invalid?

    a. 785   **e.** .486

    b. 000   **f.** +155

    c. −437820   **g.** 6

    d. 687*

Answers: 1. a, c, d, i, j. 2. TOP—10, top10, Top10, Top, Top10, Top10, TOP10: yes 3. a. BOOLEAN, b. REAL, c. INTEGER, d. CHAR, e. CHAR, f. REAL, g. STRING, h. STRING, i. BOOLEAN, j. CHAR, k. INTEGER, l. STRING 4. valid: a, b, f, g

PARTS OF A PASCAL PROGRAM

Just like any other language, Pascal has rules that must be followed. **Syntax rules** are rules that explain how the parts of a language should be put together. Syntax also involves spelling and punctuation. The syntax rules of English are present whether one is aware of them or not. Sentences are capitalized and end with a punctuation mark. Complete sentences need a subject and a verb and words must be spelled correctly. To students, these rules are automatic because they have been speaking and writing the English language for years. The syntax rules in Pascal may seem complex or awkward in the beginning, but with practice, the rules will become second nature.

The general structure of a Pascal program is shown in Figure 3-3. In the following sections, the basic syntax rules of the Pascal language will be covered.

Figure 3-3 BASIC STRUCTURE OF A PASCAL PROGRAM

```
PROGRAM program-name;

CONST
     constant_name = value;

VAR

     variable_name : data_type;

BEGIN

     statement1;
     statement2;
        .
        .
        .
     last_statement

END

(The semicolon at the end of the last_statement is optional.)
```

Program Statement

Every program must have a name. The name is given in the first line of the program, which is called the **program statement.** The program statement begins with the reserved word PROGRAM, followed by the name of the program. The syntax for the program statement is shown in Figure 3-4. Any valid Pascal identifier may be used as a program name. It is best to pick one that describes what the program does. For example, for the program converting feet to miles, the name FIND__MILES might be chosen. The following are examples of valid program statements:

```
PROGRAM AREA;
PROGRAM FindNum;
PROGRAM STARTER1;
```

Notice that program statements end with a semicolon. Listed below are some invalid program statements.

```
PROGRAM 1st;        (Program name begins with a number)
PROGRAM AVE GRADE;  (space in program name)
PROGRAM COMPUTE     (no semicolon at the end)
PROGRM SOCCER;      (program is misspelled)
```

Constant Declarations

The **constant declaration statement** starts with the reserved word CONST. It goes after the program statement, but before the variable declarations. A constant can be any of the six data types—REAL, INTEGER, LONG INTEGER, CHAR, STRING, or BOOLEAN—or it can be user-defined. In the example program FIND__MILES, the constant declaration would be stated as:

```
CONST
    FEET_MILES = 5280.0;
```

Notice that instead of a data type after the equals sign, the actual number was written. This value cannot be changed during the running of the program. Other examples of constant declarations are as follows:

```
CONST
    PI = 3.14;
    SPEED = 55;
    FLAG = FALSE;
    NAME = 'GEORGE';
    PERCENT = '%';
```

Figure 3-4 SYNTAX FOR PROGRAM STATEMENT

```
PROGRAM program__name;
```

Figure 3-5 illustrates the syntax of the constant declaration statement.

Variable Declarations

In Pascal, all variables must be declared before they can be used in the body of the program. This is done in the **variable declaration statement.** This statement comes before the reserved word BEGIN. BEGIN marks the beginning of the body of the program.

The variable declaration starts with the reserved word VAR. This is followed by any variable names and their data types. A variable declaration statement ends with a semicolon. The syntax for variable declarations is shown in Figure 3-6.

The following example shows one way of writing variable declarations:

```
VAR
     FEET    : REAL;
     MILES   : REAL;
     COUNT   : INTEGER;
     ID_NUM  : INTEGER;
```

They could also have been written as:

```
VAR
     MILES, FEET     : REAL;
     COUNT, ID_NUM : INTEGER;
```

In the second example, all of the variables of the same type are placed together. This procedure saves space and makes it easier to tell which variables are of the same data type. Notice that each variable is separated by a comma. The spaces around the colons and the commas are not necessary, but they make the program easier to read.

Figure 3-5 SYNTAX FOR CONSTANT DECLARATION STATEMENT

```
CONST
      constant_name = value;
```

Figure 3-6 SYNTAX FOR VARIABLE DECLARATION STATEMENT

```
VAR
     variable_name  :  data_type;
     variable_name  :  data_type;
```

(All variable names of the same type may be listed together and separated by commas.)

39

The whole VAR declaration statement could have been written on one line:

```
VAR FEET, MILES : REAL;  COUNT, ID_NUM : INTEGER;
```

Putting different parts of the declaration statement on separate lines makes the program easier to follow. Whichever style is chosen, it is a good idea to remain consistent throughout the program.

The format for declaring an integer to be of data type LONG INTEGER is:

```
VAR
     LARGENUM : INTEGER[N];
```

The value of N may be any positive digit up to 36. The term N indicates the number of digits that will be allowed in this integer. For example, if the declaration statement looked like:

```
VAR
     BIGGIE : INTEGER[8];
```

the largest value that could be stored in BIGGIE is 99999999.

A string declaration could look like this:

```
PERSON : STRING;
```

The length of this string will be the number of characters assigned to the string. It is also possible to state the maximum number of characters to be allowed in a string:

```
PERSON : STRING[35];
```

This string may have up to 35 characters. The number in brackets after the word STRING may be as large as 255. This allows a string to be up to 255 characters long. Here are a few examples:

```
TITLE  : STRING[95]; (TITLE may have up to 95 characters)
NATION : STRING[38]; (NATION may have up to 38 characters)
```

If no length is specified for a string in its declaration statement, the string may contain up to 80 characters.

Body of the Program

After the declaration statements comes the reserved word BEGIN. The next part of the program is where the work of the program is done. This is called the body of the program. Any needed computations are completed within the body, which can be as long as necessary. The reserved word END completes the program. The program always ends with a period.

⩔LEARNING CHECK 3-2

1. Which of the following program statements are correct?
   a. PROGRAM SEARCH;
   b. PROGRAM TELL ME;
   c. PROGRAM PhoneBill
   d. AVERAGE;
   e. PROGRAM FIND_SQUARE;
   f. PROGRAM 70PERCENT;
2. Rewrite the variable declaration statement shown below so it is more readable.

   VAR GALLON,DISTANCE,TIME:REAL; COUNT:INTEGER;

3. Which of these constant declaration statements are correct? Which data type is each?
   a. X = 4.35
   b. SCORE : 4;
   c. PRINT = 'THE CORRECT ANSWER IS:';
   d. FLAG = TRUE;

Answers:

1. a. correct, b. incorrect (space in program name), c. incorrect (no semicolon), d. incorrect (missing reserved word PROGRAM), e. correct, f. incorrect (begins with a number) 2. VAR GALLON, DISTANCE, TIME : REAL; COUNT : INTEGER; 3. a. incorrect (no semicolon): REAL, b. incorrect (has colon instead of equals sign): INTEGER, c. correct: STRING, d. correct: BOOLEAN

PROGRAM FIND_MILES

In Figure 3-7 is the Pascal program that will find the answer to the problem that has been discussed in this chapter. Note that the constant FEET_MILES is declared to be a real number. For now, it is a good idea to make all the values in a computation the same data type. Since FEET and MILES are both data type REAL, FEET_MILES was made real too. Notice the output in Figure 3-4. The value typed in for FEET was 52800.0. The answer printed to the monitor was:

THERE ARE 1.00000E1 MILES IN 5.28000E4 FEET.

The result, 1.00000E1, is written in **exponential notation,** sometimes called **scientific notation.** The number after the letter E (in this case one) indicates the number of places to shift the decimal point. If the number has a plus sign in front of it (or no sign), the

41

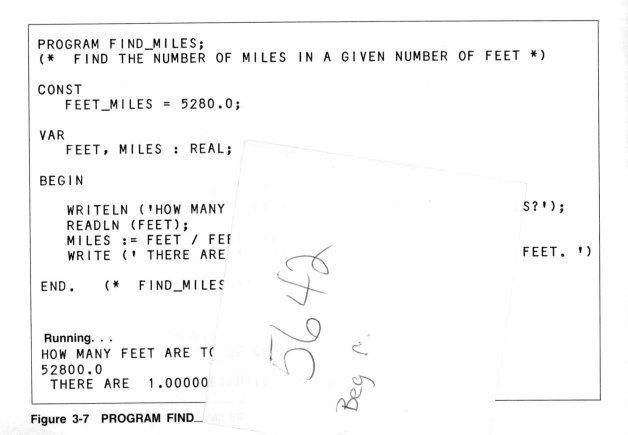

```
PROGRAM FIND_MILES;
(*  FIND THE NUMBER OF MILES IN A GIVEN NUMBER OF FEET *)

CONST
    FEET_MILES = 5280.0;

VAR
    FEET, MILES : REAL;

BEGIN

    WRITELN ('HOW MANY                              S?');
    READLN (FEET);
    MILES := FEET / FEF
    WRITE (' THERE ARE                              FEET. ')

END.    (*  FIND_MILES


 Running. . .
HOW MANY FEET ARE TC
52800.0
  THERE ARE   1.00000
```

Figure 3-7   PROGRAM FIND_

decimal point is shifted to the right. For a minus sign, the decimal point is shifted to the left. The answer could be written as the real number 10.0. Listed below are a few more examples.

2.68930E4	26893.0
1.68000E-1	0.168
4.20000E4	42000.0

In Chapter 4 it will be explained how real numbers can be formatted so that they are printed in regular decimal form.

Locate the body of the program in Figure 3-7. The body is the part between the reserved words BEGIN and END. The first statement starts with the word WRITELN. This causes the computer to write the sentence inside the parentheses and single quotation marks to the monitor. The READLN statement reads in the number that is typed to the monitor by the user. The statement

```
MILES := FEET / FEET_MILES;
```

actually computes the number of miles. Each of these types of statements will be discussed in detail later.

PUNCTUATION

One of the most confusing aspects of Pascal for the beginner is the question of where to put a semicolon. A semicolon is used to separate Pascal statements. In UCSD Pascal, a semicolon may or may not be used immediately before the reserved word END. There are no punctuation marks after the reserved words CONST and VAR. A period is always used at the end of the program. Look at the program in Figure 3-4 again. Does the punctuation in this program meet these rules? Notice that a semicolon was not used before the word END.

COMMENTS

Comments are used to explain what is going on in a program. Comments have no meaning to the computer. In Pascal, all comments must be enclosed in both parentheses and asterisks:

> (* This is a comment *)

or in braces:

> {Here is another one}

In this book, parentheses and asterisks will be used because not all keyboards have braces.

Comments may be used anywhere in a program. After the program statement, it is a good idea to include a description of what the entire program does. Comments can also be used within the program to explain what a particular section is doing. Comments may go on for as many lines as desired.

The comments in a program are called the **program documentation.** Well-documented programs make it easier not only for the programmer but for anyone else trying to understand a program. Comments are particularly useful if a program needs to be changed in the future. It is important to develop the habit of documenting programs as they are written.

LEARNING CHECK 3-3

1. Which data types are each of the following constants?
   a. NUM = 0;
   b. OFF = FALSE;
   c. STAR = '*';

43

d. DIVISOR = -61.77;

e. SPACES = '   ';

2. Write these real numbers in exponential notation.

   a. 0.06788

   b. +455.56

   c. 8000.0

   d. -123.1

3. Explain the difference between an input variable and an output variable.

SUMMARY POINTS

- This chapter has discussed the use of variable and constant names to represent storage locations. The value of a variable may change when a program is executed, but the value of a constant must remain the same. These names must be valid Pascal identifiers. Pascal identifiers must start with a letter and may contain any letter or number or the underline character.
- Six data types were discussed. They were INTEGER, REAL, CHAR, STRING, BOOLEAN, and LONG INTEGER.
- The basic parts of a Pascal program are the program statement, the constant declaration statement, the variable declaration statement, and the body of the program.
- The punctuation of a Pascal program can be confusing. Semicolons are used to separate Pascal statements. The semicolon before the reserved word END is optional. A program is always concluded with a period.

VOCABULARY LIST

Comments Statements in a computer program that explain what is being done in the program. They are ignored by the computer.

Constant An identifier whose value may not change during program execution.

Constant declaration statement The statement that tells the compiler the specified value to be associated with a constant.

Descriptive variable name A variable name that explains what the variable represents. For example, the variable AVE could be used to represent the average of a group of numbers.

Exponential notation The representation of a real number with one digit to the left of the decimal point, multiplied by a power of ten. For

example, in Pascal, 153.25 would be represented in exponential notation as 1.53250E2.

Identifier A name chosen by the programmer to represent a storage location.

Input variable A value that is placed into the computer to obtain the needed result.

Integer A whole number and its opposite.

Output variable Information the computer gives as the result of processing input.

Predefined identifiers Words that have a specific meaning to the Pascal compiler. They should not be redefined by the programmer.

Program documentation A written description of a program and what it accomplishes.

Program statement The first statement in a

Pascal program. It contains the reserved word PROGRAM followed by the name of the program.

Reserved words Words that have a specific meaning to the Pascal compiler. They may not be redefined by the programmer.

Scientific notation See **Exponential notation.**

Standard identifier See **Predefined identifier.**

Storage locations The part of the computer where information can be kept; the memory.

Syntax rules Rules that explain how the parts of a language should be put together.

Valid Use of an expression that is correct; follows the rules.

Variable A name chosen by the programmer to represent a storage location. The value of the storage location may change during program execution.

Variable declaration statement The statement that tells the compiler the variable names that will be used to represent storage locations and what their types will be.

Variable name See **Variable.**

CHAPTER TEST

VOCABULARY

Match a term from the numbered column with the description from the lettered column that best fits the term.

1. Storage locations

2. Variable

3. Syntax rules

4. Reserved words

5. Program statements

6. Identifier

7. Integer
8. Comments

a. The set of rules of a programming language that control how a program can be written.

b. Words that have a specific meaning to the Pascal compiler. They may not be redefined by the programmer.

c. A variable name that explains what the variable represents. For example, the variable AVE could be used to represent the average of a group of numbers.

d. A name chosen by the programmer to represent a storage location. The value of the storage location may change during program execution.

e. The first statement in a Pascal program. It contains the name of the program.

f. Information the computer gives as the result of processing input.

g. Correct; follows the rules.

h. Statements in a computer program that explain what is being done in the program. They are ignored by the computer.

9. Valid

    i. A name that is given to a variable, constant, program, function, or procedure.

10. Input variable

    j. The part of the computer where information can be kept; the memory.

11. Descriptive variable name

12. Output

    k. A whole number and its opposite.

    l. A value that is placed into the computer to obtain the needed results.

QUESTIONS

1. Coach Kramer wants to find out the batting average for each member of her girls' softball team. Coach Kramer figures batting averages this way:

$$\frac{\text{number of hits}}{\text{number of times at bat} - \text{number of walks}}$$

    a. Write the pseudocode for a program to find a batting average.

    b. Make a flowchart for this problem. Be sure to choose descriptive variable names.

    c. Write a program statement and variable declaration statement that would be appropriate for this problem.

2. Are these valid real numbers? If not, change them so they will be valid.

    a. $+367.0$

    b. $-.7896$

    c. 1,487.735

    d. $485.20

    e. -6.0

    f. 0.248

    g. 67%

    h. 419

3. Write the following declaration statements a different way. Try to make them as easy to read as possible.

```
a. VAR PERCENT : REAL;
       SALE_PRICE : REAL;
       NUM : INTEGER;
       DATE :  INTEGER;

b. CONST LENGTH = 25.00;
c. VAR
       CHECK:BOOLEAN;
       SCORE:INTEGER;
       INNING:INTEGER;
       NUM:INTEGER;
```

4. Write the variable and constant declaration statements for a program that finds the average of three real numbers X, Y, and Z. Write a descriptive program statement for this program.

5. What is the difference between a constant and a variable?

6. Insert the necessary punctuation marks in this program.

```
PROGRAM MILEAGE

VAR
    MILES   GALLONS   MPG   REAL

BEGIN

    WRITELN ('HOW MANY MILES DID YOU DRIVE?')
    READLN (MILES)
    WRITELN ('HOW MANY GALLONS OF GAS DID YOU USE?')
    READLN (GALLONS)
    MPG := MILES / GALLONS
    WRITELN ('YOU GOT  ', MPG, ' MILES PER GALLON OF GAS.')

END
```

CHAPTER 4

Reading and Writing Data

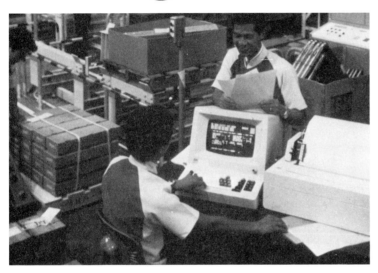

OUTLINE

LEARNING OBJECTIVES

After studying this chapter, you should be able to:

1. Explain the purpose of the WRITE and WRITELN statements.
2. Explain the differences between the WRITE and WRITELN statements in writing to the monitor.
3. Use WRITE and WRITELN statements to write prompts to the monitor.
4. Use the WRITE and WRITELN statements to output program results to the monitor.
5. Explain the purpose of the READ and READLN statements.
6. Explain the difference between the READ and READLN statements in reading from the monitor.
7. Use READ and READLN statements to read data that have been typed to the keyboard.
8. Format real numbers.
9. Format strings.

INTRODUCTION

In Chapter 3, a simple program to change feet to miles was presented. In order for the program to work, we needed a way to let the computer know the number of feet to be changed to miles. The number of feet was the input data. There had to be a way to enter these data to the computer. Also, we needed a way of finding out what answer the computer obtained. In other words, how could the computer output the answer in a readable form?

In this chapter various ways of putting data into the computer will be presented. Also, ways of commanding the computer to print results to the monitor will be explained.

THE WRITE AND WRITELN STATEMENTS

Sometimes in computer programs the programmer wants information to be printed to the monitor. The WRITE statement will accomplish this action, which is sometimes called writing to the monitor. The WRITE statement can also be used for other purposes that will be studied later in this book.

In most programs WRITE statements have two basic purposes. The first purpose is to print a **prompt** for the user. The second purpose is to print the results after a program has been run.

When a program reaches a place where the user is supposed to enter some data, a prompt should be printed to the monitor. A prompt is a sentence or sometimes a symbol that tells the user that the computer is ready for the user to enter data. It prompts the user to respond. It should also tell the user what type of data are expected. When the you see a prompt on the monitor, you should enter the data. In the FIND__MILES program, the prompt looked like this:

```
WRITELN ('HOW MANY FEET ARE TO BE CHANGED INTO MILES?');
```

This instruction tells the program user to type in the number of feet to be changed to miles. The general form of the WRITE statement is:

WRITE (output);

Whatever is to be printed to the monitor must be in parentheses. If it is of data type CHAR or STRING it must be enclosed in single quotation marks. The syntax for this statement is shown in Figure 4-1.

In the FIND__MILES program, the prompt used the word WRITELN instead of WRITE. WRITELN is read "write line." A WRITELN command looks like this:

WRITELN (output);

There is a difference between the WRITE and WRITELN statements. After the computer executes a WRITE statement, the **cursor** remains at the end of the line, where the printing stopped. The cursor is the little box that indicates where information typed to the monitor will appear on the screen. The user can then type the data starting at this spot. In a WRITELN statement, after printing to the monitor, the cursor returns to the beginning of the next line. The WRITELN statement includes a carriage return, the same as when a carriage return is used on a typewriter. Figure 4-2 contains two short programs that show the difference between the WRITE and WRITELN statements. Notice the output for the two programs is different. In the first program, a number of WRITE statements were used. The output was all printed on the same line. Any number of WRITE statements can be used. If there is room, everything will print on the same line.

Figure 4-1 SYNTAX FOR WRITE AND WRITELN STATEMENTS

```
WRITE (output);

WRITELN (output);
```

```
PROGRAM HELLO1;
(* PRINTS A MESSAGE TO THE MONITOR USING WRITE STATEMENTS *)

BEGIN

    WRITE ('HI ');
    WRITE ('THERE ');
    WRITE ('HOW ARE ');
    WRITE ('YOU DOING?');
    WRITELN

END.   (* HELLO1 *)
```

Running. . .
```
HI THERE HOW ARE YOU DOING?
```

```
PROGRAM HELLO2;
(*  PRINTS A MESSAGE TO THE  MONITOR  USING WRITELN STATEMENTS *)

BEGIN

    WRITELN ('HI');
    WRITELN ('THERE');
    WRITELN ('HOW ARE');
    WRITELN ('YOU DOING?')

END.   (* HELLO2 *)
```

Running. . .
```
HI
THERE
HOW ARE
YOU DOING?
```

Figure 4-2 TWO HELLO PROGRAMS

In the first statement in PROGRAM HELLO1

WRITE ('HI ');

there is a space between HI and the quotation mark. If spaces had not been left at the end of the strings, the output would have looked like the following:

HITHEREHOW AREYOU DOING?

The computer only leaves spaces where the programmer tells it to.

There would still be space between HOW ARE and YOU DOING because the strings were typed in with spaces between those words.

In the program HELLO1, the last statement is WRITELN. The WRITELN statement can be used alone to return to the beginning of the next line. If there had been no WRITELN statement, the cursor would have remained on the same line as the printing. It would wait right after the last character printed, in this case a question mark. Using the WRITELN statement alone leaves blank lines on the screen. This can help in spacing the output so that it is more readable. For example, if the output was to be double-spaced,

```
WRITELN;
```

could be put between each output statement.

THE READ AND READLN STATEMENTS

After the user enters data, the computer needs a way of reading those data. Also needed is a way of assigning the data to variables. The computer does this by using a READ or a READLN statement. As shown in Figure 4-3 these two statements are written this way:

```
READ (variable[s]);
READLN (variable[s]);
```

The READ or READLN statements tell the computer to stop and wait until the user enters the data. Next the computer takes the value entered and assigns it to the variable name in parentheses. The value entered must be of the same data type as the variable. This means if a variable NUM has been declared to be of data type REAL, the data typed to the monitor must be of type REAL. If there was a READ statement like this in the program:

```
READ (NUM);
```

a correct response would be to type in something like:

14.75

If we typed in

B

the computer would not accept it and the program would stop run-

Figure 4-3 SYNTAX FOR READ AND READLN STATEMENTS

```
READ (variable[s] );

READLN (variable[s] );
```

ning. When you are typing CHAR or STRING data to the monitor, it is not necessary to put quotation marks around the data.

Even though data types should match, the computer will allow an INTEGER value to be assigned to a variable that has been declared to be data type REAL. The computer will make the whole number into a real number by adding a decimal point and a zero.

Just as in the WRITELN statement, the READLN statement includes a carriage return. This means that if a READLN statement is used, the user must hit the return key after entering the data. When a READ statement is used, the computer reads the data as soon as they are typed. It is possible to have a number of variables in one READ or READLN statement. Each variable name must be separated by a comma.

In Figure 4-4, four integers are added together. The first time the program is run, all four integers are placed on one line. The program

Figure 4-4 PROGRAM ADD1

```
PROGRAM ADD1;
(* THIS PROGRAM ADDS FOUR INTEGERS TOGETHER *)

VAR
    NUM1, NUM2, NUM3, NUM4, SUM : INTEGER;

BEGIN

    WRITELN ('TYPE IN THE FOUR NUMBERS TO BE ADDED TOGETHER.');
    READLN (NUM1, NUM2, NUM3, NUM4);
    SUM := NUM1 + NUM2 + NUM3 + NUM4;
    WRITELN ('THE SUM OF ', NUM1,', ', NUM2,', ', NUM3,' AND ', NUM4, ' IS ',
        SUM)

END.    (* ADD1 *)


Running. . .
TYPE IN THE FOUR NUMBERS TO BE ADDED TOGETHER.
4 8 103 15
THE SUM OF 4, 8, 103 AND 15 IS 130


Running. . .
TYPE IN THE FOUR NUMBERS TO BE ADDED TOGETHER.
4 8 103
15
THE SUM OF 4, 8, 103 AND 15 IS 130


Running. . .
TYPE IN THE FOUR NUMBERS TO BE ADDED TOGETHER.
     4
8
         103
15
THE SUM OF 4, 8, 103 AND 15 IS 130
```

read them and added them together. The numbers are separated by spaces. The number of spaces does not matter.

The second time the program is run, three numbers are typed on one line and the fourth on the next. The computer will keep reading until it finds four numbers, even if it has to go on to the next line. The third time the program is run, every number is on a separate line and each number does not necessarily start at the left margin. The computer again simply keeps looking until it finds the numbers.

A READ statement could have been used in program ADD1 and it would have worked the same way, except for one thing. The user would not have to hit the return key after entering the last data item. Instead, the user could just type a space. With a READLN statement, the return key must be hit after the last data item is entered. When the data are read to the computer, the cursor then returns to the beginning of the next line.

In Figure 4-5, four integers are again added together. In this program, four READ statements are used, one for each integer. The first

Figure 4-5 PROGRAM ADD2

```
PROGRAM ADD2;
(* THIS PROGRAM ADDS FOUR INTEGERS TOGETHER *)

VAR
    NUM1, NUM2, NUM3, NUM4, SUM : INTEGER;

BEGIN

    WRITELN ('TYPE IN THE FOUR NUMBERS TO BE ADDED TOGETHER.');
    READ (NUM1);
    READ (NUM2);
    READ (NUM3);
    READ (NUM4);
    SUM := NUM1 + NUM2 + NUM3 + NUM4;
    WRITELN ('THE SUM OF ', NUM1, ', ', NUM2, ', ', NUM3, ' AND ', NUM4,
    ' IS ', SUM)

END.  (* ADD2 *)


  Running. . .
  TYPE IN THE FOUR NUMBERS TO BE ADDED TOGETHER.
  8 17 108 3
  THE SUM OF 8, 17, 108 AND 3 IS 136


  Running. . .
  TYPE IN THE FOUR NUMBERS TO BE ADDED TOGETHER.
  8
  17
  108
  3
  THE SUM OF 8, 17, 108 AND 3 IS 136
```

time the program was run, all four values were typed on one line. Many values can be read on one line by using a separate READ statement for each value. In a READ statement, the cursor remains on the same line after the computer reads in a data value. If there are no more values on that line, the computer will look for values on the following line. In program ADD2, the four READ statements could have been replaced with one:

```
READ (NUM1, NUM2, NUM3, NUM4);
```

Figure 4-6 illustrates an important difference between the READ and READLN statements. This program has four separate READLN statements. The first time the program is run, each integer is typed on a separate line. The program works as expected. The second time the program is run, not all of the integers are typed on a separate line.

Figure 4-6 PROGRAM ADD3

```
PROGRAM ADD3;
(* THIS PROGRAM ADDS FOUR INTEGERS TOGETHER *)

VAR
    NUM1, NUM2, NUM3, NUM4, SUM : INTEGER;

BEGIN

    WRITELN ('TYPE IN THE FOUR NUMBERS TO BE ADDED TOGETHER.');
    READLN (NUM1);
    READLN (NUM2);
    READLN (NUM3);
    READLN (NUM4);
    SUM := NUM1 + NUM2 + NUM3 + NUM4;
    WRITELN ('THE SUM OF ', NUM1, ', ', NUM2, ', ', NUM3, ' AND ', NUM4,
    ' IS ', SUM)

END.   (* ADD3 *)


Running. . .
TYPE IN THE FOUR NUMBERS TO BE ADDED TOGETHER.
19
146
2
12
THE SUM OF 19, 146, 2 AND 12 IS 179


Running. . .
TYPE IN THE FOUR NUMBERS TO BE ADDED TOGETHER.
19 208
9
102 12
44
THE SUM OF 19, 9, 102 AND 44 IS 174
```

Note the output for this program. The computer has added together the first number on each line. Any other number on the same line is ignored. Since there is only one variable in each READLN statement, the computer reads a value to that variable and then goes to the beginning of the next line. This happens because a READLN statement is being used. This difference is important to remember when using READ and READLN statements. It is important that no necessary data are skipped over when those data should have been read.

The READ statement behaves differently when data are read from files rather than from the terminal. Files will be discussed in Chapter 13 of this book.

String data may only be entered by using a READLN statement. This is because the computer does not know where the string ends. When a READLN statement is used to read in a string, everything on that line is assigned to the variable.

⚓LEARNING CHECK 4-1

1. Explain the difference between a WRITE statement and a WRITELN statement.
2. What two things does a prompt tell the user?
3. What two things does a READ statement do?
4. Why do we need to have a READ or READLN statement after a prompt?

Answers: 1. The WRITELN statement includes a carriage return. The WRITE statement does not include a carriage return. When the information is printed to the monitor in the WRITELN statement, the cursor returns to the beginning of the next line. 2. It tells the user at what point data are to be typed to the monitor and what type of data are to be typed to the monitor. 3. It reads in the data and it assigns the data value to the corresponding variable in parentheses. 4. If the READ or READLN is not present the computer will not be able to read the data value entered and assign it to a variable.

WRITING OUTPUT

After a program has computed a result, the user needs to be able to see the result. One way to find out the result is to have it printed to the monitor. In the program adding four integers together, the statement that printed the result looked like the line below.

```
WRITELN ('THE SUM OF ', NUM1, ', ', NUM2, ', ', NUM3, ' AND ', NUM4,
' IS ', SUM)
```

This is a rather complicated WRITELN statement. There are a number of parts to it. Each part is separated by a comma. The character strings are enclosed in quotes. They will be printed to the monitor exactly as they appear. Note the first string:

```
'THE SUM OF ',
```

There is a space after the word "OF." If the space was omitted, "OF" could run into the value of NUM1 when the line was printed. The variables NUM1, NUM2, NUM3, NUM4, and SUM are not in quotes, because we do not want the variable name NUM1 to be printed. Rather, we want the value that is stored in NUM1 to be printed. Notice the comma in quotes between the variables. This places a comma between each number. The string ' AND ' was put before the last number so that the word "AND" would be printed before the last number was printed, with spaces before and after it.

Spending a little extra time on writing output statements like this can make a program much more pleasant to use. It is important to remember to always place character strings in quotation marks and to separate each part of the output line by a comma.

FORMATTING OUTPUT

To make output more readable, it is **formatted.** Formatting means controlling the way in which the output will be printed. A sample program that explains this idea would be one that read six integers and printed them in columns. The integers will be called A, B, C, D, E, and F. Each column is to be 10 spaces wide. The WRITELN statement would be written as below:

```
WRITELN (A:10, B:10, C:10, D:10, E:10, F:10);
```

Each variable name is followed by a colon and the number of spaces to be allowed for that variable. A WRITELN statement could also be used to set up a heading for these columns. It might look like this:

```
WRITELN ('A':10, 'B':10, 'C':10, 'D':10, 'E':10, 'F':10);
```

This program is given in Figure 4-7. Formatting can be helpful when we want results to be printed in columns or in a table.

Formatting Real Numbers

In Chapter 3 the answer to the FIND__MILES program was written in exponential notation. The WRITELN statement looked like this:

```
WRITELN ('THERE ARE ', MILES, ' MILES IN ', FEET, 'FEET.')
```

When 52800.0 was entered as the number of feet to be changed to miles, the result printed looked this way:

```
THERE ARE 1.00000E1 MILES IN 5.28000E4 FEET.
```

Sometimes it is more convenient to have the result printed in regular

```
PROGRAM COLUMNS;
(* THIS PROGRAM PRINTS SIX INTEGERS OUT IN COLUMNS EACH TEN SPACES
WIDE *)

VAR
   A, B, C, D, E, F : INTEGER;

BEGIN

   WRITELN ('TYPE IN THE 6 INTEGERS.');
   READLN (A, B, C, D, E, F);
   WRITELN ('A':10, 'B':10, 'C':10, 'D':10, 'E':10, 'F':10);
   WRITELN (A:10, B:10, C:10, D:10, E:10, F:10);

END.  (* COLUMNS *)


Running. . .
TYPE IN THE 6 INTEGERS.
11 689 4 121 8 1093
          A         B         C         D         E         F
          11        689       4         121       8         1093
```

Figure 4-7 **PROGRAM COLUMNS**

decimal form. To do this, the WRITELN statement needs to be formatted. It could be written like the statement below;

```
WRITELN ('THERE ARE ', MILES:8:2, ' MILES IN ', FEET:8:2, ' FEET. ');
```

Now the output will look like this:

```
THERE ARE 10.00 MILES IN 52800.0 FEET.
```

To format a real number, the variable name is written, followed by a
colon(:). The first number after the colon is the total length of the
number, including the decimal point and the plus or minus sign. Even
if there is no plus or minus sign, a space should be allowed for one.
What is the total length of this number?

$$-786.43$$

It is seven. Be sure to make the length large enough for any number
that might occur in your program. If the length is larger than the
actual number, blank spaces will be left before the number.

The length number is followed by a colon and then a second
number. This second number indicates how many digits are to be
printed after the decimal point. In the FIND__MILES example, we decided to have two decimal places printed. The computer will round
the result off to two decimal places.

59

Suppose the result of a program is 3748.69812. If a WRITE statement is written like this:

```
WRITE (NUM:8:2);
```

the computer will round off the result to two decimal places. The result would be printed as

```
3748.70
```

The table below provides further examples.

Unformatted Result	WRITE Statement	Result Printed As
1.48958E2	WRITE (NUM:7:2);	148.96
1.77424E1	WRITE (NUM:8:4);	17.7424
+2.68394E1	WRITE (NUM:6:2);	+26.84
-3.18367E1	WRITE (NUM:7:3);	-31.837

Figure 4-8 shows a program that prints the real number 68.2135 using different formats. Study each format.

1. **WRITELN (R);**
   Here, R is unformatted. The result is in exponential notation.

2. **WRITELN (R:8:4);**
   This command prints the number as it is entered. Notice that there is a blank space at the beginning of the line. If there is no sign, the computer leaves a blank where the sign would have been.

3. **WRITELN (R:6:2);**
   This command prints the number with only two decimal places. The computer has rounded the answer off to two decimal places.

4. **WRITELN (R:3:2);**
   The length in this format statement is only three, which is too short for this number. Notice the number as printed has a length of six: 68.21. This result illustrates a protective device that is built into the compiler. It printed the number with two decimal places even though the length used in the format statement was too short.

5. **WRITELN (R:11:2);**
   In this example, the length is longer than the number. Notice the spaces at the beginning of the line. This happened because the computer placed the number so that the last digit would be in the 11th position on the line. The number is **right-justified.** When a number is right-justified, any blanks will be on the left side of the number. The symbol "ƀ" will be used to represent a blank.

```
PROGRAM PRINTR;
(* THIS PROGRAM READS IN A REAL NUMBER AND PRINTS IT OUT USING
DIFFERENT FORMATS *)

VAR
   R : REAL;

BEGIN

   WRITELN ('TYPE IN A REAL NUMBER');
   READLN (R);
   WRITELN (R);
   WRITELN (R:8:4);
   WRITELN (R:6:2);
   WRITELN (R:3:2);
   WRITELN (R:11:2)

END.    (* PRINTR *)



Running. . .
TYPE IN A REAL NUMBER
68.2135
  6.82135E1
 68.2135
 68.21
 68.21
      68.21
```

Figure 4-8 PROGRAM PRINTR

The number 14.73 could be written:

Program Statement	Output
WRITELN (NUM:6:2);	b14.73
WRITELN (NUM:8:2);	bbb14.73
WRITELN (NUM:11:2);	bbbbbb14.73

Formatting Integers

Integers can also be formatted. Figure 4-9 shows how this is done. The variable name is followed by a colon and then the length of the number. Notice the statement

$$WRITELN \ (I);$$

Integer values are not printed in exponential notation when they are not formatted. This is done only for real numbers. The output for the statement WRITELN (I:2); shows that the computer will not let part

```
PROGRAM PRINTI;
(* THIS PROGRAM READS IN AN INTEGER VALUE AND PRINTS IT OUT USING
DIFFERENT FORMATS *)

VAR
    I : INTEGER;

BEGIN

    WRITELN ('TYPE IN A WHOLE NUMBER');
    READLN (I);
    WRITELN (I);
    WRITELN (I:3);
    WRITELN (I:2);
    WRITELN (I:8)

END.    (* PRINTI *)


Running. . .
TYPE IN A WHOLE NUMBER
105
105
105
105
      105
```

Figure 4-9 PROGRAM PRINTI

of the number be cut off. It still printed the whole number although
the length of the number is three. In the last WRITELN statement, the
number is right-justified. All of the blanks are on the left.

Formatting Strings

Values of data type STRING may be formatted. If they are not formatted, they are printed in a field of exactly the same length as the string.
For example, the size of the field for the statement

```
WRITELN ('THIS IS A STRING.');
```

would be 17 spaces.

In Figure 4-10, the string is unformatted in the first WRITELN
statement. In the second WRITELN statement it is formatted so that
the number of spaces is the same as the length of the string. In the
third example, the size of the field is larger than the string length. In
this case, the string will be right-justified. The string is padded with
blanks on the left. There will be five blank spaces on the left. The last
example demonstrates what happens if the user places a string in a
field that is smaller than the string. The string will always be **truncated** on the right. When a value is truncated, part of the value is cut

```
PROGRAM PRINTS;
(* THIS PROGRAM PRINTS OUT A STRING USING DIFFERENT FORMATS *)

BEGIN

   WRITELN ('THIS IS A STRING.');
   WRITELN ('THIS IS A STRING.':17);
   WRITELN ('THIS IS A STRING.':22);
   WRITELN ('THIS IS A STRING.':10)

END.   (* PRINTS *)



Running. . .
THIS IS A STRING.
THIS IS A STRING.
     THIS IS A STRING.
THIS IS A
```

Figure 4-10 **PROGRAM PRINTS**

off. This part is then lost. This string will be cut off at the point where the field is filled. This is different from what happens with whole and real numbers. The computer will not allow part of a number to be cut off (except for rounding off decimal places). In the case of strings, we can cut off part of a string by placing it in a field too small for the entire length. It is important to be careful when you are formatting strings.

PROGRAM CIRCLE

A practice program follows that combines a number of things learned in this chapter. In the program, the user will be prompted to enter the diameter of a circle. From this information, the program will calculate:

1. The radius of the circle (diameter/2)
2. The circumference of the circle ($\pi \times$ diameter)
3. The area of the circle ($\pi \times$ radius^2)

This information will be printed in columns that are each 15 spaces wide. Figure 4-11 shows this program. First the diameter is entered and assigned to the variable DIAMETER. From this information, the radius, circumference, and area are calculated. This information is printed by using one WRITELN statement. Each value will be rounded off to two decimal places. Each real number will be right-justified in a field containing 15 spaces. Notice that a header was also written for this information. The statement generating the header looks like this:

```
PROGRAM CIRCLE;
(* THIS PROGRAM READS THE DIAMETER OF A CIRCLE IN INCHES.  FROM THESE
DATA THE RADIUS, CIRCUMFERENCE, AND AREA OF THE CIRCLE ARE THEN COMPUTED. *)

CONST
   PI = 3.14;

VAR
   DIAMETER, RADIUS, CIRCUM, AREA : REAL;

BEGIN

   WRITELN ('WHAT IS THE DIAMETER OF THE CIRCLE IN INCHES?');
   READLN (DIAMETER);
   RADIUS := DIAMETER / 2;
   CIRCUM := DIAMETER * PI;
   AREA := PI * RADIUS * RADIUS;
   WRITELN ('DIAMETER':15, 'RADIUS':15, 'CIRCUMFERENCE':15, 'AREA':15);
   WRITELN (DIAMETER:15:2, RADIUS:15:2, CIRCUM:15:2, AREA:15:2)

END.   (* CIRCLE *)


Running. . .
WHAT IS THE DIAMETER OF THE CIRCLE IN INCHES?
12
        DIAMETER         RADIUS  CIRCUMFERENCE              AREA
          12.00           6.00          37.68            113.04
```

Figure 4-11 PROGRAM CIRCLE

```
WRITELN ('DIAMETER':15, 'RADIUS':15, 'CIRCUMFERENCE':15, 'AREA':15);
```

Each of these labels will be placed in fields 15 spaces wide so that
each label will print above the correct number. It is important to label
results so that the user can easily understand them.

◹LEARNING CHECK 4-2

1. How will this number be output to the terminal given the formats in a–e: −28.3765? Be sure to
   indicate any blank spaces by using a "b̸."
   a. NUM:5:1
   b. NUM:7:3
   c. NUM:2:2
   d. NUM:11:2
   e. NUM:6:2
2. Write a WRITELN statement that will print eight integers in columns six spaces wide.
3. Explain what right-justified means.

SUMMARY POINTS

- Chapter 4 examined ways a program can be written to allow the user to type data to the monitor. The program can use these data to obtain the needed answers. By using WRITE or WRITELN statements, prompts can be printed on the screen. The WRITE and WRITELN statement are also used to print results on the monitor. The prompt tells the user to enter data. Also explained in this chapter were the READ and READLN statements, which are used to assign values to variables.
- Formatting output was covered. Formatting can be used to line items up in columns and to round off real numbers to the number of decimal places desired. Formatting makes program output easier to read.

VOCABULARY LIST

Cursor A box that indicates where information entered to the monitor will appear on the screen.

Format To control the way in which output will be printed.

Prompt A sentence or symbol printed on the monitor that tells the user that data should be entered at this point.

Right-justified Used of information that is lined up on the right side of the field. Any blank spaces will be on the left side of the field.

Truncate To cut off a part of a value. For example, if 17.23 was truncated at the decimal point the result would be 17.

CHAPTER TEST

VOCABULARY

Match a term from the numbered column with the description from the lettered column that best fits the term.

1. Constant

2. Right-justified

3. Variable declaration statement

a. A sentence printed to the monitor that tells the user data should be entered at this point.

b. To control the way in which output will be printed.

c. The written description of a program and what it accomplishes.

4. Format

    d. A Pascal statement that declares a variable name and its data type.

5. Truncate

    e. A box that indicates where typed material will appear on the screen.

6. Prompt

    f. A name chosen by the programmer to represent a storage location. The value of the storage location may not change during program execution.

7. Exponential notation

    g. Information is lined up on the right side of the field. Any blank spaces will be on the left side of the field.

8. Program documentation

    h. Conventions that explain how the parts of a language should be put together.

9. Syntax rules

    i. The representation of a real number in base ten.

10. Cursor

    j. A Pascal statement that defines a program constant.

11. Constant declaration statement

    k. To cut off.

QUESTIONS

1. Why can't a READ statement be used to read a string?
2. The numbers below are in exponential notation. How would they be printed if they were formatted like this: NUM:7:2?
    a. 2.57834E2
    b. -3.162891E1
    c. a.97384E2
    d. $+1.24765$E1
    e. 4.00000E2
3. Tell where the cursor will be located after each of these statements is executed.
    ```
    a. WRITELN ('TYPE IN A LETTER.');
    b. WRITE ('WHAT IS THE SECOND NUMBER?');
    c. WRITE ('WHAT IS YOUR AGE?');
    d. WRITELN ('ENTER ACCOUNT NUMBER.');
    ```
4. How will these strings be printed? Be sure to indicate any blanks with a "b."
    ```
    a. WRITELN ('THERE IS A MONKEY IN THE TREE.':15);
    b. WRITELN ('LOOK DOWN HERE.':15);
    c. WRITELN ('WHAT IS YOUR MIDDLE NAME?':30);
    d. WRITELN ('ANSWER THE DOOR.');
    e. WRITELN ('MARY HAD A LITTLE LAMB.':10);
    ```
5. Look at this program segment:
    ```
    READ (X);
    READ (Y);
    READ (Z);
    ```

Tell what the values of X, Y, and Z will be in each part below if the data are entered as shown.

   a. 4 16 10
      108 7
      32
   b. 16
      81
      1182
   c. 109
      63 70
      2871 532

6. Look at this program segment:

```
READLN (A);
READLN (B);
READLN (C);
```

Tell what the values of A, B, and C will be in each part below if the data are entered as shown.

   a. 77 32 0
      188
      16 2871
   b. 44
      18 97
      100 82

7. Here's another program segment:

```
READLN (L, M, N);
```

What will the values of L, M, and N be, given the data below?

   a. 4 15 82
      91 0
      12
   b. 66
      17 18

8. What is formatting? Why do programmers format output?
9. What will these program statements print to the monitor? (Be sure to indicate blanks.)

```
WRITE ('THAT''S');
WRITE (' ALL');
WRITELN;
WRITELN;
WRITELN ('FOLKS!');
```

PROGRAMMING PROBLEMS

1. Look at the two programs in Figure 4-1. Can you write a program that places each of the words "HI THERE HOW ARE YOU DOING?" on a separate line?
2. Write a program that prints the following:
First line: your name.
Second line: your age.
Third line: blank.
Fourth line: your address.

67

3. Write a program that reads five real numbers. Print each number in a field of length seven so that it has two decimal places.

4. Read four integers. Print them so they are in columns each ten spaces wide. Make a header for the columns. Here is a sample of how the output might look:

```
FIRST           SECOND          THIRD           FOURTH

  5               16              101              10
```

Leave a blank line between the header and the integers.

CHAPTER 5

Simple Pascal Statements

OUTLINE

VOCABULARY LIST

CHAPTER TEST
   Vocabulary • Questions

PROGRAMMING PROBLEMS

LEARNING OBJECTIVES

After studying this chapter, you should be able to:

1. Define and explain the purpose of an assignment statement.
2. Write valid Pascal assignment statements.
3. Define the terms:
   arithmetic operators
   relational operators
   operand
   expression
   control statement
4. Name the six arithmetic operators and explain what function each performs.
5. Write statements using the unary plus and minus signs.
6. Write assignment statements using the six arithmetic operators.
7. List the order of operations in Pascal.
8. Write statements using parentheses to control the order in which operations will be performed.
9. Write program segments using the IF/THEN and IF/THEN/ELSE control statements.
10. Explain the meaning of each of the relational operators.
11. Explain the purpose of a control statement.

INTRODUCTION

In Chapter 3, the different data types were explained. In this chapter, you will learn how to take a variable of a specific data type and give it a value. We will also discuss how to do arithmetic in Pascal. In the conclusion of the chapter, two Pascal statements that will be helpful in writing programs will be explained. These statements allow the programmer to determine whether or not a certain part of a program will be executed.

ASSIGNMENT STATEMENTS

Computer programs solve problems for us. In the program converting feet to miles in Chapter 3, we needed a way to create a new vari-

able, called MILES, to hold the result of the computation
FEET / FEET__MILE. This was done by using an **assignment statement.** The assignment statement in the FIND__MILES program is:

```
MILES := FEET / FEET_MILE;
```

The result of the computation FEET / FEET__MILE is assigned to the
variable MILE. This statement should be read "MILES is assigned the
value of FEET divided by FEET__MILE." The symbol := should not be
thought of as an equals sign. As many assignment statements as necessary may be used in a program. Assignment statements are used often in computer programs. The general syntax of an assignment statement, as also shown in Figure 5-1, is:

variable := expression;

An **expression** can be made up of a variable, constant, or any valid
combination of variables, constants, or operators. An **operator** is a
symbol that stands for a process. In this case, the symbol := stands
for the process of placing the result of the expression on the right
side of the statement into the variable on the left side of the statement.

If you want to find the average of three whole numbers, this calculation can be performed in two steps. First, the sum of the three
numbers must be found. This sum will be divided by three (the number of items being averaged). The first assignment statement could be
written:

```
SUM := A + B + C;
```

The sum of A + B + C is now stored in the variable SUM. The second
assignment statement could look like this:

```
AVE := SUM / 3;
```

Figure 5-2 is the data table for this program. What type of number will
AVE be? It could be a whole number, but more than likely it will be a
real number. AVE will be declared to be of data type REAL. Figure
5-3 gives the complete program for this problem.

An assignment statement does not always include an arithmetic
operation. It can be used to copy a value from one variable to another:

```
TEMP := SUM;
```

Figure 5-1 SYNTAX FOR ASSIGNMENT STATEMENT

variable := expression;

71

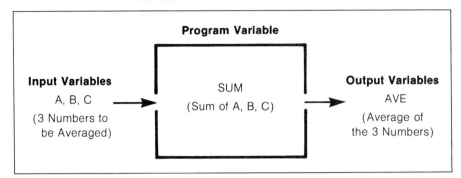

Figure 5-2 DATA TABLE FOR PROGRAM AVERAGE

```
PROGRAM AVERAGE;
(* FINDS THE AVERAGE OF 3 NUMBERS *)

VAR
    SUM, A, B, C : INTEGER;
    AVE          : REAL;

BEGIN

    WRITE ('WHAT ARE THE 3 NUMBERS? ');
    READLN (A, B, C);
    SUM := (A + B + C);
    AVE := SUM / 3;
    WRITELN ('THE AVERAGE IS ', AVE:7:2)

END.    (* AVERAGE *)

Running. . .
WHAT ARE THE 3 NUMBERS? 4 12 18
THE AVERAGE IS    11.33
```

Figure 5-3 PROGRAM AVERAGE

After this statement is executed, the value of TEMP is the same as the value of SUM. The value of SUM remains the same. This type of statement can often be useful.

An assignment statement can be used to find the opposite of a number:

$$A := -A;$$

Suppose the beginning value of A is -105. The value of $-A$ will then be 105. This value, 105, will then be stored in A. This statement is the same as multiplying A by -1. Here's another assignment statement:

```
SUM := SUM + 1;
```

This increases the value of SUM by 1. Such a statement is useful for counting how many there are of a certain item.

It is not necessary to have a variable name on the right side of an assignment statement. If COUNT is declared to be of data type INTEGER, this statement would be valid:

```
COUNT := 10;
```

Would the statement below be a valid assignment statement?

```
COUNT := 1.5;
```

No, because 1.5 is a real number and COUNT has been declared to be of data type INTEGER. For the same reason this statement is invalid:

```
COUNT := COUNT + 2.75;
```

What if COUNT had been declared to be of data type REAL? Could there be an assignment statement like the one below?

```
COUNT := 14;
```

Yes, because the computer can convert the whole number into a real number.

Assignment statements can also be used with STRING and CHAR data types. Here's a program segment:

```
PROGRAM ASSIGN;

VAR
    STAR : CHAR;
    NAME, NEWNAME : STRING;

BEGIN

    STAR := '*';
    NAME := 'JONATHAN DAVID';
```

The value of STAR is now *. The variable NAME now contains the value JONATHAN DAVID. Remember that in CHAR and STRING data types the value assigned to the variable must be in single quotation marks. Since the variables NAME and NEWNAME are both of the same data type (STRING), an assignment statement could be written like this:

```
NEWNAME := NAME;
```

73

NAME is not enclosed in quotation marks because it is a variable name and not a character string. Now both NAME and NEWNAME contain the character string JONATHAN DAVID. The next statement would be invalid:

$$STAR\ :=\ NEWNAME;$$

The data type CHAR can contain only one character.

The data type BOOLEAN can be assigned only one of two values: true or false. If ANSWER is declared to be of type BOOLEAN the assignment statement could look like this:

$$ANSWER\ :=\ TRUE;$$

or like this:

$$ANSWER\ :=\ FALSE;$$

In all these examples of assignment statements, the computer finds the value of the expression on the right side of the assignment statement. This result is then assigned to the variable on the left side of the assignment statement.

LEARNING CHECK 5-1

1. Explain why the computer can convert a whole number to a real number. Why can't a real number be converted to a whole number?
2. All of the variables below have been declared to be of data type REAL. Which of these assignment statements are valid?
   a. PERCENT := 0.75;
   b. COST = -14.85;
   c. NUM := 51;
   d. FIRST := LAST;
   e. HEIGHT := HEIGHT - 4.51;
   f. SCORE + 1 := SCORE;
   g. 451 := HEIGHT * WIDTH;
   h. SIZE := LENGTH / 12;
3. Given the following declaration statement, which of the assignment statements below are valid?

```
VAR
    SCORE, NUM, TOTAL : INTEGER;
```
   a. SCORE := 1.5;
   b. TOTAL := SCORE * NUM;
   c. NUM := NUM + 1;
   d. SCORE := NUM / TOTAL;
   e. NUM * 2 := TOTAL;
   f. TOTAL := SCORE - NUM;

ARITHMETIC OPERATORS

There are six **arithmetic operators** in Pascal. An arithmetic operator is a symbol that stands for a particular arithmetic process, such as addition or subtraction. The first four arithmetic operators are familiar to us:

$$+ \quad \text{add}$$
$$- \quad \text{subtract}$$
$$* \quad \text{multiply}$$
$$/ \quad \text{divide}$$

The symbols, and their meanings, are shown in Figure 5-4. Each one of these will be examined individually.

Addition

In addition, the value of the first **operand** is added to the value of the second operand. An operand is a value upon which an arithmetic operation is performed. In this case, we are adding the two operands together. In this example

$$14 + 12$$

the operands are 14 and 12. The arithmetic operator is the plus sign. When whole numbers are added together, the result will be a whole number:

```
A := 1 + 4;
```

Although the answer will always be a whole number, variable A may be declared to be of data type INTEGER or of data type REAL. The

Figure 5-4 ARITHMETIC OPERATORS

Aritmetic Operator	Meaning	Example
+	add	A + B
−	subtract	A − B
*	multiply	A * B
/	divide	A / B

75

computer will convert the whole number to a real number. Figure 5-5 lists two programs that illustrate addition. In both programs, X and Y are whole numbers that are added together. In FIND__TOT1 the result, SUM, is a whole number. In FIND__TOT2 the result is a real number. The computer has taken the whole number 21 and converted it to the real number 21.00.

When two real numbers are added together, the result must always be of data type REAL. If the result of adding two real numbers together was assigned to an INTEGER variable, it would cause an error when the program was run. The computer cannot change a real number into a whole number. Here are some examples of addition with variables of data type REAL:

Figure 5-5 TWO ADDITION PROGRAMS

```
PROGRAM FIND_TOT1;
(* ADD TWO INTEGERS TOGETHER AND PLACE THE RESULT IN AN INTEGER VARIABLE *)

VAR
    X, Y, SUM : INTEGER;

BEGIN

    WRITE ('TYPE IN THE TWO NUMBERS TO BE ADDED TOGETHER: ');
    READLN (X, Y);
    SUM := X + Y;
    WRITELN ('THE SUM IS ', SUM)

END.    (* FIND_TOT1 *)


Running. . .
TYPE IN THE TWO NUMBERS TO BE ADDED TOGETHER: 14 7
THE SUM IS 21




PROGRAM FIND_TOT2;
(* ADD TWO INTEGERS TOGETHER AND PLACE THE RESULT IN A REAL VARIABLE *)

VAR
    X, Y : INTEGER;
    SUM  : REAL;

BEGIN

    WRITE ('TYPE IN THE TWO NUMBERS TO BE ADDED TOGETHER: ');
    READLN (X, Y);
    SUM := X + Y;
    WRITELN ('THE SUM IS ', SUM:7:2)

END.    (* FIND_TOT2 *)

Running. . .
TYPE IN THE TWO NUMBERS TO BE ADDED TOGETHER: 14 7
THE SUM IS    21.00
```

```
        POINT := 100.00 + TEST1;

        DIAMETER := 35.75 + 0.68;

        DISTANCE1 := DISTANCE1 + 5.0;
```

A whole number and a real number may be added together. The result should always be placed in a real variable.

Subtraction

In subtraction, the value of the second operand is subtracted from the value of the first. The rules concerning the use of INTEGER and REAL data types are the same as for addition. Look at these examples:

Statement	Data Type
COUNT := COUNT - 1;	INTEGER
YARDS := 108 - 16;	INTEGER
COST := PRICE - 1.85;	REAL
BILL := 486.85 - 115.23;	REAL

Multiplication

The arithmetic operator for multiplication is the asterisk (*). It is the only sign that may be used for multiplication. In multiplication, the value of the first operand is multiplied by the value of the second. The result of two whole numbers being multiplied together will always be a whole number. As in subtraction and addition, this result may be placed in a variable of either data type INTEGER or REAL. The result of two real numbers being multiplied together will always be of data type REAL. Some examples:

Statement	Data Type
SQUARE := 4 * 4;	INTEGER
SCORE := TD * 6;	INTEGER
AREA := HEIGHT * 12.34;	REAL

Division

Division is not as simple as the arithmetic operations we have looked at so far. In Pascal, the arithmetic operator for division is the slash sign (/). The operand is divided by the second.

The result of a whole number being divided by another whole number must always be assigned to a REAL variable. This is because the result will usually be a real number. Two real numbers may be divided by each other. Again, the result will be a real number. In these examples all of the variables on the left side of the assignment statement have been declared to be of data type REAL:

```
PERCENT := SUM / 80.5;
FRACTION := 10 / 3;
HEIGHT := FEET / 36;
```

As in arithmetic, division by zero is not allowed. The statement below is not valid:

```
NUM := SCORE / 0;
```

DIV and MOD

The two arithmetic operators DIV and MOD can be used with whole numbers only. The result will always be a whole number. The DIV operation truncates the result of a division problem. This means it cuts the number off. In this case, it cuts the number off at the decimal point. Below are some examples.

$$
\begin{array}{r}
4 \\
6\overline{)27} \\
24 \\
\hline
3
\end{array}
$$

In the statement below, A is of data type INTEGER:

```
A := 27 DIV 6;
```

After this statement is executed, the value of A will be four. There is never a decimal point in the result of a DIV operation. Here's another example:

```
X := 105 DIV 12;
```

The division problem looks like this:

$$
\begin{array}{r}
8 \\
12\overline{)105} \\
96 \\
\hline
9
\end{array}
$$

The value of X will be eight.
Here is the same problem using the MOD operator:

$$REM \; := \; 105 \; MOD \; 12;$$

The value of REM is nine. MOD assigns the value of the remainder to REM. The variable REM must be declared to be data type INTEGER. Look at the problems below and see if you agree with the answers given.

Problem	Answer
8 DIV 3	2
10 MOD 3	1
140 DIV 12	11
140 MOD 12	8
160 DIV 8	20
160 MOD 8	0

As in regular division, the divisor in a DIV or MOD operation may not be equal to zero. Both of these statements are invalid:

$$A \; DIV \; 0$$
$$B \; MOD \; 0$$

The MOD function may not be used with data type LONG INTEGER.

Unary Plus and Minus

The **unary plus** and **minus** signs are used alone with a number. The plus sign leaves the number unchanged whereas the minus sign results in the opposite number. For example:

$$-47 \quad +83 \quad -Y \quad +Z \quad -0.385$$

In arithmetic expressions, two arithmetic operators may not be next to each other. This would be an invalid expression:

$$A \; := \; X \; + \; -Y \; + \; Z;$$

Instead, the expression must be written this way:

$$A \; := \; X \; + \; (-Y) \; + \; Z;$$

The parentheses separate the $-Y$ from the addition sign. Look at Figure 5-6 for some examples.

$$LARGE \; := \; -14 \; / \; (+A)$$

$$MIDDLE \; := \; Z \; + \; 16 \; * \; (-104)$$

$$A \; := \; B \; DIV \; (-C)$$

LARGE := −14 / (+A)

MIDDLE := Z + 16 * (−104)

A := B DIV (−C)

Figure 5-6 CORRECT USE OF UNARY PLUS AND MINUS SIGNS

☟LEARNING CHECK 5-2

1. Explain why the result of dividing two whole numbers must be assigned to a variable of data type REAL.
2. Write an assignment statement that will square B and place the result in variable X.
3. Which of these DIV and MOD expressions are valid?
   a. 12.5 DIV 6
   b. 10 DIV 0
   c. 12 MOD 8
   d. 205 MOD 0.5
4. Add parentheses to these expressions so that they are valid Pascal expressions:
   a. −148 / −14
   b. 68 * +ZERO
   c. 18 + −16 + +28
   d. +A / −B + C * −D
5. Assume X has been declared as data type INTEGER. Tell what the value of X will be in each case:
   a. X := 100 MOD 3;
   b. X := 92 DIV 8;
   c. X := 14 MOD 13;
   d. X := X MOD 1;

Answers: 1. The result of dividing two numbers will usually be a real number. Therefore, the result would be assigned to a real variable. 2. X := B * B; 3. a. invalid (only integer operands allowed), b. invalid (division by zero not allowed), c. valid, d. invalid (only integer operands allowed), 4. a. (−148) / (−14) (first set of parentheses is optional), b. 68 * (+ZERO), c. 18 + (−16) + (+28), d. (+A) / (−B) + C * (−D) (first set of parentheses is optional) 5. a. 1, b. 11, c. 1, d. 0

ORDER OF OPERATIONS

In Pascal, arithmetic expressions can be written that contain many operations. Here is an example:

$$4 * 18 + 20 / 5 - 3$$

In this expression several steps must be executed to find the answer. Which step should be performed first? To answer this question it is necessary to know the **order of operations.** This is a set of rules that determine the order in which the arithmetic will be done. The order of operations says that multiplication and division are done before addition and subtraction. Any operations that are on the same level are done from left to right. Figure 5-7 lists these rules. In the expression above, 4 * 18 and 20 / 5 are both at the same level. First, 4 is multiplied by 18 since we are going from left to right. Then 20 will be divided by 5. After all of the multiplication and division steps are complete, then the addition and subtraction are performed. We will work from left to right since addition and subtraction are both on the same level. The steps for the expression above will be:

1. 4 * 18 = 72
2. 20 / 5 = 4
3. 72 + 4 = 76
4. 76 − 3 = 73

The value of this expression is 73.

In the example above, what if we needed to subtract three from five before completing the rest of the problem? Parentheses can be used to control the order in which arithmetic operations are performed. Parentheses are often used for the same purpose in algebra. The expression above could be written:

$$4 * 18 + 20 / (5 - 3)$$

In this case the steps will be:

1. 5 − 3 = 2
2. 4 * 18 = 72
3. 20 / 2 = 10
4. 72 + 10 = 82

The value of the expression is now 82. Any expressions in parentheses are always evaluated first. If two expressions are nested (one inside the other), the innermost one will be evaluated first.

$$1500 / (10 * (14 - 4))$$

The steps in evaluating this expression will be:

1. 14 − 4 = 10

Figure 5-7 ORDER OF OPERATIONS

> 1. Evaluate anything in parentheses.
> 2. *, /, DIV, and MOD are evaluated before + and −.
> 3. Arithmetic operators at the same level (such as * and DIV) are evaluated left to right.

2. 10 * 10 = 100

3. 1500 / 100 = 15

The result is 15. Below is the same problem with no parentheses:

$$1500 / 10 * 14 - 4$$

The steps would now be:

1. 1500 / 10 = 150

2. 150 * 14 = 2100

3. 2100 − 4 = 2096

Changing the order of the steps gives a very different answer. If you have any doubts about how an expression you have written will be evaluated, always use parentheses. This way you will know exactly in what order the arithmetic will be done. Adding parentheses when they are not necessary cannot hurt anything. Parentheses can also make a program easier to understand.

ALGEBRAIC EQUATIONS

Algebraic equations often look like this:

$$\frac{A \times B}{N - 1} \times \frac{X + Y^2}{N + 1}$$

How would this be written in Pascal? Again, parentheses will be needed to control the order in which the arithmetic is performed. The left side would be written:

$$A * B / (N - 1)$$

It is not necessary to put A * B in parentheses, but it might help keep things clear. The right side would look like this:

$$(X + Y * Y) / (N + 1)$$

Notice that Y is multiplied by itself to square it. Next the two sides are multiplied together:

$$(A * B / (N - 1)) * ((X + Y * Y) / (N + 1))$$

There are parentheses around each entire term. All of the operations in each term must be performed before the two sides are multiplied together. Be careful when you are using parentheses inside other sets of parentheses. It is very easy to leave one off or put it in the wrong place. This can cause an error when your program is run.

✐ LEARNING CHECK 5-3

1. Use this program segment to write the following Pascal statements and answer the questions below.

```
PROGRAM COMPUTE;

VAR
      NUM1, NUM2, A, B, C : REAL;

BEGIN

      A := 15.0;
      B := 3.0;
      C := 27.0;
```

   a. Subtract A from B. Then multiply the result by 2. Assign this value to the variable NUM1. What will the value of NUM1 be?
   b. Divide C by B. Then divide the result by 2. Assign the result to NUM2. What will the value of NUM2 be?
   c. Add A and C together. Divide this result by B. Assign the result to A. What will the value of A be?
   d. Subtract B from C. Square the result. Then assign the result to NUM1. Figure out what the value of NUM1 will be.

2. Evaluate the following expressions and give the result:
   a. 4 − 6 / 2
   b. 6.5 + 8.5 − 4.3
   c. 18 + (− 16) / 4
   d. 280 / 7 * 6
   e. 73.5 / 2.5 * 16.75
   f. 73.5 / (2.5 * 16.75)
   g. 6 − 15 DIV 4
   h. 85 MOD 3 − 18
   i. 85 MOD (3 − 18)
   j. (16 + 32) / 2
   k. 38 * 20 − 8

Answers:

1. a. NUM1 := (B − A) * 2; NUM1 = −24.0 b. NUM2 := (C / B) / 2; NUM2 = 4.5; C. A:= (A + C) / B A = 14.0, d. (C − B); NUM1 = 576.0 2. a. 1.0, b. 10.7, c. 14.0, d. 240.0, e. 492.45, f. 1.76 (rounded to two decimal places), g. 3, h. − 17, i. 10 (Note that although the quotient is negative, the remainder will be positive because the dividend is positive), j. 24.0, k. 752

IF/THEN STATEMENTS

In real life, people are constantly making decisions. Many decisions are based on a particular situation. Past experiences are often taken into account. You start making decisions when you awaken in the morning. Is there time for a shower and breakfast? If it's raining outside, what coat should you wear? If you do not feel well, should you stay in bed or not?

Computer programs also need to be able to handle decisions. Programs do this by evaluating conditions. For example, is variable A larger than zero? If so, something may be done to A that would not be done if A was less than or equal to zero. Such decisions can be coded by using an IF/THEN statement. The IF/THEN statement tests to see if a given condition is true. It looks like this:

IF condition THEN
   statement;

If the condition is true, the next part of the statement is executed. If the condition is false, the program goes on to the following statement. The IF/THEN statement is all one Pascal statement. A semicolon appears only at the end of the statement. There is no semicolon after THEN. We could write the statement all on one line:

IF condition THEN statement;

Putting it on two lines and indenting the second line makes the program easier to read (Figure 5-8).

In order to use the IF/THEN statement, we need a way of comparing two operands. This is done by using **relational operators.** Relational operators are operators that compare one operand with another. The relational operators in Pascal are listed in Figure 5-9. These same operators are used in mathematics, although some of the symbols are slightly different. Below is an example of an IF/THEN statement:

```
IF  Z  =  Y  THEN
      Z  :=  Z  +  10;
```

This is read "If Z is equal to Y then assign the value of Z plus 10 to Z." In this example, Z will be increased by 10 only if Z is equal to Y.

Figure 5-8 SYNTAX FOR IF/THEN STATEMENT

IF condition THEN
   statement;

Operator	Meaning	Example
=	equals	X = Y
<>	not equal to	X <> Y
>	greater than	X > Y
>=	greater than or equal to	X >= Y
<	less than	X < Y
<=	less than or equal to	X <= Y

Figure 5-9 RELATIONAL OPERATORS

This statement could be changed to the opposite:

```
IF  Z  <>  Y  THEN
    Z  :=  Z  +  10;
```

In this case, the value of Z will be increased by ten only if it is *not* equal to Y. If Z is equal to Y, the program will simply skip to the next statement.

Relational operators may also be used with character and string data. Look at the expressions below and how they evaluate.

Expression	Evaluates As
'A' < 'D'	true
'JIMINY' > 'JIMN'	false
'PARTRIDGE' = 'PARTRIDGE'	true
'P' <> 'Q'	true

Now we will write a program using an IF/THEN statement. The local record store is having a sale. All of the albums are marked down to $5. If you buy six or more albums, ten percent is deducted from the total price. The flowchart for this program is illustrated in Figure 5-10. First, the number of albums to be bought needs to be read. This number will be multiplied by the price per album, $5. Now we need to determine whether the number of albums being bought is greater than or equal to six. If it is, the price charged will be only 90 percent of the total (100% − 10% = 90%). For this segment, the IF/THEN statement could look like this:

```
IF  ALBUMS  >=  6  THEN
    COST  :=  COST  *  0.90;
```

It could also be written like this:

```
IF  ALBUMS  >  5  THEN
    COST  :=  COST  *  0.90;
```

Either way, 10 percent is taken off of the total price if six or more albums are being bought. Figure 5-11 shows the complete program.

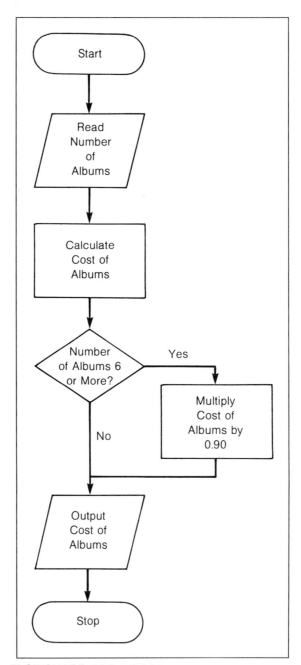

Figure 5-10 FLOWCHART FOR PRICE1

IF/THEN/ELSE STATEMENTS

The IF/THEN statement is called a single-alternative IF statement. There is only one choice. The condition is either true or false, and if it is false, nothing is done. Suppose the discount on the records is a little different. Suppose the prices were like this:

```
PROGRAM PRICE1;
(* FIND THE TOTAL COST OF THE RECORD ALBUMS.  THE ALBUMS ARE $5.00 EACH.
IF 6 OR MORE ARE BOUGHT, THERE IS A 10% DISCOUNT *)

VAR
    ALBUMS : INTEGER;
    COST   : REAL;

BEGIN

    WRITE ('HOW MANY ALBUMS ARE BEING BOUGHT? ');
    READLN (ALBUMS);
    COST := ALBUMS * 5.00;

    IF ALBUMS >= 6 THEN
       COST := COST * 0.90;

    WRITELN ('THE COST OF THE ALBUMS IS $', COST:6:2)

END.   (* PRICE1 *)


Running. . .
HOW MANY ALBUMS ARE BEING BOUGHT? 7
THE COST OF THE ALBUMS IS $ 31.50
```

Figure 5-11 PROGRAM PRICE1

one to five albums: $5.00 each
six or more albums: $4.85 each

Look at the flowchart for this problem in Figure 5-12. The easiest way to write this program would be to use a double-alternative IF statement (Figure 5-13).

IF condition THEN
   statement
ELSE
   statement;

In this case, if the first condition is true, the statement following the condition is executed. If it is not true, the statement following the ELSE is executed. One or the other of the statements will always be excuted. Notice that there is a semicolon only at the very end of the statement. The IF/THEN/ELSE statement is a single Pascal statement. For the problem computing the cost of the albums the IF/THEN/ELSE statement could look like this:

```
IF ALBUMS <= 5 THEN
   COST := ALBUMS * 5.00
```

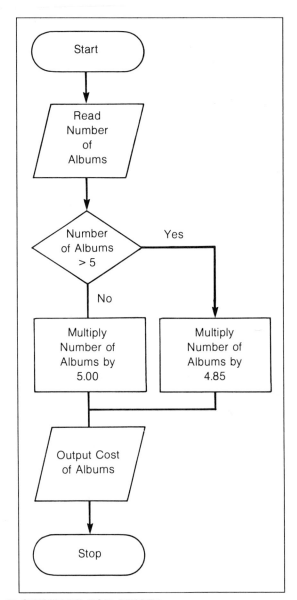

Figure 5-12 FLOWCHART FOR PRICE2

```
ELSE
    COST := ALBUMS * 4.85;
```

We could change this around and obtain the same results:

```
IF ALBUMS > 5 THEN
    COST := ALBUMS * 4.85
ELSE
    COST := ALBUMS * 5.00;
```

Figure 5-14 is the complete program for this problem.

The IF/THEN and IF/THEN/ELSE statements are called **control**

```
IF condition THEN
    statement
ELSE
    statement;
```

Figure 5-13 SYNTAX FOR IF/THEN/ELSE STATEMENT

statements. A control statement allows the programmer to determine whether or not a statement (or group of statements) will be executed and how many times they will be executed. In the IF/THEN statement, a condition is evaluated. If the condition is true, the rest of the statement is executed. Otherwise the program skips to the following statement. There are other control statements in Pascal that will be introduced later in this book. Listed below in Figure 5-14 is a program segment.

How is an expression containing both arithmetic operators (+, −, *, /, DIV, and MOD) and relational operators evaluated? For example, how would the expression below be evaluated?

$$IF \ A \ * \ B \ = \ C \ THEN$$

The arithmetic operations are always performed before the relational operations. First, the value of A * B is found and then this value is compared to C. Listed below is a program segment:

Figure 5-14 PROGRAM PRICE2

```
PROGRAM PRICE2;
(* FIND THE TOTAL COST OF THE RECORD ALBUMS.  IF 1-5 ALBUMS ARE BOUGHT,
THE PRICE IS $5.00 EACH.  IF 6 OR MORE ALBUMS ARE BOUGHT, THEY ARE
$4.85 EACH  *)

VAR
    ALBUMS : INTEGER;
    COST   : REAL;

BEGIN

    WRITE ('HOW MANY ALBUMS ARE BEING BOUGHT? ');
    READLN (ALBUMS);

    IF ALBUMS > 5 THEN
        COST := ALBUMS * 4.85
    ELSE
        COST := ALBUMS * 5.00;

    WRITELN ('THE COST OF THE ALBUMS IS $', COST:6:2)

END.   (* PRICE2 *)


Running. . .

HOW MANY ALBUMS ARE BEING BOUGHT? 6
THE COST OF THE ALBUMS IS $ 29.10
```

```
VAR
    A, B, C, LARGEST, SMALLEST : INTEGER;

BEGIN

    A := 4;
    B := 10;
    C := 6;
```

Look at these expressions below to see if you agree with the results.

Expression	*Evaluates As*
IF A > B THEN	false (4 is not greater than 10)
IF A + C = B THEN	true (4 + 6 = 10)
IF C <= B * 2 THEN	true (6 is less than or equal to 10 * 2)
IF 10 < B THEN	false (10 is not less than 10)

LEARNING CHECK 5-4

1. The program shown in Figure 5-2 has two assignment statements:

```
SUM := A + B + C;
AVE := SUM / 3;
```

Write these two statements as one, using parentheses.

2. Write the following mathematical expressions in Pascal.

a. $X = \dfrac{Y^2}{2}$

b. $A = Y + Z \times 3$

c. $B = \dfrac{X + 10}{4 \times 8} + 2$

d. $Z = 12 + (-A) - \dfrac{A + B}{X}$

3. Given the following program segment, tell whether the expressions below it will evaluate as true or false.

```
PROGRAM ONE;

VAR
    I, J, K : INTEGER;
    ANSWER, MORE : BOOLEAN;
    ADDRESS : STRING;

BEGIN

    I := 10;
```

```
J := 12;
K := 0;
ANSWER := TRUE;
MORE := FALSE;
ADDRESS := '101 S. MAIN';
```

a. I >= J
b. ANSWER <> MORE
c. K < I
d. ADDRESS = '101 S. MAIN'
e. J = 12
f. MORE = TRUE
g. J = K + 1

Answers:

1. SAVE := (A + B + C) / 3; 2. a. X := Y * Y / 2; b. A := Y + Z * 3; c. B := (X + 10) / (4 * 8) + 2; d. Z := 12 + (−A) − (A + B) / X; 3. a. false, b. true, c. true, d. true, e. true, f. false, g. false

---

SUMMARY POINTS

- A number of valuable features of Pascal have been reviewed in this chapter. The assignment statement is used to assign a value to a variable. The value of an arithmetic expression is found by following a certain order of operations, which determines in what order arithmetic operations will be performed. The order in which operations are performed can be controlled by using parentheses.
- The IF/THEN and IF/THEN/ELSE statements are control statements that test a condition. With IF/THEN statements, if the condition tested is true, the next part of the statement is executed. If it is not true, this step is skipped. IF/THEN/ELSE statements provide one option if the condition is true, another if it is false. In this way, the programmer can control whether or not a certain step will be executed. Control statements will be important in virtually every Pascal program.

VOCABULARY LIST

Arithmetic operator A symbol that stands for an arithmetic process, such as addition or subtraction.

Assignment statement A statement that allows a value to be stored in a variable.

Control statement A statement that allows the programmer to determine whether or not a statement (or a group of statements) will be executed and how many times they will be executed.

Expression Any valid combination of variable(s), constant(s), operator(s), or parentheses.

Operand A value upon which an arithmetic operation is performed.

Operator A symbol that stands for a process.

Order of operations The sequence in which expressions are evaluated.

Relational operators Operators that compare one operand with another.

Unary minus sign A symbol (−) used alone with a number which gives the opposite of the number.

Unary plus sign A symbol (+) used alone with a number which leaves the number unchanged.

CHAPTER TEST

VOCABULARY

Match a term from the numbered column with the description from the lettered column that best fits the term.

1. Unary minus sign

2. Operator

3. Relational operators

4. Unary plus sign

5. Operand

6. Arithmetic operator

7. Assignment statement

8. Expression

a. A statement that allows a value to be stored in a variable.

b. Operators that compare one operand with another.

c. A symbol that stands for a process.

d. A symbol used alone with a number which gives the opposite of the number.

e. A variable, constant, or any valid combination of variables, constants, or operators.

f. A value upon which an operation is performed.

g. A symbol used alone with a number which leaves the number unchanged.

h. A symbol that stands for an arithmetic process, such as addition or subtraction.

QUESTIONS

1. Explain in your own words what an assignment statement does.
2. Evaluate each expression listed below. What data type will the result be?
   a. 10 / 4
   b. 14 + 18 + 32
   c. 5 DIV 2
   d. 5 MOD 2
   e. 16.5 * 18.3
   f. 414 − 318
   g. 162 DIV 11
   h. 162 MOD 11
   i. 162 / 11
3. List each of the relational operators and tell what each one does.

4. What is the difference between an IF/THEN statement and an IF/THEN/ELSE statement? Give appropriate examples of each.

PROGRAMMING PROBLEMS

1. Write a program that finds the result of the following expression.

$$\frac{16.8 - 8.0}{3.3} + \frac{7.0 + 2}{12.5 \times 2}$$

2. Sally wants to buy a new outfit. The items she would like to buy are:

> SWEATER—$35.00
> SKIRT—$28.50
> BLOUSE—$22.95
> BRACELET—$12.25

The clothing store is having a sale next Tuesday. Everything will be 15 percent off, except for jewelry. Write a program to tell Sally how much the items listed above would cost now. Also figure out how much the items would cost if Sally waited until they were on sale. Both amounts should be printed at the end of the program.

3. Write a program that will determine the cost of a movie ticket. The customer's age is typed to the keyboard. If the age is 12 or less, the cost of the ticket is $2. If the customer's age is 13 or more, the cost is $3.50. Write the cost of the ticket to the monitor with appropriate labeling.

4. WJCR 1414 Radio is giving $140 to the 14th person to call in. Billie needs the money for her new ten-speed bike. She has figured that each call takes 6.4 seconds to be answered after it begins ringing at the radio station. It then takes 12.8 seconds for the radio stations to answer the phone and tally the call. How many seconds should she wait before calling the radio station? It will take her 5.8 seconds to dial the call.

5. Write a program segment that will print an integer only if it is even. (Hint: think about how the MOD operator could be used to do this.)

CHAPTER 6

Statements: Control and Compound

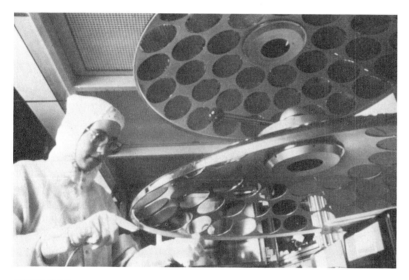

OUTLINE

LEARNING OBJECTIVES

After studying this chapter, you should be able to:

1. Define a compound statement.
2. Write compound IF/THEN/ELSE statements.
3. Explain how nested IF/THEN/ELSE statements work.
4. Write correctly nested IF/THEN/ELSE statements.
4. Write ELSE IF control statements.
6. Write CASE statements.
7. Determine which of the control statements studied up to this point is the most appropriate for a given programming problem.

INTRODUCTION

Control statements are an important part of computer programs. Control statements allow the programmer to determine two things:

1. Whether or not a particular section of a program will be executed.
2. How many times a section of a program will be executed.

The last part of Chapter 5 introduced IF/THEN and IF/THEN/ELSE statements. In this chapter, more control statements will be discussed. These new statements will also determine whether or not a part of a program will be executed. Each of these types of control statements can be useful when writing a program.

COMPOUND STATEMENTS

So far the programs in this book have contained simple Pascal statements. What if it was necessary to write an IF/THEN statement that did more than one thing? Below is an IF/THEN statement that checks to see if a whole number is positive. If the number is positive, it will be squared. The IF/THEN statement looks like this:

```
IF X >= 0 THEN
    X := X * X;
```

How could we instruct the computer to print this result only if X is a positive number?

We could achieve the desired result by using two separate IF/THEN statements:

```
IF  X  >=  0  THEN
    X  :=  X  *  X;
IF  X  >=  0  THEN
      WRITELN  (X);
```

But a simpler way would be to write a **compound statement.** In this case, the compound statement would look like this:

```
IF  X  >=  0  THEN
    BEGIN
        X  :=  X  *  X;
        WRITELN  (X)
    END;
```

The general syntax for the compound IF/THEN statement is shown in Figure 6-1.

The compound IF/THEN statement for the problem squaring only positive numbers is illustrated in Figure 6-2. Notice that the final value of X is printed only if X is a positive number. If X is negative, nothing is done. A compound statement must always start with the reserved word BEGIN and conclude with the reserved word END. A compound statement can include any number of individual statements. The compound statement above consists of two simple statements:

```
X  :=  X  *  X;
```

and

```
WRITELN  (X)
```

No semicolon has been put after the second statement. This is because the statement is followed by END. No semicolon is needed here although one may be used if desired.

Figure 6-1 SYNTAX FOR COMPOUND IF/THEN STATEMENT

```
IF condition THEN
  BEGIN
    statement1;
    statement2;
      .
      .
      .
    last_statement
  END

(A semicolon is optional after last_statement.)
```

```
PROGRAM SQUARE;
(* THIS PROGRAM SQUARES A NUMBER IF IT IS POSITIVE.   THE RESULT IS
THEN PRINTED ONLY IF IT IS A POSITIVE NUMBER *)

VAR
   X : INTEGER;

BEGIN

   WRITE ('TYPE IN AN INTEGER. ');
   READLN (X);

   (* DETERMINE IF X IS POSITIVE *)
   IF X >= 0 THEN
      BEGIN
         X := X * X;
         WRITELN (X)
      END

END.   (* SQUARE *)


Running. . .
TYPE IN AN INTEGER. 8
64


Running. . .
TYPE IN AN INTEGER. -17
```

Figure 6-2 **PROGRAM SQUARE**

You may recall that the body of a Pascal program starts with BE-GIN and finishes with END. The body of a Pascal program is one compound statement. It is possible to have many compound statements in a program. Some compound statements may be inside of others. It is important to have a BEGIN and an END for each one. Otherwise the computer will not know where each compound statement starts and finishes. The program in the next section will demonstrate the use of compound statements.

PROGRAM SEWING

The purpose of the program SEWING is to tell students how much fabric they will need to complete a home economics project. Each student has a choice of making an apron or a vest. Aprons take 2.0 yards of fabric and vests take 3.25 yards. The flowchart for this program is in Figure 6-3. First, the students are asked to enter the name of the item that they are making. An IF/THEN/ELSE statement is used to determine which item has been chosen. The amount of fabric needed is assigned to the variable YARDS. The amount is then printed

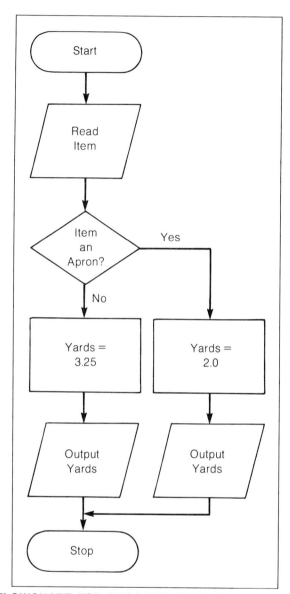

Figure 6-3 FLOWCHART FOR PROGRAM SEWING

for the students to read. The complete program is shown in Figure 6-4. There are two compound statements in this program. The first compound statement follows the expression IF ITEM = 'APRON' THEN. This compound statement is made up of two simple statements:

```
YARDS := 2.0;
WRITELN ('YOU WILL NEED ', YARDS:7:2, ' YARDS OF FABRIC FOR YOUR APRON.')
```

Be careful not to put a semicolon after the reserved word END before the ELSE portion of an IF/THEN/ELSE statement. Remember that the IF/THEN/ELSE is all one statement. When the prompt, 'WHICH PROJECT ARE YOU MAKING, AN APRON OR A VEST?' is printed to the

```
PROGRAM SEWING;
(* THIS PROGRAM TELLS HOME ECONOMICS STUDENTS HOW MUCH FABRIC THEY WILL
NEED FOR THEIR SEWING PROJECT.   THE PROJECTS TAKE:
      1. APRON : 2.0 YARDS
      2. VEST : 3.25 YARDS *)

 VAR
     ITEM  : STRING;
     YARDS : REAL;

 BEGIN

     WRITELN ('WHICH PROJECT ARE YOU MAKING, AN APRON OR A VEST?');
     READLN (ITEM);

     (* COMPUTE AMOUNT OF FABRIC NEEDED FOR THE ITEM *)
     IF ITEM = 'APRON' THEN
        BEGIN
           YARDS := 2.0;
           WRITELN ('YOU WILL NEED ', YARDS:7:2, ' YARDS FOR YOUR APRON.')
        END
     ELSE
        BEGIN
           YARDS := 3.25;
           WRITELN ('YOU WILL NEED ', YARDS:7:2, ' YARDS FOR YOUR VEST.')
        END


 END.   (* SEWING *)



Running. . .
WHICH PROJECT ARE YOU MAKING, AN APRON OR A VEST?
APRON
YOU WILL NEED     2.00 YARDS FOR YOUR APRON.
```

Figure 6-4   PROGRAM SEWING

monitor, the user must type in APRON in capital letters in order for the expression IF ITEM = 'APRON' to evaluate as true. Any other response will cause the ELSE portion of the statement to be executed.

NESTED IF/THEN/ELSE STATEMENTS

It is possible to place one IF/THEN/ELSE statement inside of another one. Sometimes this is necessary when several conditions must be checked. For example, how would a program be written to find the largest of three numbers? The numbers need to be compared with one another in an orderly way to determine the largest number. One way is to use **nested statements.** The flowchart for this program is in Figure 6-5. Look at program LARGE in Figure 6-6. First A is compared with B. If A is larger than B, then A is compared to C. If A is larger than C, the value of A is assigned to the variable BIGGEST. Otherwise, C is assigned to BIGGEST. The ELSE portion of the program is exe-

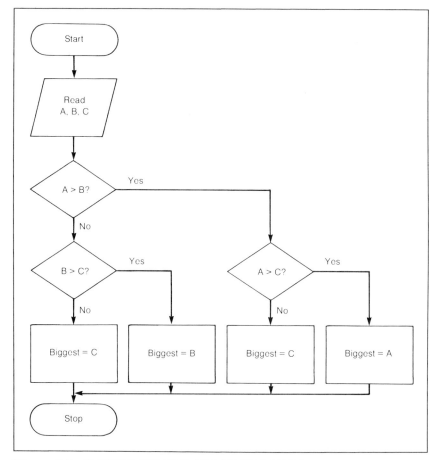

Figure 6-5 FLOWCHART FOR PROGRAM LARGE

cuted only if B is larger than A. Here B is compared to C and the
larger of the two is assigned to the variable BIGGEST. Notice that
there is an IF/THEN/ELSE statement nested within the IF/THEN part of
the statement and there is another IF/THEN/ELSE statement nested
within the ELSE part. The inner IF/THEN/ELSE must be nested completely within one portion of the outer IF/THEN/ELSE. It may not
overlap like this:

```
IF  A  >  B  THEN
     IF  A  >  C  THEN
          BIGGEST  :=  A
     ELSE
ELSE
     BIGGEST  :=  B
```

Logically, this makes no sense. The computer would not accept the
second ELSE since the inner IF/THEN/ELSE is not completely resolved.

How does the computer know which ELSE goes with which
IF/THEN? The computer starts from the innermost IF/THEN and

```
PROGRAM LARGE;
(* THIS PROGRAM READS IN THREE REAL NUMBERS AND PRINTS OUT THE LARGEST
OF THE THREE *)

VAR
    A, B, C, BIGGEST : REAL;

BEGIN

    WRITELN ('TYPE IN THE THREE REAL NUMBERS');
    READLN (A, B, C);

    (* DETERMINE WHICH IS THE LARGEST NUMBER *)
    IF A > B THEN
       IF A > C THEN
          BIGGEST := A
       ELSE
          BIGGEST := C
    ELSE
       IF B > C THEN
          BIGGEST := B
       ELSE
          BIGGEST := C;


    WRITELN ('THE LARGEST OF THE THREE NUMBERS ', A:7:2, ', ', B:7:2, ',',
    ' AND ', C:7:2, ' IS ', BIGGEST:8:2)

END.   (* LARGE *)


Running. . .

TYPE IN THE THREE REAL NUMBERS
6.9  123.8  34.6
THE LARGEST OF THE THREE NUMBERS     6.90,  123.80, AND   34.60 IS    123.80
```

Figure 6-6 PROGRAM LARGE

matches it to the ELSE that is closest to it. It works from the inside
out, matching each IF/THEN with the corresponding ELSE. Figure 6-7
shows three nested IF/THEN/ELSE statements. Each IF/THEN is bracketed with its matching ELSE. Carefully indenting each IF/THEN helps
to keep the matching ELSE easier to locate. They should both start in

Figure 6-7 NESTED IF/THEN/ELSE STATEMENTS

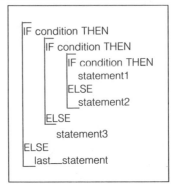

the same column. In the next section, a program will be written that combines a number of the items introduced so far in this chapter.

LEARNING CHECK 6-1

1. What is a compound statement?
2. Why is the body of a Pascal program a compound statement?
3. What is a nested IF/THEN/ELSE statement?

Answers: 1. A compound statement is a sequence of statements or other compound statements bracketed by BEGIN and END. 2. The body of a Pascal program is one compound statement because it starts with BEGIN and finishes with END. 3. A nested IF/THEN/ELSE statement is an IF/THEN/ELSE statement that is inside of another IF/THEN/ELSE statement; it must be entirely inside of either the IF/THEN or the ELSE portions of the other statement.

PROGRAM PIZZA

Smiley's Pizza Pub needs a program to calculate the cost of pizzas for its customers. Pizzas come in three sizes:

> 9 inch—$3.50
> 12 inch—$4.75
> 16 inch—$6.50

If the customer wants a thick-crusted pizza, it costs 50 cents extra regardless of the size of the pizza. Each extra topping costs:

> 9 inch—$0.40
> 12 inch—$0.55
> 16 inch—$0.75

First the cost of the basic pizza will be determined. This depends on the size of the pizza. This could be found by writing a series of IF/THEN statements:

```
IF  SIZE = 9 THEN
    COST := 3.50;
IF  SIZE = 12 THEN
    COST := 4.75;
IF  SIZE = 16 THEN
    COST := 6.50;
```

Three single-alternative IF statements have been used. Each pizza will fall into one of these categories since these are the only sizes of pizza

103

available. The same result could be accomplished by using nested IF/THEN/ELSE statements:

```
IF SIZE = 9 THEN
    COST := 3.50
ELSE
IF SIZE = 12 THEN
    COST := 4.75
ELSE
    COST := 6.50;
```

It is important that a semicolon be placed only at the end of this entire statement.

ELSE IF STATEMENTS

A simpler way of writing program PIZZA would be to use an ELSE IF statement. It would look like this:

```
IF SIZE = 9 THEN
    COST := 3.50
ELSE IF SIZE = 12 THEN
    COST := 4.75
ELSE IF SIZE = 16 THEN
    COST := 6.50;
```

Figure 6-8 illustrates the syntax of the ELSE IF statement. Again, remember there is only one semicolon. Figure 6-9 shows the flowchart for the PIZZA program. Each ELSE IF is executed only if the condition stated is true; otherwise the program goes on to the next ELSE IF. If none of the stated conditions are true, then none of the statements following the conditions will be executed. Nothing will be changed. If the programmer would like something to be done even if none of the statements are true, a final ELSE statement can be used. The ELSE statement will be executed if none of the conditions above it are true.

Figure 6-8 SYNTAX FOR ELSE IF STATEMENT

```
IF condition1 THEN
    statement1
ELSE IF condition2 THEN
    statement2
    .
    .
    .
ELSE
    last_statement;

(The last ELSE and the statement following it are optional.)
```

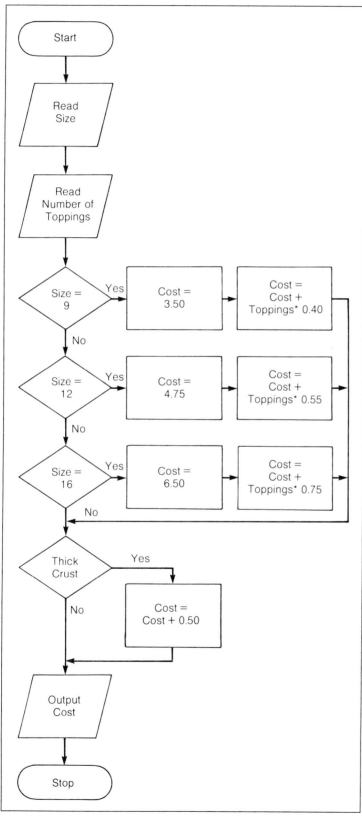

Figure 6-9 FLOWCHART FOR PROGRAM PIZZA

An appropriate ELSE statement for the PIZZA program would be:

```
ELSE
     WRITELN ('NO PIZZA IS AVAILABLE IN THAT SIZE.')
```

If the user typed in 14 for the pizza size, the following message would be printed on the monitor:

```
NO PIZZA IS AVAILABLE IN THAT SIZE.
```

If this happened, we would need to go back to the beginning of the program to allow the user to reenter the size of the pizza correctly. Such techniques will be covered later in the book. Checking for incorrect data is one of the signs of a well-written program. Spend some time studying PROGRAM PIZZA in Figure 6-10.

PROGRAM WEEK

When the user is asked to type data to the monitor, it is best to make entering the data as easy as possible. One way of doing this is to use codes that stand for something else. An example would be assigning a number to represent each day of the week:

1—Sunday
2—Monday
3—Tuesday
4—Wednesday
5—Thursday
6—Friday
7—Saturday

It is much simpler for the user to type a 5 than to type THURSDAY. There is less chance for a typing error, and time is saved.

In the program itself, the programmer will probably need to assign the corresponding day to a variable so that the day of the week and not a number will be printed. This can be done by using an ELSE IF statement. In the program in Figure 6-11, the variable D has been declared to be of data type INTEGER and DAY of data type STRING. The program reads an integer and assigns it to variable D. The corresponding value is assigned to the variable DAY.

CASE STATEMENTS

Program WEEK 1 could also be written by using a CASE statement. The CASE statement checks each label; if the value of the variable

```
PROGRAM PIZZA;
(* THIS PROGRAM COMPUTES THE COST OF PIZZAS FOR SMILEY'S PIZZA
PARLOR.   THE COST OF A PIZZA IS:
      9 INCH - $3.50
     12 INCH - $4.75
     16 INCH - $6.50
EACH EXTRA TOPPING COSTS:
      9 INCH - $0.40
     12 INCH - $0.55
     16 INCH - $0.75
PIZZAS WITH A THICK CRUST ARE $0.50 EXTRA, REGARDLESS OF THE SIZE.

THE VARIABLES USED ARE:
   COST       - THE COST OF EACH PIZZA
   SIZE       - THE SIZE OF EACH PIZZA
   TOPPINGS - NUMBER OF TOPPINGS DESIRED ON THE PIZZA
   CRUST      - WHETHER OF NOT A THICK CRUST IS DESIRED *)

VAR
   COST : REAL;
   SIZE, TOPPINGS : INTEGER;
   CRUST : STRING;

BEGIN

   WRITELN ('WHAT SIZE PIZZA DO YOU WANT?');
   WRITELN ('THE CHOICES ARE : 9, 12, OR 16 INCHES');
   READLN (SIZE);

   WRITELN ('HOW MANY TOPPINGS WOULD YOU LIKE?');
   WRITELN ('TYPE IN A WHOLE NUMBER UP TO 6.');
   READLN (TOPPINGS);

   (* DETERMINE COST OF PIZZA WITH DESIRED NUMBER OF TOPPINGS *)
   IF SIZE = 9 THEN
      BEGIN
         COST := 3.50;
         COST := COST + (TOPPINGS * 0.40)
      END
   ELSE IF SIZE = 12 THEN
      BEGIN
         COST := 4.75;
         COST := COST + (TOPPINGS * 0.55)
      END

   ELSE IF SIZE = 16 THEN
      BEGIN
         COST := 6.50;
         COST := COST + (TOPPINGS * 0.75)
      END;


   (* ADD $0.50 IF THICK-CRUSTED *)
   WRITELN ('DO YOU WANT A THICK CRUST?');
   WRITELN ('ANSWER YES OR NO.');
   READLN (CRUST);
```

Figure 6-10   PROGRAM PIZZA

Continued next page

```
    IF  CRUST  =  'YES'  THEN
        COST  :=  COST  +  0.50;

    (*  PRINT  OUT  TOTAL  COST  OF  PIZZA  *)
    WRITELN  ('THE  COST  OF  YOUR  PIZZA  IS  $',  COST:7:2)

END.    (*  PIZZA  *)
```

Running. . .

```
WHAT  SIZE  PIZZA  DO  YOU  WANT?
THE  CHOICES  ARE  :  9,  12,  OR  16  INCHES
9
HOW  MANY  TOPPINGS  WOULD  YOU  LIKE?
TYPE  IN  A  WHOLE  NUMBER  UP  TO  6.
3
DO  YOU  WANT  A  THICK  CRUST?
ANSWER  YES  OR  NO.
YES
THE  COST  OF  YOUR  PIZZA  IS  $     5.20
```

Figure 8-10 (con't.)

matches the label, the statement following the colon is executed. The CASE statement for this program would be:

```
CASE  D  OF
1  :  DAY  :=  'SUNDAY';
2  :  DAY  :=  'MONDAY';
3  :  DAY  :=  'TUESDAY';
4  :  DAY  :=  'WEDNESDAY';
5  :  DAY  :=  'THURSDAY';
6  :  DAY  :=  'FRIDAY';
7  :  DAY  :=  'SATURDAY'
END
```

The syntax for the CASE statement is illustrated in Figure 6-12 on page 110. Figure 6-13 shows the complete program using the CASE statement.

Notice that each statement is followed by a semicolon. Also, the CASE statement concludes with an END. This is true even though there is no BEGIN. Case statements are handy in many situations. The example below shows how an appropriate message can be printed, depending on the value of the variable GRADE. The variable GRADE has been declared to be of data type CHAR.

```
CASE  GRADE  OF
    'A'  :  WRITELN  ('ALL  RIGHT!');
    'B'  :  WRITELN  ('GOOD  JOB.');
    'C'  :  WRITELN  ('NOT  BAD.');
    'D',  'F'  :  WRITELN  ('YOU  BLEW  IT.')
END;  (*  CASE  *)
```

```
PROGRAM WEEK1;
(* THIS PROGRAM TRANSLATES A CODE NUMBER INTO A DAY OF THE WEEK.  THE
CODES AND THEIR CORRESPONDING DAYS ARE:
     1 - SUNDAY
     2 - MONDAY
     3 - TUESDAY
     4 - WEDNESDAY
     4 - THURSDAY
     5 - FRIDAY
     6 - SATURDAY    *)

VAR
   D   : INTEGER;   (* INTEGER CODE FOR DAY OF WEEK *)
   DAY : STRING;  (* STRING CONTAINING NAME OF DAY OF WEEK *)

BEGIN

   WRITELN ('WHAT IS THE CODE FOR THE DAY?');
   WRITELN ('ENTER AN INTEGER 1-7');
   READLN (D);

   (* ASSIGN CORRESPONDING DAY *)
   IF D = 1 THEN
     DAY := 'SUNDAY'
   ELSE IF D = 2 THEN
     DAY := 'MONDAY'
   ELSE IF D = 3 THEN
     DAY := 'TUESDAY'
   ELSE IF D = 4 THEN
     DAY := 'WEDNESDAY'
   ELSE IF D = 5 THEN
     DAY := 'THURSDAY'
   ELSE IF D = 6 THEN
     DAY := 'FRIDAY'
   ELSE IF D = 7 THEN
     DAY := 'SATURDAY';

   WRITELN ('THE DAY IS ', DAY, '.')

END.   (* WEEK1 *)


Running. . .
WHAT IS THE CODE FOR THE DAY?
ENTER AN INTEGER 1-7
3
THE DAY IS TUESDAY.
```

Figure 6-11 PROGRAM WEEK1

More than one value may be listed on a line. An example of this is the
statement

```
        'D', 'F' : WRITELN ('YOU BLEW IT.')
```

This statement will be executed if the value of GRADE is either D or
F.

```
CASE expression OF
   value1 : statement1;
   value2 : statement2;
           .
           .
           .
   last_value : last_statement
END

(A semicolon may or may not be used before the END.)
```

Figure 6-12 SYNTAX FOR CASE STATEMENT

Figure 6-13 PROGRAM WEEK2

```
PROGRAM WEEK2;
(* THIS PROGRAM TRANSLATES A NUMBER CODE INTO A DAY OF THE WEEK.  THE
CODES WITH THEIR CORRESPONDING DAYS OF THE WEEK ARE:
       1 - SUNDAY
       2 - MONDAY
       3 - TUESDAY
       4 - WEDNESDAY
       5 - THURSDAY
       6 - FRIDAY
       7 - SATURDAY      *)

VAR
    D   : INTEGER;  (* INTEGER CODE REPRESENTING DAY OF WEEK *)
    DAY : STRING;   (* STRING CONTAINING DAY OF THE WEEK *)

BEGIN

    WRITELN ('WHAT IS THE CODE FOR THE DAY?');
    WRITELN ('ENTER AN INTEGER 1-7.');
    READLN (D);

    (* ASSIGN CORRESPONDING DAY *)
    CASE D OF
       1 : DAY := 'SUNDAY';
       2 : DAY := 'MONDAY';
       3 : DAY := 'TUESDAY';
       4 : DAY := 'WEDNESDAY';
       5 : DAY := 'THURSDAY';
       6 : DAY := 'FRIDAY';
       7 : DAY := 'SATURDAY'

    END;    (* CASE *)


Running. . .
WHAT IS THE CODE FOR THE DAY?
ENTER AN INTEGER 1-7.
5
THE DAY IS THURSDAY.
```

1. Look at the program segment below:

```
IF OUNCES = 40 THEN
    SIZE := 'JUMBO'
ELSE IF OUNCES = 25 THEN
    SIZE := 'LARGE'
ELSE IF OUNCES = 18 THEN
    SIZE := 'REGULAR'
ELSE
WRITELN ('THIS PRODUCT DOES NOT COME IN ', OUNCES, 'OUNCE SIZE.');
```

What will the value of SIZE be if OUNCES is equal to each of the values below?
a. 18
b. 40
c. 20
d. 50
e. 25

2. How does the computer determine which IF/THEN goes with which ELSE when there are nested IF/THEN/ELSE statements?

3. Give two examples of programming problems where the CASE statement would be useful.

Answers:

1. a. REGULAR, b. JUMBO, c. Value of SIZE is undefined; the program will print: THIS PRODUCT DOES NOT COME IN 20 OUNCE SIZE, d. Value of SIZE is undefined; the program will print: THIS PRODUCT DOES NOT COME IN 50 OUNCE SIZE, e. LARGE 2. The computer starts with the innermost IF/THEN and matches it to the ELSE closest to it. Working from the inside out, it matches each IF/THEN with its corresponding ELSE. 3. The CASE statement could be used to assign names of months if the month has been entered as a number; it also could be used to assign a price to an item if the item has been given a price code.

SUMMARY POINTS

- In this chapter, compound statements have been explained. Compound statements start with BEGIN and conclude with END. They can contain any number of statements, including other compound statements.
- Nested IF/THEN/ELSE statements allow the programmer to check for a number of conditions. It is very important to make certain that the nesting is done properly. Indenting each set of IF/THEN/ELSE statements makes it easier to check for correct nesting.
- An ELSE IF statement can be used to check for a number of conditions. Each ELSE IF is executed only if the condition given is true. The CASE statement is used to compare a variable to a list of values. If the variable matches one of the values, the statement following that value is executed.
- One of the best features of Pascal is its wide variety of control statements. There is a control statement for practically any purpose. The control state-

ments in this chapter enable the programmer to determine whether or not a certain part of a program will be executed. Control statements that allow the programmer to repeat parts of a program as many times as desired will be introduced in the next chapter.

VOCABULARY LIST

Compound statement A series of statements that starts with BEGIN and concludes with END.

Nested statement A statement that is contained within another statement.

CHAPTER TEST

VOCABULARY

Match a term from the numbered column with the description from the lettered column that best fits the term.

1. Nested statement

   a. A statement that is contained within another statement.

2. Order of operations

   b. A statement that allows the programmer to determine whether or not a statement (or a group of statements) will be executed and how many times it will be executed.

3. Compound statement

   c. A series of statements that starts with BEGIN and concludes with END.

4. Control statement

   d. The sequence in which expressions are evaluated.

QUESTIONS

1. Rewrite this program segment using one compound statement instead of three IF/THEN statements.

```
IF LETTER = 'A' THEN
    VOWELS := VOWELS + 1;
IF LETTER = 'A' THEN
    CONT := TRUE;
IF LETTER = 'A' THEN
    WRITELN ('THIS LETTER IS A VOWEL.');
```

2. Rewrite the following program segment so that it is properly indented. Bracket the IF/THEN/ELSE statements that go together.

```
IF  INCHES > 64 THEN
IF  INCHES > 72 THEN
IF  INCHES > 76 THEN
HEIGHT := 'HUGE'
ELSE
HEIGHT := 'TALL'
ELSE
HEIGHT := 'AVERAGE'
ELSE
HEIGHT := 'SHORT';
```

3. Rewrite the program segment in Problem 2 using an ELSE IF statement.

4. Write a CASE statement that will assign a color when a code letter is used. The code table is listed below:

Code	Color
R	RED
G	GREEN
B	BROWN
O	ORANGE
W	WHITE
P	PURPLE
Y	YELLOW

5. Look at the program segment below:

```
CASE KIND OF
    1 : FISH := 'BASS';
    2 : FISH := 'CARP';
  3,4 : FISH := 'TROUT';
    5 : FISH := 'PERCH';
  6,7 : FISH := 'WALLEYE'
END;
WRITELN (FISH);
```

What will the value of KIND be in each of the assignment statements below?

```
a.KIND := 1 + 5;
b.KIND := 2 * 2;
c.KIND := 1;
d.KIND := 7;
```

PROGRAMMING PROBLEMS

1. Mrs. Hasselschartz, the librarian, would like a program to calculate library fines. Fines are charged on the following basis:

general books
    paperbacks: 15¢/day
    other general books: 20¢/day
magazines: 25¢/day
reference books
    encyclopedias: 50¢/day
    other reference books: 35¢/day

Write this program using nested IF/THEN/ELSE statements.

2. Write a program that reads the length and width of a rectangle or a square. The length and width will be entered in inches. Then determine if the figure is a square. If it is a square, print the area of the square. If it is a rectangle, print the perimeter of the rectangle. Print the results with appropriate labels.

3. Pat Nabel's father will only allow her to make $10.00 worth of long-distance phone calls a month. She would like a program to figure out the cost of each of her calls. Below is a code number for each type of call Pat makes and the cost of each per minute.

Code	Call To	Cost per Minute
1	her grandmother in Santa Clara	.22
2	her brother in Pittsburgh	.14
3	her boyfriend in Hamburg	.73

Use a CASE statement to read in a 1, 2, or 3 and assign the appropriate charge. The output should be formatted like this:

THE COST OF THIS CALL IS $2.83

4. Mickey Koth likes to go on cross-country bike trips. She needs a way of calculating the amount of time a particular bike trip will take. The distance she can travel in an hour depends on the weather conditions. They are as follows:

E—excellent conditions: 25 miles/hour
G—good conditions: 20 miles/hour
P—poor conditions: 13 miles/hour

Write a program that will allow Mickey to type in the distance in miles and then enter a code (E, G, or P) for the weather conditions. The amount of time the trip will take her should then be printed in hours.

5. Steve Cavanaugh works for Uptown Lumber Company on weekends and evenings. He receives $3.60 an hour except when he works more than 15 hours a week; then he is paid $3.75 an hour. State income tax is taken out of his weekly check as follows:

6 percent state tax is taken out if he makes $50.00 or less a week.
7 percent state tax is taken out if he makes more than $50.00 a week.

114

Write a program that will calculate how much Steve's weekly paycheck will be. Write it so that Steve can type in the number of hours he works in a given week. The amount of his paycheck will be printed so that he can read it.

6. Write a program that will calculate what coins could be given out in change. The amount of money will always be less than a dollar. For example, if the amount entered is 43, the program should print:

QUARTERS	DIMES	NICKELS	PENNIES
1	1	1	3

CHAPTER 7

Loops

OUTLINE

LEARNING OBJECTIVES

After studying this chapter, you should be able to:

1. Explain what is meant by a loop.
2. Write a loop using the REPEAT/UNTIL control statement.
3. Write a loop using the WHILE control statement.
4. Explain two differences between the REPEAT/UNTIL loop and the WHILE loop.
5. Write programs using the FOR loop.
6. List three things done automatically by the FOR loop.
7. Write programs that check input data to make certain they are usable in the program.
8. Explain why GOTO statements should not be used in Pascal programs unless there is no alternative.
9. List the three BOOLEAN operators and explain the purpose of each.
10. Use BOOLEAN operators in programs.
11. Evaluate expressions using BOOLEAN operators.
12. Explain what is meant by a scalar data type.

INTRODUCTION

In Chapter 4, a program was written that calculated the radius, circumference, and area of a circle. It probably would have been faster to figure these results by hand than to write this program. But, suppose it was necessary to calculate these values for a thousand circles. This is an example of a situation where the computer can really save time. The computer can easily do the same job over and over again.

This chapter will introduce some new types of control statements. These control statements are called **loops.** Loops allow the programmer to repeat a particular section of a program as many times as needed. A loop contains a series of instructions that will be executed repeatedly as long as specified conditions are not changed. This means that each time through a loop a condition will be evaluated. The condition must evaluate as true or false. How this condition evaluates will determine if the loop will be executed. In this chapter, three types of loops will be explained.

THE REPEAT/UNTIL LOOP

The first type of loop control statement that will be examined is the REPEAT/UNTIL loop. The syntax for the REPEAT/UNTIL loop is shown in Figure 7-1. The loop starts with the word REPEAT. Every statement between the REPEAT and the UNTIL is executed. These statements are the loop body. The condition following the word UNTIL is then

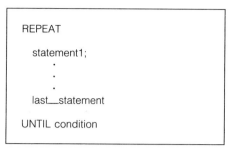

```
REPEAT

    statement1;
         ·
         ·
         ·
    last__statement

UNTIL condition
```

Figure 7-1 SYNTAX FOR REPEAT/UNTIL LOOP

evaluated. If the condition evaluates as false, the program returns to the REPEAT statement and executes the following statements again. If the condition evaluates as true, the statement following the UNTIL is executed. The loop is not executed again. Figure 7-2 shows how the REPEAT/UNTIL loop is represented in a flowchart.

Study the program segment below. How many times will this loop be executed?

```
NUM := 2;
REPEAT
    NUM := NUM + 1
UNTIL NUM = 4;
```

This loop will be executed two times. Going into the loop the first time, the value of NUM will be two. The statement NUM := NUM + 1 is executed, making the value of NUM three. The condition NUM = 4 will evaluate as false, since three is not equal to four. The loop is executed again. One more is added to NUM this time through the

Figure 7-2 FLOWCHART FOR REPEAT/UNTIL LOOP

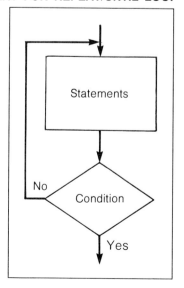

119

loop, making NUM equal to four. Since NUM = 4 is now true, the loop will not be executed again. Instead, the statement following the loop will be executed. In the next section, a complete program will illustrate the use of the REPEAT/UNTIL statement.

Program FACTORIAL

The purpose of the next program is to compute the factorial of a positive number. The general formula for computing a factorial is:

$$N * (N - 1) * (N - 2) * . . . * 1$$

The factorial of six would be:

$$6 * 5 * 4 * 3 * 2 * 1 = 720$$

The factorial of one is one.

The flowchart for the program is represented in Figure 7-3. Study the program shown in Figure 7-4. First, the value of N is typed to the keyboard and read. This value is assigned to the variable TEMP. This is so the original value of N can be printed in the WRITELN statement at the end of the program. Since the value of N will be changed when the program is executed, it is important to store the original value in another variable. In this case, TEMP has been used for this purpose. The variable name TEMP stands for temporary. TEMP is used to temporarily hold the value of N.

Next, an IF/THEN/ELSE statement is used to determine if the value of N is one. If N is equal to one, the value of FACT is set to one. If N is not equal to one, the ELSE portion of the IF/THEN/ELSE statement is executed. FACT is set to the value of N before the loop starts. In the loop, N is first decreased by one, and then FACT is multiplied by this new value of N. This value of N is then compared to one. As long as N is not equal to one, the loop will be executed. Once the value of N is equal to one, the loop is not executed again. The statement after the loop will then be executed. Suppose the integer five is used for the value of N. Trace through the program and see if you agree with the values below. The values listed are the values of N and FACT at the end of each repetition of the loop.

Number of Times Through the Loop	N	FACT
1	4	20
2	3	60
3	2	120
4	1	120

Why was the factorial of one not set in the WHILE loop like the other

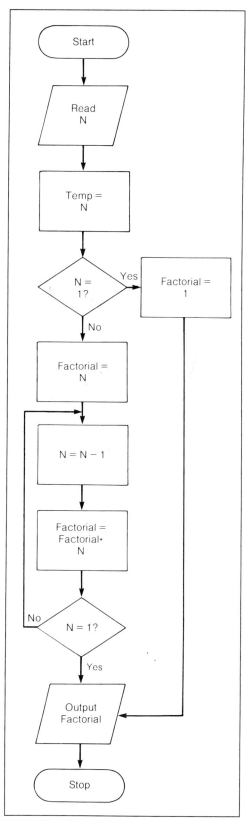

Figure 7-3 FLOWCHART FOR PROGRAM FACTORIAL

```
PROGRAM FACTORIAL;
(* THIS PROGRAM COMPUTES THE FACTORIAL OF A POSITIVE INTEGER *)

VAR
    N, TEMP : INTEGER;
    FACT : INTEGER[10];

BEGIN

    WRITELN ('WHAT IS THE INTEGER?');
    READLN (N);
    TEMP := N;

(* IF N = 1, FACTORIAL = 1 *)
    IF N = 1 THEN
        FACT := 1
    ELSE
    (* LOOP TO COMPUTE FACTORIAL *)
        BEGIN
            FACT := N;

            REPEAT
                N := N - 1;
                FACT := FACT * N
            UNTIL N = 1

        END;    (* ELSE *)

    WRITELN ('THE FACTORIAL OF ', TEMP, ' IS ', FACT)

END.    (* FACTORIAL *)

Running. . .
WHAT IS THE INTEGER?
8
THE FACTORIAL OF 8 IS 40320
```

FIGURE 7-4 PROGRAM FACTORIAL

factorials? The program segment below shows what would happen in the loop if the value assigned to N was one.

```
FACT := N;                    (FACT is assigned the value of
REPEAT                         one)

    N := N - 1;               (N := 0)
    FACT := FACT * N          (FACT := 0)
```

The statement

$$FACT := FACT * N$$

will assign zero to FACT. The factorial of one is actually one. So, by using the loop, the program would have obtained the incorrect result for the factorial of one. There is another serious problem with using one for the value of N in this loop. What will this condition evaluate as at the end of the loop?

UNTIL N = 1

The condition will evaluate as false because N is now equal to zero. The next time through the loop the value of N will be − 1. The value of N will never be one. Instead, it will become a larger and larger negative number. This loop will never stop. This is called an **infinite loop.** It is important that the programmer be careful not to let this happen when writing programs. Careful testing of possible data values can help avoid this problem.

Notice that FACT has been declared to be of data type LONG INTEGER. This is because factorials become large numbers very quickly. The factorial of eight is 40,320. The data type INTEGER cannot contain an integer larger than 32,767. The following declaration allows FACT to contain an integer up to 9999999999.

FACT : INTEGER[10];

LEARNING CHECK 7-1

1. Why are loops useful in computer programs?
2. Describe a job you do that involves repeating a task over and over again until a certain condition is met.
3. How many times will the loop in the following program segment be executed? What will the value of I be at the end of the loop each time through?

```
PROGRAM EX1;

VAR
     I : INTEGER;

BEGIN

     I := 1;
     REPEAT
         I := I + 1;
         WRITELN (I)
     UNTIL I >= 10;
```

Answers:

1. Loops are useful in computer programs because they allow a series of instructions to be repeated as many times as is necessary. 2. Some choices might be training for a sport (swimming or running laps, doing situps, etc.); washing dishes; delivering on a paper route; solving math problems. 3. The loop will be repeated nine times.

Loop #	*Value of I*
1	2
2	3
3	4
4	5
5	6
6	7
7	8
8	9
9	10

THE WHILE LOOP

The WHILE loop is similar to the REPEAT/UNTIL loop. The syntax for the WHILE loop is shown in Figure 7-5. Unlike the REPEAT/UNTIL loop, the WHILE loop must contain a BEGIN and an END if there is more than one statement in the loop body. In the WHILE loop, a condition is tested before the body of the loop is executed. A flowchart of a WHILE loop is shown in Figure 7-6. The program segment below shows how a WHILE loop might be used in a program.

```
COUNT := 1;
WHILE COUNT < 16 DO
   BEGIN
      READLN (CLASS);
      WRITELN (CLASS);
      COUNT := COUNT + 1
   END;
```

This program segment could be used to read and write a list of classes. The value of COUNT is set to one before the loop is entered. This is called **initializing** the variable. The value of COUNT was initialized

Figure 7-5 SYNTAX FOR WHILE LOOP

```
WHILE condition DO
  BEGIN
    statement1;
        .
        .
        .
    last_statement
  END
```

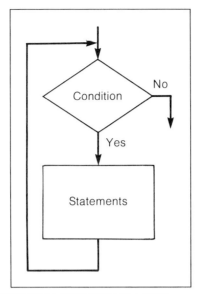

Figure 7-6 FLOWCHART FOR WHILE LOOP

to one. If the value of COUNT had not been initialized, the statement COUNT := COUNT + 1 would be meaningless. It is impossible for the computer to increase the value of a variable if the original value of the variable has not been set. COUNT is called a **loop control variable** (LCV for short). This is because COUNT is used to control how many times the loop will be executed. Each time through the loop the value of COUNT is increased by one until the condition COUNT < 16 is false. Then the program will skip down to the statement following the END.

The loop in the example above will be executed 15 times. It could be used to read and write a list of 15 classes. What if the variable COUNT had been initialized to 16 rather than one? The first time the expression

```
WHILE COUNT < 16 DO
```

was evaluated, it would be false. The loop would not have been executed at all.

This is different from the REPEAT/UNTIL loop. Since the condition in the REPEAT/UNTIL loop is evaluated at the end of the loop, the REPEAT/UNTIL loop will always be executed at least once. Another difference is that the WHILE loop is executed while a condition is true, whereas the REPEAT/UNTIL loop is executed while a condition is false.

Program FIVES

The WHILE loop will now be used to count by fives. The flowchart for this program is presented in Figure 7-7. The variable COUNT is

125

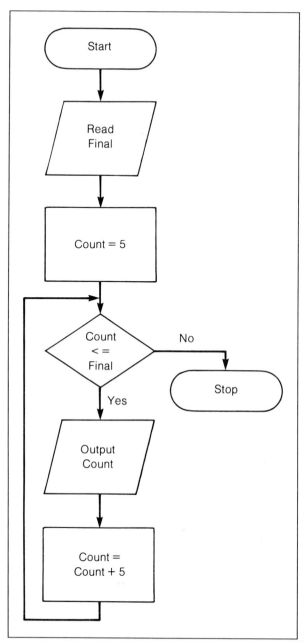

Figure 7-7 FLOWCHART FOR PROGRAM FIVES

initialized to five. Then the condition COUNT <= FINAL is evaluated. If it is true, the loop is executed. The value of COUNT is printed. Then five is added to COUNT. The loop then branches back to the condition COUNT <= FINAL. The loop will be executed until COUNT is not less than or equal to FINAL. Then the program stops. Figure 7-8 shows the complete program. What if the value of FINAL is not a multiple of five? Will this program still work? Yes, it will. For example, if the value of FINAL is set to 18, the last time through the loop the

```
PROGRAM FIVES;
(* THIS PROGRAM COUNTS BY FIVES FROM FIVE TO THE VALUE OF FINAL *)

VAR
    COUNT, FINAL : INTEGER;

BEGIN

    WRITELN ('HOW FAR DO YOU WANT TO COUNT BY FIVES?');
    WRITELN ('TYPE IN AN INTEGER.');
    READLN (FINAL);
    COUNT := 5;

    (* LOOP TO ADD FIVE TO COUNT UNTIL VALUE OF FINAL IS REACHED *)
    WHILE COUNT <= FINAL DO
        BEGIN
            WRITELN (COUNT);
            COUNT := COUNT + 5
        END    (* WHILE *)

END.  (* FIVES *)
```

Running. . .
```
HOW FAR DO YOU WANT TO COUNT BY FIVES?
TYPE IN AN INTEGER.
45

5
10
15
20
25
30
35
40
45

HOW FAR DO YOU WANT TO COUNT BY FIVES?
TYPE IN AN INTEGER.
28

5
10
15
20
25
```

Figure 7-8 PROGRAM FIVES

value of COUNT will be 20 and value of FINAL will be 18. The expression being evaluated will look like this:

$$WHILE\ 20\ <=\ 18\ DO$$

The condition will be false and the loop will not be executed again.

The program will stop. Trace through the loop to make sure that you understand this point.

THE FOR LOOP

The FOR loop is a useful loop control statement. The syntax is shown in Figure 7-9. This loop could be used in a program segment like this:

```
FOR I := 1 TO 7 DO
    WRITELN ('WE ARE ON LOOP', I);
```

This loop will be repeated seven times. Notice that no BEGIN or END is needed in the example above. This is a single statement. If there was more than one statement in the loop, then a BEGIN and an END would be needed. In this example of the FOR loop, three steps have been done automatically:

1. I has been initialized to 1.
2. Each time through the loop the expression I < = 7 is evaluated. If it evaluates as true, the loop will be executed.
3. One is added to the value of I each time through the loop.

Figure 7-9 SYNTAX FOR THE FOR LOOP

FOR LOOP USING ''TO'' FORMAT

FOR loop__control__variable : = beginning__value TO end__value DO

  BEGIN

    statement1;
    .
    .
    .
    last__statement

  END

FOR LOOP USING ''DOWNTO'' FORMAT

FOR loop__control__variable : = beginning__value DOWNTO end__value DO

  BEGIN

    statement1;
    .
    .
    last__statement

  END

(The value of the loop control variable may not be changed inside the loop body.)

In a FOR loop, the loop control variable may not be changed in the body of the loop.

Figure 7-10 presents four examples of FOR loops. Program EX1 gives the example already discussed, showing what the results look like when the program is run.

Figure 7-10 PROGRAMS WITH FOR LOOPS

```
PROGRAM EX1;

VAR
    I : INTEGER;

BEGIN

  FOR I := 1 TO 7 DO
     WRITELN ('WE ARE ON LOOP ', I)

END.  (* EX1 *)
```

Running. . .
```
WE ARE ON LOOP 1
WE ARE ON LOOP 2
WE ARE ON LOOP 3
WE ARE ON LOOP 4
WE ARE ON LOOP 5
WE ARE ON LOOP 6
WE ARE ON LOOP 7
```

```
PROGRAM EX2;

VAR
    I : INTEGER;

BEGIN

   FOR I := 27 TO 33 DO
     WRITELN ('WE ARE ON LOOP ',I)

END.  (* EX2 *)
```

Running. . .
```
WE ARE ON LOOP 27
WE ARE ON LOOP 28
WE ARE ON LOOP 29
WE ARE ON LOOP 30
WE ARE ON LOOP 31
WE ARE ON LOOP 32
WE ARE ON LOOP 33
```

Continued next page   **129**

```
PROGRAM EX3;

VAR
    LETTER : CHAR;

BEGIN

    FOR LETTER := 'A' TO 'G' DO
        WRITELN ('WE ARE ON LOOP ', LETTER)

END.    (* EX3 *)
```

Running. . .
```
WE ARE ON LOOP A
WE ARE ON LOOP B
WE ARE ON LOOP C
WE ARE ON LOOP D
WE ARE ON LOOP E
WE ARE ON LOOP F
WE ARE ON LOOP G
```

```
PROGRAM EX4;

VAR
    I : INTEGER;

BEGIN

    FOR I := 7 DOWNTO 1 DO
        WRITELN ('WE ARE ON LOOP ', I)

END.    (* EX4 *)
```

Running. . .
```
WE ARE ON LOOP 7
WE ARE ON LOOP 6
WE ARE ON LOOP 5
WE ARE ON LOOP 4
WE ARE ON LOOP 3
WE ARE ON LOOP 2
WE ARE ON LOOP 1
```

Figure 7-10   (con't.)

The loop control variable does not have to start at one. This loop would also be executed seven times:

```
FOR I := 27 TO 33 DO
    WRITELN ('WE ARE ON LOOP ', I);
```

The loop control variable may also be of data type CHAR. The loop

```
FOR LETTER := 'A' TO 'G' DO
    WRITELN (LETTER);
```

will again be executed seven times. Programs EX2 and EX3 in Figure 7-10 show these two programs. Any expression that evaluates as data type INTEGER or CHAR may be used as a loop control variable. This is because these are **scalar data types.** A scalar data type is a data type where all of the values may be listed. Sometimes these are called **ordinal data types.** For example, it is possible to list the values between 16 and 105 or the values between G and Z. REAL and STRING are not scalar data types. How could all of the values between 10.8 and 47.65 be listed? They are infinite. Likewise, if NAME is of data type STRING, an expression such as

```
FOR NAME := MARY TO SARAH DO
```

is meaningless. In chapter 10 another scalar data type will be studied, the user-defined scalar data type.

The data type BOOLEAN is also a scalar data type. Its values are true and false. But, since it only has two values, it is not generally useful as a loop control variable in a FOR loop.

Expressions may be used in the FOR loop as long as they evaluate as a scalar data type. For example,

```
FOR X := (2 * 10) TO (200 - 50) DO
    WRITELN (X);
```

is a valid FOR loop. It would be the same as writing

```
FOR X := 20 TO 150 DO
    WRITELN (X);
```

There is another way of writing a FOR loop. Its syntax is illustrated at the bottom of Figure 7-9. It looks like this:

```
FOR I := 7 DOWNTO 1 DO
    WRITELN ('WE ARE ON LOOP', I);
```

The value of I is initialized to seven. Each time through this loop the value of I will be decreased by one. The loop will be executed as long as the expression $I >= 1$ evaluates as true. Program EX4 in Figure 7-10 contains this program and its output.

⚓LEARNING CHECK 7-2

1. Write a FOR loop that reads in 20 numbers and adds them together.
2. Name three things that are done automatically in the FOR statement.
3. Read the program segment below. How many times will the WHILE loop be executed? What will the value of Y be at the end of each loop execution? What will the value of X be?

```
Y := 0;
X := Y;

WHILE Y < 11 DO
      BEGIN
          Y := Y + X;
          X := X + 1;
          WRITELN (X, Y)
      END
```

Answers:

CHECKING FOR INCORRECT DATA

It is important for the programmer to make certain that the data typed to the keyboard by the user can be used in the program. The factorial problem shown earlier in this chapter is a good example. Suppose the user had entered an integer that was less than one. The program would have been caught in an infinite loop. This is the kind of error the programmer needs to check for. When an error is caught, the user can be asked to reenter the data.

Figure 7-11 shows how the factorial program could be rewritten to check for incorrect data. A WHILE loop has been used. This is an example of an excellent use for a WHILE loop. If the value of N is less

```
PROGRAM FACTORIAL;
(* THIS PROGRAM COMPUTES THE FACTORIAL OF A POSITIVE INTEGER *)

VAR
   N, TEMP : INTEGER;
   FACT : INTEGER[10];

BEGIN

   WRITELN ('WHAT IS THE INTEGER?');
   READLN (N);

   (* LOOP TO MAKE CERTAIN N IS GREATER THAN ZERO *)
   WHILE N < 1 DO
      BEGIN
         WRITELN ('THE INTEGER MUST BE GREATER THAN ZERO.');
         WRITELN ('PLEASE TYPE IN THE INTEGER.');
         READLN (N)
      END;    (* WHILE *)

   TEMP := N;

(* IF N = 1, FACTORIAL = 1 *)
   IF N = 1 THEN
      FACT := 1
   ELSE
   (* LOOP TO COMPUTE FACTORIAL *)
      BEGIN
         FACT := N;

         REPEAT
            N := N - 1;
            FACT := FACT * N
         UNTIL N = 1

      END;    (* ELSE *)

   WRITELN ('THE FACTORIAL OF ', TEMP, ' IS ', FACT)

END.    (* FACTORIAL *)
```

Running. . .
```
WHAT IS THE INTEGER?
-14
THE INTEGER MUST BE GREATER THAN ZERO.
PLEASE TYPE IN THE INTEGER.
0
THE INTEGER MUST BE GREATER THAN ZERO.
PLEASE TYPE IN THE INTEGER.
5
THE FACTORIAL OF 5 IS 120
```

Figure 7-11 CATCHING AN ERROR IN INPUT DATA

than one, the loop will be executed. The loop prints an error message telling the user that N must be greater than zero. The user is then asked to reenter N. If this time N is greater than zero, the program will go on to the next statement following the loop. If N is still incorrect, the loop will be repeated.

A REPEAT/UNTIL loop would not have worked well here. Remember that the REPEAT/UNTIL loop is always executed at least once. In this case, the loop should not be executed at all if the value of N is greater than zero. A REPEAT/UNTIL loop is useful when a loop must be executed at least once.

A FOR loop also would not be useful for the type of error checking used in the factorial program. It is not possible to know whether or not the loop will be executed or how many times the loop will be executed. The FOR loop is useful when it can be determined how many times a loop will be executed.

THE GOTO STATEMENT

The GOTO statement allows program execution to branch to another part of a program. Here is an example:

```
12 : WRITELN ('TYPE IN A NEGATIVE NUMBER.');
READ (X);
IF X <= 0 THEN
    GOTO 12;
```

The program will branch back up to the statement

```
12 : WRITELN ('TYPE IN A NEGATIVE NUMBER.');
```

if X is less than or equal to zero. The "12" is a label. It marks the statement so that the computer will know where to branch. A label may be any integer up to 999. It must be declared in a label declaration statement like this:

```
LABEL 12;
```

The GOTO statement is not a structured programming statement. It is always better to use a structured control statement rather than a GOTO statement. In the example above, it would be much better to write the program segment this way:

```
REPEAT
    WRITELN ('TYPE IN A NEGATIVE NUMBER.');
    READLN (X)
UNTIL X > 0;
```

GOTO statements often cause program errors. They make the logic of a program much harder to follow. None of the programs in this book require the use of the GOTO statement. It is recommended that it not be used in writing Pascal programs unless absolutely necessary.

BOOLEAN OPERATORS

So far, the arithmetic operators (+, −, *, /, DIV, and MOD) and the relational operators (=, <>, <, >, <=, >=) have been covered. Now a third type of operator will be discussed. These are the BOOLEAN operators. The BOOLEAN operators are used for BOOLEAN expressions only. Remember that BOOLEAN expressions are expressions that evaluate as true or false. The three BOOLEAN operators are NOT, AND, and OR.

NOT is a unary operator. This means that it is used alone with a BOOLEAN expression. For example, if the variable A was of data type INTEGER, the expression

```
WHILE NOT (A > 0) DO
```

would evaluate as true if A > 0 was false. If A was equal to one, the expression

```
WHILE NOT (1 > 0) DO
```

would evaluate as false.

AND is used to combine two BOOLEAN expressions. For example, the expression

```
IF (HEIGHT > 72) AND (WEIGHT > 150) THEN
```

will evaluate as true only if HEIGHT > 72 and WEIGHT > 150 are both true. Both of these expressions must be true for the entire expression to be true.

OR is also used to combine two BOOLEAN expressions. In this case, only one of the expressions needs to evaluate as true for the entire expression to evaluate as true. In the expression

```
IF (HEIGHT > 72) OR (WEIGHT > 150) THEN
```

if either HEIGHT > 72 or WEIGHT > 150 is true, the entire expression will evaluate as true. With some compilers, parentheses must be used when you are using relational operators with BOOLEAN expressions. The BOOLEAN operators are evaluated in this order:

1. NOT
2. AND
3. OR

This means an expression using NOT will be evaluated first, then AND, and lastly OR. Here is an example of a BOOLEAN expression:

```
NOT (10 < 12) OR (10 * 3 = 30)
```

This expression would be evaluated in this order:

1. Expressions in parentheses are evaluated left to right. $(10 < 12)$ evaluates as true; $(10 * 3 = 30)$ evaluates as true $(30 = 30)$.
2. NOT is evaluated before OR; NOT (TRUE) evaluates as false; (FALSE) OR (TRUE) evaluates as true.

The expression

```
NOT (10 < 12) OR (10 * 3 = 30)
```

evaluates as true. When you are evaluating a complex BOOLEAN expression, it is important to be careful to perform each step in the correct order. Breaking the expression down into small parts makes it simpler.

The programmer can use parentheses to change the order in which the expression will be evaluated. This is done the same way as with arithmetic and relational operators. If the programmer wanted the OR operation to be evaluated before the NOT, the expression could be written:

```
NOT ((10 < 12) OR (10 * 3 = 30))
```

The steps to evaluate this expression would be:

```
1. NOT ((TRUE) OR (TRUE))
2. NOT (TRUE) = FALSE
```

This expression would evaluate as false. The parentheses have changed the entire meaning of the expression.

A program will now be written that uses BOOLEAN operators. This program will be used to write the appropriate activity for a given day. The program is shown in Figure 7-12. Two questions are asked of the user:

```
IS TODAY A SCHOOLDAY?
```

and

```
IS TODAY SUNNY?
```

```
PROGRAM ACTIVITY;
(* THIS PROGRAM DETERMINES WHAT ACTIVITY WILL BE DONE ON A PARTICULAR DAY. *)

VAR
    ANSW1, ANSW2 : STRING;
    SCHOOLDAY, SUNNY : BOOLEAN;

BEGIN

    WRITELN ('IS TODAY A SCHOOLDAY?');
    WRITELN ('TYPE IN YES OR NO.');
    READLN (ANSW1);

    IF ANSW1 = 'YES' THEN
        SCHOOLDAY := TRUE
    ELSE
        SCHOOLDAY := FALSE;

    WRITELN ('IS TODAY SUNNY?');
    WRITELN ('TYPE IN YES OR NO.');
    READLN (ANSW2);

    IF ANSW2 = 'YES' THEN
        SUNNY := TRUE
    ELSE
        SUNNY := FALSE;

    IF SCHOOLDAY AND SUNNY THEN
        WRITELN ('GO TO SCHOOL TODAY.');

    IF SCHOOLDAY AND NOT SUNNY THEN
        WRITELN ('WEAR RAINCOAT TO SCHOOL TODAY.');

    IF NOT SCHOOLDAY AND NOT SUNNY THEN
        WRITELN ('WATCH TV TODAY.');

    IF NOT SCHOOLDAY AND SUNNY THEN
        WRITELN ('PLAY BALL TODAY!')

END.  (* ACTIVITY *)
```

Running. . .
```
IS TODAY A SCHOOLDAY?
TYPE IN YES OR NO.
NO
IS TODAY SUNNY?
TYPE IN YES OR NO.
NO
WATCH TV TODAY.

IS TODAY A SCHOOLDAY?
TYPE IN YES OR NO.
NO
IS TODAY SUNNY?
TYPE IN YES OR NO.
YES
PLAY BALL TODAY!
```

Figure 7-12 PROGRAM ACTIVITY

There are four different combinations of answers to these two questions:

```
SCHOOLDAY AND SUNNY
SCHOOLDAY AND NOT SUNNY
NOT SCHOOLDAY AND SUNNY
NOT SCHOOLDAY AND NOT SUNNY
```

Each of these conditions is tested for. A different sentence is printed depending on which of the conditions is true. Look at the expression

```
IF SCHOOLDAY AND SUNNY THEN
```

You may wonder why this expression isn't written

```
IF (SCHOOLDAY = TRUE) AND (SUNNY = TRUE) THEN
```

This is because SCHOOLDAY itself has the value of true or false. This value has already been assigned to it in the expressions SCHOOLDAY := TRUE or SCHOOLDAY := FALSE.

Study the BOOLEAN expressions below and make certain that you understand how each is evaluated.

Expression	*Evaluates To*
NOT (1 * 4 = 5)	TRUE
(18 < 16) OR (7 + 2 = 9)	TRUE
(18 < 16) AND (7 + 2 = 9)	FALSE
(2 + 8 <= 11) AND (17 * 2 = 34)	TRUE
NOT (12 > 8 - 2)	FALSE

✎LEARNING CHECK 7-3

1. What is a BOOLEAN operator? What are the three BOOLEAN operators? In what order are they evaluated?
2. What is meant by an infinite loop?
3. What is a scalar data type? What are the three scalar data types that have been covered so far?

Answers:

1. A BOOLEAN operator is an operator used with a BOOLEAN expression; the BOOLEAN operators are NOT, AND, and OR. 2. An infinite loop is a loop in which the condition controlling loop repetition will never contain the value needed to stop the loop. 3. A scalar data type is a data type whose values can be listed; the three scalar data types studied so far are: INTEGER, CHAR, and BOOLEAN.

SUMMARY POINTS

- This chapter introduced a new type of control statement, the loop. The loop allows the programmer to repeat a series of instructions as many times as is needed. There are three basic types of loops: the RE-PEAT/UNTIL loop, the WHILE loop, and the FOR loop. In the WHILE loop, a condition is evaluated at the beginning of the loop. While that condition is true, the loop is executed. In a REPEAT/UNTIL loop, the condition is evaluated at the end of the loop. Until that condition is true, the loop is repeated. The FOR loop is useful when it can be determined how many times a loop is to be executed.
- Checking to make sure that data the user enters will work with a particular program is very important. If the data are not correct for the program, an error message should be printed to the monitor and the user should be allowed to reenter the data.
- The BOOLEAN operators are NOT, AND, and OR. They are used with BOOLEAN expressions; that is, expressions that evaluate as true or false.

VOCABULARY LIST

Infinite loop A loop in which the condition controlling loop repetition will never contain the value needed to stop the loop.

Initialize To set a variable to a starting value.

Loop A control statement that allows a series of instructions to be executed repeatedly as long as specified conditions are constant.

Loop control variable A variable whose value is used to control the repetition of a loop.

Ordinal data type See **Scalar data type.**

Scalar data type A data type where all of the values of that data type may be listed. INTEGER, CHAR, BOOLEAN, and USER-DEFINED are all scalar data types.

CHAPTER TEST

VOCABULARY

Match a term from the numbered column with the description from the lettered column that best fits the term.

1. Initialize

2. Loop

3. Infinite loop

a. A control statement that allows a series of instructions to be executed repeatedly as long as specified conditions are constant.

b. To set a variable to a starting value.

c. A step in solving a problem where a comparison is made. The step that will be done next de-

4. Loop control variable

    pends on the results of that comparison.

    d. A loop in which the condition controlling loop repetition will never contain the value needed to stop the loop.

5. Decision step

    e. A variable whose value is used to control the repetition of a loop.

QUESTIONS

1. Explain how a REPEAT/UNTIL loop works.
2. How many times will the loop below be executed? What will the value of NUM be at the end of the loop each time through?

```
PROGRAM EX2;

VAR
    NUM : INTEGER;

BEGIN

    NUM := 12;

    REPEAT
        NUM := NUM - 2;
        WRITELN (NUM)
    UNTIL NUM < 0;
```

3. How is a WHILE loop different from a REPEAT/UNTIL loop?
4. Rewrite the program below using a WHILE loop instead of the REPEAT/UNTIL loop.

```
PROGRAM EXAMPLE;

VAR
    COUNT : INTEGER;
    NAME : STRING;

BEGIN

    COUNT := 1;

    REPEAT
        WRITELN ('TYPE IN A NAME.');
        READLN (NAME);
        COUNT := COUNT + 1
    UNTIL COUNT >= 8

END.
```

5. Rewrite the program segment in question 4 using a FOR loop.
6. Why is it important for the programmer to write a program that checks to make sure the user has entered data that will work with the program?
7. Using the program segment below, evaluate the BOOLEAN expressions that follow.

```
VAR
     ANSWER : BOOLEAN;
     X,Y,Z : INTEGER;

BEGIN

     ANSWER := TRUE;
     X := 4;
     Y := 3;
     Z := 12;
```

a. NOT ANSWER
b. (X * Y = Z) AND (X = 4)
c. (X + Z = 10) OR (4 * 4) = 10
d. ANSWER AND (X + Y * 10 = 14)

PROGRAMMING PROBLEMS

1. Write a program that will read five numbers and print the largest of the five. Use a FOR loop the first time you write the program. Then rewrite it using a WHILE loop.
2. Write a program that reads an integer, I, and calculates I + (I − 1) + (I − 2) + . . . + 1. For example, if the integer read was 6, the calculation would look like this:

$$6 + 5 + 4 + 3 + 2 + 1 = 21$$

Use an appropriate type of loop to do this problem. Print the result to the monitor.
3. Write a program that will read the number of miles a person runs each day for a week (seven days). Use a FOR loop to allow the user to input the number of miles run on day 1, 2, and so on. Then calculate and print to the monitor the total number of miles run per week and the average number of miles run per day.
4. Write a program that allows a grocer to take inventory. The program should ask the user what the inventory number of the current item is (for example, 1 = cheese, 2 = lettuce, 3 = steak) and the amount of each item on hand. Use a REPEAT/UNTIL loop to allow the grocer to enter a new item. (Hint: Use a CASE statement to tell the program that item number 1 means cheese or item number 2 means lettuce.)

CHAPTER 8

Programming Style and Debugging

OUTLINE

LEARNING OBJECTIVES

After studying this chapter, you should be able to:

1. Explain what good programming style is and why it is important.
2. List the three characteristics of a program with good style.
3. Write good beginning program documentation and good documentation within the body of the program.
4. List the two places in a program where indentation can make a program easier to understand.
5. Use spacing and blank lines to make programs easier to understand.
6. Use meaningful variable names when writing programs, and explain why this is important.
7. Identify the two basic steps in the debugging process.
8. List and describe syntax, run-time, and logic errors.
9. List some common syntax errors.
10. Describe and use a basic debugging procedure for syntax errors.
11. List some common run-time errors.
12. Describe how program tracing can be used to debug run-time errors.
13. Use program tracing to debug run-time errors.
14. Use program tracing and hand simulation to debug logic errors.

INTRODUCTION

This chapter will first discuss **programming style.** A program's style refers to the way it is written to make it easier to read and understand. The style of a program has nothing to do with the actual Pascal statements. The computer can execute a program that has poor style just as easily as a program that has good style.

A program with good style has the following characteristics:

1. It is well documented.
2. Indentation and blank spaces are used to make the program easier to read and understand.
3. The variables have meaningful names.

Each of these three points will be discussed in this chapter.

Computer programming is often difficult. Programmers from beginners to professionals find program errors, or bugs, in many of their programs. Program errors are a fact of life for most programmers. The process of finding and correcting program errors is called **debugging.** The first step in debugging a program is locating and identifying the program error. Then, various debugging techniques can be used to correct the error. A key to successful debugging is a good understanding of the different types of program errors, how they affect the computer and the program. This chapter will help you to identify and debug program errors.

DOCUMENTATION

Documentation is the comments that explain what is being done in a computer program. These comments are used to make the program easier for users to understand. The comments mean nothing to the computer. Comments must be enclosed like this:

```
(* A COMMENT *)
```

or like this:

```
{ANOTHER COMMENT}
```

This tells the computer to ignore what comes between these symbols. When writing comments, the programmer should try to make them as brief and clear as possible. Documentation appears in two basic places in a program:

1. After the program statement (beginning documentation).
2. Within the body of the program.

Beginning Documentation

After the program statement comes the documentation that explains the program as a whole. The purpose of the program is stated here. This is where any input the program needs is described. For example, a comment like:

```
(* THE USER ENTERS AN INTEGER TO THE KEYBOARD. *)
```

explains the type of data that must be entered. The output produced by the program should also be explained here. All of the input in programs so far in this book has been read from the keyboard and all of the output has been printed to the monitor. Later on, this will not necessarily be true. For example, input may come from a diskette and output may go to a printer. As programs become more complex, it is important to state exactly where input comes from and where output will be going. This is very important to people who are not familiar with the program but who want to use it.

The programs written so far have used only a few variables. As programs become more complex, it is important that the major variables be listed at the beginning of the program and that the purpose of each be explained. Study the program in Figure 8-1. This program calculates the cost of an order at a fast-food restaurant. Each of the variables used in this program has been listed in the beginning documentation. Following the variable name, a brief explanation of each variable's purpose is given. This is especially helpful to people unfamiliar with the program.

Beginning documentation may include any codes that are used in the program. In the sample program there is a table that lists each food item, its code number, and the cost of that item. These code numbers are used in the CASE statement in the body of the program.

Figure 8-1 PROGRAM MEAL

```
PROGRAM MEAL;
(* THIS PROGRAM CALCULATES THE COST OF A PURCHASE AT A FAST-FOOD
RESTAURANT.  THE USER ENTERS AN INTEGER TO THE  MONITOR THAT
REPRESENTS THE COST OF A SPECIFIC ITEM.  THE USER THEN ENTERS
HOW MANY OF THAT ITEM ARE DESIRED.  THE COST OF THE ITEM
IS THEN CALCULATED.  THE USER IS THEN ALLOWED TO ENTER ANOTHER
ITEM.  WHEN THE USER IS DONE ENTERING AN ORDER, THE TOTAL COST OF
THE ORDER IS PRINTED TO THE  MONITOR.

THE CODE USED TO ENTER FOOD ITEMS IS AS FOLLOWS:

      CODE NUMBER      ITEM            COST OF ITEM

      ------------------------------------------------
          1            HAMBURGER       $0.75
          2            CHEESEBURGER    $0.90
          3            FRENCH FRIES    $0.55
          4            FRUIT PIE       $0.60
          5            DRINK           $0.50

          6   USED TO INDICATE END OF THE ORDER.


      ------------------------------------------------

MAJOR VARIABLES USED:
      FOOD    - CODE NUMBER TO INDICATE A PARTICULAR ITEM.
      COST    - COST OF AN ITEM.
      NUMBER  - HOW MANY OF A PARTICULAR ITEM ARE DESIRED.
      TOTCOST - THE TOTAL COST OF AN ORDER.
      ------------------------------------------------
*)

VAR
      FOOD, NUMBER  : INTEGER;
      COST, TOTCOST : REAL;
```

Continued next page

Figure 8-1 (con't.)

```
BEGIN

    (* INITIALIZE TOTAL COST TO ZERO *)
    TOTCOST := 0;

    (* READ IN CODE NUMBER OF FIRST ITEM *)
    WRITELN ('ENTER CODE NUMBER FOR FOOD ITEM.');
    WRITELN ('IF ORDER IS COMPLETE, TYPE IN THE NUMBER 6.');
    READLN (FOOD);

    (* LOOP TO READ IN EACH FOOD ITEM AND ASSIGN COST *)
    WHILE FOOD <> 6 DO
        BEGIN
            (* INITIALIZE COST OF AN ITEM TO ZERO *)
            COST := 0.0;

        (* LOOP TO ALLOW USER TO REENTER CODE NUMBER IF AN
        INCORRECT NUMBER HAS BEEN ENTERED. *)
        WHILE (FOOD < 1) OR (FOOD > 6) DO
            BEGIN
                WRITELN ('CODE NUMBER MUST BE BETWEEN 1 AND 6.');
                WRITELN ('PLEASE REENTER CODE NUMBER.');
                READLN (FOOD)
            END;    (* WHILE *)

        (* CASE STATEMENT TO ASSIGN APPROPRIATE COST TO EACH FOOD
        ITEM *)
        CASE FOOD OF
            1 : COST := 0.75;
            2 : COST := 0.90;
            3 : COST := 0.55;
            4 : COST := 0.60;
            5 : COST := 0.50
        END;    (* CASE *)

        (* DETERMINE HOW MANY OF A PARTICULAR ITEM ARE DESIRED
        AND COMPUTE TOTAL COST *)
        WRITELN ('HOW MANY OF THIS ITEM ARE DESIRED.');
        READLN (NUMBER);
        COST := COST * NUMBER;
        TOTCOST := TOTCOST + COST;

        (* READ IN CODE NUMBER OF NEXT ITEM *)
        WRITELN ('ENTER CODE NUMBER FOR FOOD ITEM.');
        WRITELN ('IF ORDER IS COMPLETE, TYPE IN THE NUMBER 6.');
        READLN (FOOD)

    END;    (* WHILE *)

    (* PRINT TOTAL COST OF THE ORDER TO THE  MONITOR *)
    WRITELN ('THE TOTAL COST OF THIS ORDER IS $ ', TOTCOST:7:2)

END. (* MEAL *)
```

Running. . .
```
ENTER CODE NUMBER FOR FOOD ITEM.
IF ORDER IS COMPLETE, TYPE IN THE NUMBER 6.
4
```

```
HOW MANY OF THIS ITEM ARE DESIRED.
3
ENTER CODE NUMBER FOR FOOD ITEM.
IF ORDER IS COMPLETE, TYPE IN THE NUMBER 6.
9
CODE NUMBER MUST BE BETWEEN 1 AND 6.
PLEASE REENTER CODE NUMBER.
1
HOW MANY OF THIS ITEM ARE DESIRED.
2
ENTER CODE NUMBER FOR FOOD ITEM.
IF ORDER IS COMPLETE, TYPE IN THE NUMBER 6.
6
THE TOTAL COST OF THIS ORDER IS $     3.30
```

Figure 8-1 (con't.)

Documentation Within the Program Body

Documentation within the program body is comments that are placed inside the body of the program. These comments are usually brief, not over a few lines in length. Comments should be placed before control statements explaining the purpose of the control statement. Look at the comment before the second WHILE loop in program MEAL. It explains the purpose of the loop:

```
(* LOOP TO ALLOW USER TO REENTER CODE NUMBER IF AN INCORRECT NUMBER
HAS BEEN ENTERED. *)
```

This comment explains briefly what the loop does. The loop checks to make sure the code number is valid. The comment also explains that the loop allows the user to reenter a code number if an invalid number has been entered.

It is a good idea to also have comments before READ and WRITE statements unless the meaning of the statement is absolutely clear. Comments following the reserved word END can help in matching up an END with its BEGIN. For example:

```
            WHILE FOOD <> 6 DO
                BEGIN
                    statement;
                        .
                        .
                        .
                END (* WHILE *)
```

Comments within the body of a program may be placed on separate lines like this:

`(* CASE STATEMENT TO ASSIGN APPROPRIATE COST TO EACH FOOD ITEM *)` or after a Pascal statement, like this:

```
READLN (NUM); (* READ NUMBER OF ITEMS *)
```

INDENTATION AND SPACING

Imagine an essay written for an English class that had no paragraphs, margins, or blank lines. The essay would be a sheet of paper filled with sentence after sentence. It would probably not be easy to read or understand. Certainly it would not be enjoyable to read and wouldn't receive a good grade. A programmer should attempt to make a program as easy to read as a well-written English essay. Although the use of indentation and spacing make no difference to the computer, they can make following a program much more pleasant for people.

Indentation

Indentation refers to blank spaces left at the beginning of Pascal statements. There are two places where indentation helps to make a program more readable:

1. To separate a control statement from the rest of a program.
2. To separate a compound statement from the rest of the program

An IF/THEN/ELSE statement could be written this way:

```
IF X <> Y THEN SUM := SUM + X
ELSE WRITELN (X, ' IS A DUPLICATE NUMBER.');
```

It also could be written like this:

```
IF X <> Y THEN
SUM := SUM + X
ELSE
WRITELN (X, ' IS A DUPLICATE NUMBER.');
```

But, in this book it will be written this way:

```
IF X <> Y THEN
    SUM := SUM + X
ELSE
    WRITELN (X, ' IS A DUPLICATE NUMBER.');
```

All three of these examples would be treated the same by the computer. The last example makes it easier to read and follow the logic of the program. The same is true for indenting compound statements. Indentation makes it easy to see which statements are a part of the compound statement. In program MEAL, this program segment is indented twice:

149

```
WHILE (FOOD < 1) OR (FOOD > 6) DO
    BEGIN
        WRITELN ('CODE NUMBER MUST BE BETWEEN 1 AND 6.');
        WRITELN ('PLEASE REENTER CODE NUMBER.');
        READLN (FOOD)

    END; (* WHILE *)
```

The first indentation is to set off the WHILE loop statements. The second indentation shows that the statements between the BEGIN and the END are all part of a compound statement.

Spacing

Spaces are left in Pascal statements to make the statements more readable. It is not necessary to leave spaces between variables and operators. The examples on the left side of the table below have no spaces around the operators or after the word READLN. The right side shows these same statements with spaces. This is a matter of personal preference. Generally, leaving spaces helps to separate each part of the statement and make it more readable.

Without Spaces

```
READLN(X,Y,Z);
COST:=COST+(COST*PERCENT);
WHILE(COUNT<>100) OR (X*Y>10) DO
```

With Spaces

```
READLN (X, Y, Z);
COST := COST + (COST * PERCENT);
WHILE (COUNT <> 100) OR (X * Y > 10) DO
```

Blank Lines

Blank lines can be used to separate different sections of the program from the rest. It is a good idea to use blank lines around control statements. A blank line before and after a loop make it easy to see where the loop begins and ends. In program MEAL, blank lines have been used to separate sections of the program.

LEARNING CHECK 8-1

1. What is meant by good programming style?
2. What three things will be true of a program with good style?
3. Why are program statements indented?
4. Name two types of statements that may be indented to set them apart from the rest of the program.

USING MEANINGFUL NAMES

Meaningful names should be used to represent variables and constants in Pascal programs. In program MEAL, the variable name TOTCOST is a meaningful name. It stands for the words "total cost." It is easy to figure out that this variable represents the total cost of the meal. Names in Pascal programs should be chosen to describe the variables they represent.

Sometimes it isn't possible to find a meaningful name, as in the case of a loop control variable. Then it is usually best to choose a simple name such as I (for integer) or COUNT.

Meaningful names are particularly useful in helping people other than the programmer to understand a program.

PROGRAM ERRORS

Three types of errors can occur in a program. They are syntax, run-time, and logic errors. **Syntax errors** are violations of the grammatical rules of a programming language. These are also called **compile-time errors.** They occur during the translation of the program by the compiler. A common syntax error is forgetting to place a semicolon between Pascal statements. **Run-time errors** cause abnormal program behavior during the execution of the program. Run-time errors often cause the program to stop running early. **Logic errors** are flaws in a program's algorithms, formulas, or logic that cause incorrect program output. They occur during the execution of the program, but the program will usually run normally and will have output. A common logic error is incorrectly translating an arithmetic formula. For example, the average of 4 and 2 is the sum of 4 and 2, or 6, divided by 2. A logic error would occur if the average was calculated in a program by the formula 4 + 2/2. The program would output 5, not the correct answer 3. Figure 8-2 illustrates syntax, run-time, and logic errors.

It is important to remember the differences between syntax, runtime, and logic errors. The computer will react differently to each type of program error. This in turn means that the programmer needs different debugging techniques for each type of error. The programmer, program error, and computer are part of a debugging cycle. Figure 8-3 illustrates a way of looking at the debugging cycle. Through careful structured programming you can reduce the amount of time you spend in this cycle.

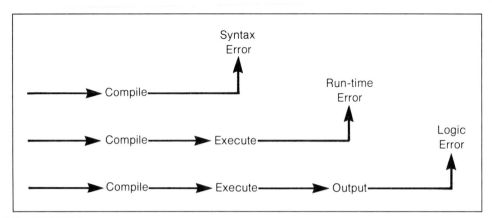

Figure 8-2 ERRORS

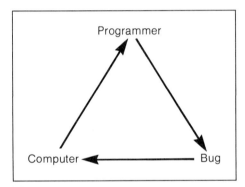

Figure 8-3 DEBUGGING CYCLE

SYNTAX ERRORS

Syntax errors are the most frequent type of program error. Fortunately, they are also the easiest program error to find. Syntax errors are a result of incorrect usage of the UCSD Pascal language.

Syntax errors are discovered when a program is compiled. The Pascal compiler will report each syntax error as it is found in the program. You then have the option to immediately enter the program and correct the error or to continue compiling the program. Any syntax error in a UCSD Pascal program is a fatal error. A program cannot be executed until all syntax errors are corrected. You will not be able to run any program that contains syntax errors!

In most versions of UCSD Pascal, syntax errors will be flagged by an error message from the compiler. The error message may vary from just a number to a short description. Some common syntax errors and error messages are illustrated in Figure 8-4.

```
PROGRAM COUNT;                                    Error
                                                 Message
    CONST MILE : 5280                 ' = ' expected
    VAR
        I : INTEGER                   ' ; ' expected (possibly on line
        SUM : REAL;                       above)

    BEGIN                             ')' expected
        WRITE (MILES RUN TODAY: ;     undeclared identifier
        READLN (TODAY);               undeclared identifier
        I := TODAY                    ': =' expected
        SUM = I * MILE
        WRITELN ('FEET RUN: ', SUM)   ')' expected (integer expected)
        WRITELN ('MILES RUN: ', I:3,2); unexpected end of
                                      input
```

Figure 8-4 PROGRAM COUNT

Debugging Syntax Errors

Attention to program detail and careful typing will help you avoid many syntax errors. A good debugging strategy for syntax errors is to correct each syntax error as it is flagged by the compiler. Why? First, if you enter the edit option when a syntax error is flagged, the editor will mark the part of the statement in the program that was flagged. Second, often an early syntax error will cause several other syntax errors later in the program. Editing syntax errors as they are flagged may eliminate some later errors. Figure 8-5 illustrates the suggested procedure for debugging syntax errors.

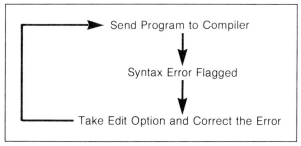

Figure 8-5 DEBUGGING SYNTAX ERRORS

The procedure should be followed until all syntax errors are corrected.

LEARNING CHECK 8-2

1. What are the two basic steps in the debugging process?
2. How does the UCSD Pascal compiler react to syntax errors?
3. List a few common syntax errors.

RUN-TIME ERRORS

Run-time errors cause abnormal program behavior during execution. The end-result of most run-time errors is that a program will not be completely executed by the computer. Run-time errors are described by the compiler. Run-time error messages are usually less descriptive and more difficult to understand than syntax error messages. In many cases, the appendix of your Pascal user's manual will more fully describe run-time errors. An important difference between the computer's response to run-time and syntax errors is that the programmer must find run-time errors. The computer will not automatically locate a run-time error, as it will do for syntax errors. Run-time error messages will note in what procedure or function the error occurred.

Run-time errors can be caused by the program or by the data used by the program. If data do not match the type of the calling variables, a run-time error will occur. Some common run-time errors and error messages are listed in Figure 8-6.

Debugging Run-Time Errors

Run-time errors are more difficult to find and fix than syntax errors. Run-time errors will always occur after all syntax errors are found and fixed. **Program tracing** is a technique that can be used to find run-time errors. Program tracing has four steps. First, read the error message and note the type of error. Second, enter Edit mode and, starting at the top of the program, move down looking for any statements that

Figure 8-6 COMMON RUN-TIME ERRORS

1. Division by zero
2. Using a variable in a program before assigning a value to it.
3. Assigning a value to a variable that is larger than the specified bounds of the variable.

```
PROGRAM ERROR;
    VAR
        I : INTEGER;

BEGIN

    WHILE I <= 12 DO
        BEGIN
            I := I + 1;
            READLN (NAME)
        END

    END.
```

Figure 8-7 A RUN-TIME ERROR

Before	After

AVE := MILES / DAYS;	IF DAYS > 0 THEN
	    AVE := MILES / DAYS
	ELSE
	    WRITELN ('DAYS EQUALS ZERO';

Figure 8-8 DEFENSIVE PROGRAMMING

may have caused the error. Third, when a possible error-causing state-ment is found, insert a WRITELN statement to print the value of the variables in the statement. Fourth, compile and execute the program. Look at the values printed by the WRITELN statement(s) you inserted. They should help you determine if the run-time error is occurring at that point in the program. In Figure 8-7, a READLN statement is used to read a list of 12 names. Do you see the run-time error in the pro-gram? The variable I has not been initialized. It should have been ini-tialized to zero before the loop was entered. A run-time error will occur when the program attempts to increment I by one.

Defensive programming means that a program is written so that program errors are trapped by the program. In Figure 8-8 an IF statement is used to protect the variable MILES from being divided by zero. Though defensive programming requires extra effort, it saves the programmer time in finding and correcting program errors.

LOGIC ERRORS

Logic errors are flaws in the algorithms, formulas, or logic used in a program. Logic errors always occur after both syntax and run-time errors. A program with a logic error will compile and execute, but

155

will output the wrong information. Logic errors are the most difficult of all to find and correct. No error messages will appear if a logic error occurs. In general, only the output of the program will indicate that a logic error exists.

Debugging Logic Errors

Logic errors are usually the last program errors to be discovered in a program. Debugging logic errors is much easier if the program is well structured and organized. If the program is written clearly, the program logic will be easier to follow. Errors will then be easier to find. As a program grows larger, program documentation becomes more important. Each logical group in a program should be briefly described. Program documentation helps the programmer follow the logic of a program.

Program tracing is a good way of locating logic errors. Inserting WRITELN statements into the program at various points allows the programmer to determine what the actual value of different variables is. This can help to pinpoint logic errors. Hand-simulating a program is also helpful in finding logic errors. **Hand simulation** means that the programmer pretends to be the computer. The programmer reads through the program and performs all the operations normally done by the computer.

When you suspect that your program has a logic error, try to print your program. If you have access to a printer, UCSD Pascal allows you to easily print a program file. First, save the program on a diskette. Second, use the FILER and the TRANSFER command to move the program file from the diskette to the printer. Figure 8-9 illustrates the procedure. A printout of a program is usually very useful in debugging program errors.

All programmers spend time debugging programs. Your goal should be to make debugging as painless as possible. This chapter should help you find and correct many common program errors.

Figure 8-9 PRINTING OUT A PROGRAM

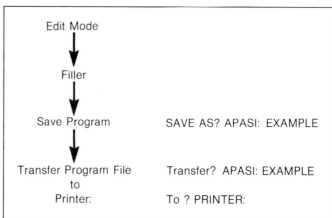

Structured programming will reduce the number of program errors in your programs. Also, careful attention to the writing and typing of a program will help eliminate many syntax, run-time, and logic errors.

LEARNING CHECK 8-3

1. When do run-time errors occur?
2. How do run-time errors usually affect a program?
3. When are logic errors usually detected in a program?
4. Why are logic errors difficult to locate?

Answers: 1. Run-time errors occur during the execution of the program. 2. Run-time errors will usually cause the program to stop executing. 3. Logic errors are usually detected in the program output. 4. Logic errors are difficult to locate because the computer does not flag logic errors. Also, the program will usually output some information.

SUMMARY POINTS

- Using good programming style means writing a program so that it is as easy as possible for people to read and understand. Programs that have good style are well documented and use indentation and blank spaces to make the program easier to follow. Meaningful names are used to identify variables.
- Documentation should be used both at the beginning and within the body of a program. The documentation at the beginning should contain a general description of the program. The documentation in the body of the program should be used to explain specific sections of the program.
- Control statements and compound statements should be indented to set them apart from the rest of the program. Using blank spaces around operators makes statements easier to read. Blank lines, like indentation, are used to separate a section of a program from the rest of the program.
- It is important to use meaningful names for Pascal variables and constants. This makes it easier to remember what a particular variable represents.
- Computer programs are written not just for the computer. They are also written for people. Using good programming style makes it easier for people to understand and use a program.
- Most programmers find program errors in the majority of their programs.
- Syntax errors are the most frequent type of error. Syntax errors are violations of the rules of the Pascal language. Syntax errors are usually found when the program is compiled.
- Run-time errors cause abnormal program behavior and will not allow the program to run properly. They are usually found during the execution of a program. Program tracing is a good debugging technique for run-time errors.
- Logic errors are flaws in the algorithms, formulas, or logic of a program. They cause incorrect program output. Logic errors are the most difficult

157

program error to debug. Program tracing and hand simulation are often necessary to debug a logic error.

VOCABULARY LIST

Compile-time errors See **Syntax errors.**

Debugging The process of finding and correcting program errors.

Defensive programming The anticipation of potential program errors and the inclusion of program statements that keep track of the variable values and flag program errors.

Hand simulation A debugging technique where the programmer pretends to be the computer. The programmer performs by hand all the operations normally done by the computer in a program.

Logic errors Flaws in a program's algorithms, formulas, or logic that cause incorrect program output.

Program tracing A debugging technique that can be used to find run-time and logic errors. WRITE and WRITELN statements are inserted into a program to allow the programmer to examine the variable values and follow the program logic.

Run-time errors Flaws in a program that often cause the program to stop running early.

Programming style Writing a program in a way that will make it easier for people to read and understand the program.

Syntax errors Violations of the grammatical rules of a programming language that make it impossible for a program to be compiled.

CHAPTER TEST

VOCABULARY

Match a term from the numbered column with the description from the lettered column that best fits the term.

1. Programming style

2. Program tracing

3. Run-time errors

4. Hand simulation

5. Defensive programming

a. Flaws in a program's algorithms, formulas, or logic that cause incorrect program output.

b. Flaws in a program that often cause the program to stop running early.

c. A debugging technique that can be used to find run-time and logic errors: WRITELN statements are inserted into a program to allow the programmer to examine the variable values and follow the program logic.

d. The process of finding and correcting program errors.

e. The anticipation of potential program errors and the inclusion of program statements that keep track of the variable values and flag program errors.

6. Logic errors

f. A debugging technique where the programmer pretends to be the computer.

7. Debugging

g. The way in which a program is written to make it easier for people to read and understand.

QUESTIONS

1. What should be included in beginning program documentation? What should be included in documentation in the program body?
2. Rewrite the following Pascal statements, using blank spaces to make the statements more readable:
   a. `WRITELN('THE SUM OF ', X,Y,Z, 'IS',SUM);`
   b. `PERCENT:=(NUM1+NUM2+NUM3)/TOTAL;`
   c. `SCORE:=10*12+50*10;`
3. What is meant by using meaningful variable names? Give three examples of meaningful variable names.
4. Describe syntax, run-time, and logic errors. When do each occur?
5. Describe how the programmer, computer, and program error interact.
6. Describe a general debugging strategy for syntax errors.
7. List a few common run-time errors.
8. Describe the technique of program-tracing.
9. What is defensive programming? How can it save the programmer time?
10. Describe the process of hand-simulating a program.
11. How can structured programming and good program documentation help debug logic errors?

PROGRAMMING PROBLEMS

1. The Tuesday evening bowling league would like a program to compute the average bowling score of each of its players. The program should read each bowler's name and the scores of her last five games. The average of these five scores should then be calculated. The output should be similar to this:

```
SALLY DOE HAS AN AVERAGE SCORE OF 173.5
```

The program must be well documented and use meaningful variable names.
2. Write a program that will read the length and width of a rectangle. The length and width should be given in inches. The program should then calculate the perimeter and area of the rectangle. These results should be printed to the monitor. The program must be well documented and use meaningful variable names.
3. Write a program that will read a list of ten last names. The program should

159

determine which of the names comes first and which of the names comes last alphabetically. The output should be similar to this:

```
THE NAME WHICH COMES FIRST ALPHABETICALLY IS ABBOT.
THE NAME WHICH COMES LAST ALPHABETICALLY IS WYNMANN.
```

4. Write a program to calculate an individual's typing speed. The program should read the following information:
   a. Name.
   b. Number of words typed.
   c. Number of minutes spent typing.
   d. Number of errors.

The formula for calculating words typed per minute is:

$$\text{WPM} = \frac{\text{number of words typed} - (\text{number of errors} * 5)}{\text{number of minutes spent typing}}$$

Print the number of words typed per minute to the monitor. Use meaningful variable names. Document the program thoroughly.

5. The program below contains several syntax errors. Type in the program on your computer and debug it.

```
PROGRAM P_SYNTAX

   CONST DAYS : ;

   VAR
       I : INTEGER:
       FOR : CHAR;
       WEEK = ARRAY[1..DAYS] OF STRING[10];

   BEGIN

       FOR I = 1 TO DAYS DO
          WRITE ('THE FIRST DAY OF THE WEEK IS :);
          READLN (DAY);
          WEEK[I] := DAY
          END;

       WRITELN;
       WRITELN (THE DAYS OF THE WEEK ARE:')

       FOR I = 1 TO DAYS DO
           WRITELN (WEEK[I])

   END.   (* P_SYNTAX *)
```

Functions and Procedures

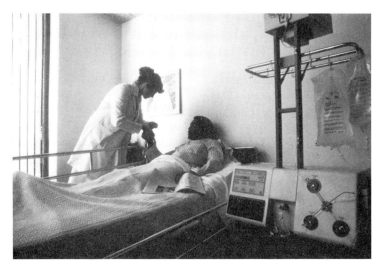

OUTLINE

LEARNING OBJECTIVES

After studying this chapter, you should be able to:

1. List the advantages of using functions and procedures in programs.
2. Explain the differences between functions and procedures.
3. Correctly write functions and function calls.
4. Correctly write procedures and procedure calls.
5. Identify global and local variables in programs and explain the difference between the two.
6. Explain the difference between value and variable parameters.
7. Use value and variable parameters correctly when writing subprograms.
8. Explain why variable parameters must be represented by a variable name and not an expression in a procedure call.
9. Write functions and procedures that are well documented.

INTRODUCTION

An important characteristic of structured programming languages is that they allow large programs to be broken down into smaller subprograms. There are two types of subprograms in Pascal—**functions** and **procedures.** Writing a function or a procedure is very similar to writing a complete Pascal program. This chapter will examine the rules for writing functions and procedures. Using functions and procedures makes large, complex programs easier to write and understand after they are written.

FUNCTIONS

A function is a subprogram that is used to determine a single value. Figure 9-1 shows the format of a function. A function begins with the function heading. The function heading starts with the reserved word FUNCTION followed by the name of the function. The name may be any valid Pascal identifier and should describe the purpose of the function.

The next part of the function heading contains the **formal parameter** list. **Parameters** are used to communicate between the subprogram and the calling program. They are used to pass values between the two programs. The calling program contains an expression that causes the subprogram to be executed. At this point, program control branches to the subprogram, executes it, and branches back to the calling program. A formal parameter is a variable that stands for a value that will be passed to the function or procedure from the program calling that function or procedure. The formal parameter list

```
                                        Name of Part
                                        of the Function

FUNCTION function_name (formal parameter list) : data_type;    (function heading)

VAR
    variable_name : data_type;                        (local variable
    variable_name : data_type;                        declarations)

BEGIN
    statement1;

       .                                              (body of the
       .                                              function)
    last_statement
END;
```

Figure 9-1   FORMAT OF A FUNCTION

is enclosed in parentheses. The data type of each formal parameter is also listed. After the formal parameter list comes a colon and the data type of the function.

Some examples of function headings are:

```
FUNCTION SAME (X, Y, Z : CHAR; NUM : INTEGER) : BOOLEAN;
FUNCTION CODE (LETTER : CHAR) : CHAR;
FUNCTION CODE (NUM2 : REAL) : REAL;
FUNCTION CALC : REAL;
```

FUNCTION SAME is of data type BOOLEAN. It has four formal parameters: X, Y, Z, and NUM. The parameters X, Y, and Z are of data type CHAR. The parameter NUM is of data type INTEGER. Notice that if there is more than one parameter of the same type, these parameters may be declared in the same statement. Declaration statements are separated by semicolons. Look at the last function heading:

```
            FUNCTION CALC : REAL;
```

This is an example of a function that has no parameters. A function is not required to have parameters. If there are no parameters, then all that is needed in the function heading is the function name and the data type of that function.

Below is a function that converts a Celsius temperature to the corresponding Fahrenheit temperature:

```
        FUNCTION F_TEMP (C_TEMP : REAL) : REAL;
            BEGIN
                F_TEMP := 1.8 * C_TEMP + 32.0
            END; (* F_TEMP *)
```

The name of this function is F_TEMP. The data type of the function

163

is REAL. The only parameter in this function is C_TEMP, which is also of data type REAL. There is only one statement in the body of this function. The body of a function must contain at least one statement that assigns a value to the function. In this example the statement

$$F\_TEMP := 1.8 * C\_TEMP + 32.0$$

is used to assign a value to F_TEMP. Notice that the reserved word END is followed by a semicolon and not a period, because it is not at the end of the main program.

Function Calls

Function F_TEMP can be executed by using a **function call.** A function call is an expression that causes the function to be executed. Its format is shown in Figure 9-2. A function may be called from the main program, a procedure, or another function. In this chapter, all functions will be called from a main program.

The following would be valid function calls for F_TEMP:

```
FAHREN := F_TEMP (48.5);
FAHREN := F_TEMP (X + 2);
FAHREN := F_TEMP (CELSIUS);
```

In the function calls listed above, the result of F_TEMP will be assigned to FAHREN. FAHREN must be declared to be of the same data type as F_TEMP. In this case, FAHREN must be of data type REAL.

The parameters in the function call are referred to as the **actual parameters.** The actual parameters are the values that will replace the variable names in the formal parameter list when the function is executed. In function calls, the actual parameters are listed in parentheses. If there is more than one actual parameter, they are separated by commas. The actual parameters may be any valid expression, but the expression must evaluate to the same data type as the formal parameter in the function. There must be the same number of actual parameters as there are formal parameters. The order of the parameters must be the same in both parameter lists.

Look at the last function call listed above:

```
FAHREN := F_TEMP (CELSIUS);
```

The variable CELSIUS is an actual parameter. CELSIUS must be de-

Figure 9-2   FORMAT OF A FUNCTION CALL

```
Variable := function_name (actual parameter list);
```

clared as data type REAL (or INTEGER). CELSIUS must have a value assigned to it before the function F_TEMP is called. The value of CEL-SIUS will be substituted for the formal parameter C_TEMP. Figure 9-3 shows how this substitution takes place when the function is called.

Any functions or procedures in a program are placed at the beginning of the program after the declaration statements. The short program that contains FUNCTION F_TEMP is illustrated in Figure 9-4. In this example, it would have been easier to simply place the statement converting the temperature in the main program. When functions grow long and complex, however, it is easier to write them separately from the rest of the program. Also, this function can be called as many times as it is needed from the main program.

For example, it might be necessary to convert a Celsius temperature to Fahrenheit near the beginning of a program and then do the same thing again later on in the same program. Coding the function separately spares the programmer from writing the same statements over and over. Figure 9-5 contains more examples of function headings and calls that illustrate how the actual parameters will be passed to the formal parameters when the function is called.

Global and Local Variables

Variables in Pascal programs are either **local** or **global variables.** A global variable is one that is declared in the main program. A global variable may be used anywhere in the program, including any procedures or functions within the program. In program SUMS (Figure 9-6) the global variables are E_SUM, O_SUM, NUM, TOTAL, I, and EVEN.

Program SUMS reads a list of integers. All of the integers that are odd will be added together and all of the integers that are even will

Figure 9-3 SUBSTITUTION OF ACTUAL PARAMETER FOR FORMAL PARAMETER

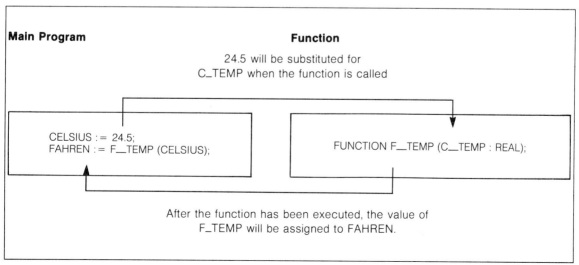

```
PROGRAM CONVERT;
(* THIS PROGRAM READS A CELSIUS TEMPERATURE FROM THE KEYBOARD.
THE PROGRAM THEN CALLS FUNCTION F_TEMP WHICH CONVERTS THE TEMPERATURE
TO FARENHEIT.  THIS RESULT IS THEN PRINTED TO THE  MONITOR. *)

VAR
    CELSIUS, FAHREN : REAL;

(*************************************************************************)
FUNCTION F_TEMP (C_TEMP : REAL) : REAL;
(* THIS FUNCTION CONVERTS A TEMPERATURE FROM CELSIUS TO FARENHEIT. *)

BEGIN    (* F_TEMP *)

    F_TEMP := 1.8 * C_TEMP + 32.0

END;    (* F_TEMP *)
(*************************************************************************)

BEGIN    (* CONVERT *)

    WRITELN ('WHAT IS THE CELSIUS TEMPERATURE TO BE CONVERTED?');
    READLN (CELSIUS);
    FAHREN := F_TEMP (CELSIUS);
    WRITELN ('THE TEMPERATURE IN FAHRENHEIT IS ', FAHREN:7:2)

END.    (* CONVERT *)
```

Running. . .

```
WHAT IS THE CELSIUS TEMPERATURE TO BE CONVERTED?
  35.60
THE TEMPERATURE IN FAHRENHEIT IS   96.08
```

Figure 9-4   **PROGRAM CONVERT**

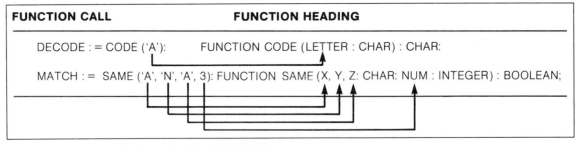

Figure 9-5   **FUNCTION CALLS AND HEADINGS**

be added together. These two sums will be printed at the end of the program. This complete program is shown in Figure 9-6. It uses FUNCTION FIND to determine if a number is odd or even. After the function heading there is a variable declaration:

```
VAR
    REM : INTEGER;
```

Figure 9-6   PROGRAM SUMS

```
PROGRAM SUMS;
(* THIS PROGRAM READS A LIST OF INTEGERS TYPED TO THE KEYBOARD ONE AT
A TIME.  FOR EACH INTEGER READ, FUNCTION FIND IS CALLED TO DETERMINE IF
THE NUMBER IS ODD OR EVEN.  THEN ALL OF THE ODD NUMBERS ARE ADDED
TOGETHER AND ALL OF THE EVEN NUMBERS ARE ADDED TOGETHER.  THESE
TWO SUMS ARE PRINTED TO THE MONITOR . *)

VAR
    E_SUM, O_SUM, NUM, TOTAL, I : INTEGER;
    EVEN : BOOLEAN;

(*********************************************************************)
FUNCTION FIND (X : INTEGER) : BOOLEAN;
(* DETERMINE IF THE INTEGER IS ODD OR EVEN. *)

    VAR
       REM : INTEGER;

    BEGIN   (* FIND *)

       REM := X MOD 2;

       IF REM = 0 THEN
          FIND := TRUE
       ELSE
          FIND := FALSE

    END;   (* FIND *)
(*********************************************************************)

BEGIN   (* SUMS *)

    E_SUM := 0;
    O_SUM := 0;

    WRITELN ('HOW MANY NUMBERS ARE THERE?');
    READLN (TOTAL);
    WRITELN ('ENTER THE NUMBERS.');

    (* LOOP TO READ IN EACH NUMBER AND ASSIGN IT TO THE APPROPRIATE SUM *)
    FOR I := 1 TO TOTAL DO
       BEGIN
          READ (NUM);
          EVEN := FIND (NUM);
          IF EVEN THEN
             E_SUM := E_SUM + NUM
          ELSE
             O_SUM := O_SUM + NUM
       END;   (* FOR *)

    WRITELN;
    WRITELN ('THE SUM OF THE EVEN NUMBERS IS ', E_SUM);
    WRITELN ('THE SUM OF THE ODD NUMBERS IS ', O_SUM)

END. (* SUMS *)



Running. . .

HOW MANY NUMBERS ARE THERE?
8
```

Continued next page

```
ENTER THE NUMBERS.
15
44
33
55
67
99
0
78

THE SUM OF THE EVEN NUMBERS IS 122
THE SUM OF THE ODD NUMBERS IS 269
```

Figure 9-6 (con't.)

This is a local variable declaration statement. REM is a local variable. Local variables are variables that are declared in subprograms. They have no meaning outside of the subprogram in which they are declared. If this statement was inserted in the main program

$$\text{REM} := \text{REM} * 2;$$

it would cause an error because REM is undeclared in the main program.

LEARNING CHECK 9-1

1. Which of the following function headings are correctly formatted?
   a. FUNCTION SUM (X, Y : REAL) : REAL;
   b. FUNCTION FIND (A, B, C, NUM ; INTEGER) : BOOLEAN;
   c. FUNCTION DOUBLE : REAL;
   d. LARGE (ITEM1, ITEM2, ITEM3 : CHAR; COUNT : INTEGER);
2. Write a function call that would be valid for each of the function headings below.
   a. FUNCTION LETTER (CODE1, CODE2, CODE3 : CHAR) : CHAR;
   b. FUNCTION PAYCHECK (HOURS, RATE, TAX : REAL) : REAL;
   c. FUNCTION SIZE (OUNCES : REAL) : INTEGER;
3. What is the difference between a global and a local variable?

Answers: 1. a. Formatted correctly. b. Formatted incorrectly. There is a semicolon separating the formal parameters and their data type. There should be a colon. c. Formatted correctly. d. Formatted incorrectly. The function has no data type and the reserved word FUNCTION has been omitted. 2. The answers should be similar to the following: a. ALPHA := LETTER ('M', 'O', 'E'); b. MONEY := PAYCHECK (40.8, 8.32, 0.04); c. PACKAGE := SIZE (48); 3. A global variable is a variable that has been declared in the main program. A global variable may be used anywhere in a program. A local variable is a variable that has been declared in a subprogram. It is undeclared outside of that subprogram.

PROCEDURES

A function is a subprogram that is used to determine one value and return this value to the calling program. A **procedure** is a subprogram that is used to perform a specific task. An example would be adding sales tax to the price of an item. If a subprogram is needed to determine more than one value, a procedure should be used. A procedure doesn't have to return any values to the calling program. It may be used simply to read or write data.

The format for a procedure is shown in Figure 9-7. The procedure heading begins with the reserved word PROCEDURE and the name of the procedure. This is followed by the formal parameter list. The formal parameter list is written the same way as for a function. Notice that the procedure has no data type. Unlike a function, the procedure name will not return a value to the calling program. The purpose of the procedure name is only to identify the procedure so that it may be referred to from the calling program. If the procedure is to return any values to the calling program, these values must be represented by variables in the formal parameter list.

Procedures, like functions, are useful for two basic reasons:

1. The subprogram may be called any number of times. This means that if the same operations need to be performed more than once in a program, using a subprogram to do these operations will make the program shorter.
2. Procedures help to break down a large, complex program into more manageable subprograms. Since each subprogram has a specific task, this makes the logic of a program easier to follow.

Procedure Calls

Procedures, like functions, may be called from a main program, another procedure, or a function. The **procedure call** contains the name of the procedure and the actual parameter list. The format of

Figure 9-7 FORMAT FOR A PROCEDURE

```
                                                    Name of Part
                                                    of the Procedure

PROCEDURE procedure_name (formal parameter list);    (procedure heading)

VAR
    variable_name : data_type;                       (local variable dec-
    variable_name : data_type;                       larations)

BEGIN

    statement1;                                      (body of the proce-
       .                                             dure)
       .
       .
    last_statement

END;
```

the procedure call is shown in Figure 9-8. Here are some examples of procedure calls:

```
AMOUNT (X, 109.98, PRICE);
ANSWER (AVE1, AVE2, AVE3, GRADE);
```

Sample Program

We will now write a program to calculate and print statistics for members of a basketball team. This program is shown in Figure 9-9. PROCEDURE STATS is used to print each player's statistics. The name, total points scored, average points per game, and the highest number of points scored in one game are printed for each player. The procedure also prints a heading for this information. No calculations are performed by this procedure and no results are passed back to the main program.

Figure 9-8 FORMAT OF A PROCEDURE CALL

Procedure__name (actual parameter list);

Figure 9-9 PROGRAM B__BALL

```
PROGRAM B_BALL;
(* THIS PROGRAM COMPUTES THE STATISTICS FOR A PLAYER ON A BASKETBALL
TEAM.  THE PLAYER'S NAME AND THE NUMBER OF POINTS SCORED IN EACH GAME
BY THAT PLAYER ARE READ FROM THE KEYBOARD.  THE TOTAL NUMBER OF
POINTS SCORED AND THE AVERAGE NUMBER OF POINTS SCORED PER GAME
ARE CALCULATED.  THE MOST NUMBER OF POINTS SCORED IN A SINGLE
GAME IS DETERMINED.  PROCEDURE STATS IS THEN CALLED TO PRINT
THESE RESULTS. *)

VAR
    NAME : STRING;
    AVE : REAL;
    POINTS, HIGH, TOT, I : INTEGER;
(**********************************************************************)
PROCEDURE STATS (PL_NAME : STRING;  PL_AVE : REAL; PL_TOT, PL_HIGH : INTEGER);
(* THIS PROCEDURE PRINTS OUT THE STATISTICS FOR AN INDIVIDUAL
PLAYER *)

BEGIN

    WRITELN;
    WRITELN ('PLAYER''S':20, 'TOTAL':10, 'AVE PER':10, 'MOST POINTS' :15);
    WRITELN ('NAME':17, 'POINTS':13, 'GAME':10, 'IN ONE GAME':15);
    WRITELN ('_____');
    WRITELN (PL_NAME:20, PL_TOT:10, PL_AVE:10:2, PL_HIGH:15);

END;   (* STATS *)
(**********************************************************************)

BEGIN    (* B_BALL *)

    HIGH := 0;
    TOT := 0;
    WRITELN ('ENTER PLAYER''S NAME');
```

Continued next page

Figure 9-9 (con't.)

```
        READLN (NAME);
        WRITELN ('ENTER NUMBER OF POINTS MADE IN EACH OF THE 8 GAMES');

        (* LOOP TO READ SCORE FOR EACH GAME AND DETERMINE TOTAL POINTS
        SCORED AND MOST POINTS SCORED IN A SINGLE GAME *)
        FOR I := 1 TO 8 DO
            BEGIN
                READ (POINTS);
                TOT := POINTS + TOT;
                IF POINTS > HIGH THEN
                    HIGH := POINTS
            END;    (* FOR *)

        (* DETERMINE AVERAGE POINTS SCORED PER GAME *)
        AVE := TOT / 8;

        (* CALL PROCEDURE STATS TO PRINT RESULTS *)
        STATS (NAME, AVE, TOT, HIGH);

    END.    (* B_BALL *)
```

Running. . .

```
ENTER PLAYER'S NAME
GINNY ELLING
ENTER NUMBER OF POINTS MADE IN EACH OF THE 8 GAMES
3
2
5
0
6
2
8
3

        PLAYER'S      TOTAL    AVE PER    MOST POINTS
          NAME        POINTS    GAME      IN ONE GAME
    _____
        GINNY ELLING    29      3.63           8
```

VALUE AND VARIABLE PARAMETERS

So far all of the parameters used in the subprograms in this chapter have been **value parameters.** Value parameters are parameters that only work in one direction. Value parameters pass values to subprograms. They cannot pass a value back to the calling program. This means that if the value of a parameter is changed in a subprogram, the value will not be changed in the calling program. PROGRAM TOTAL1 in Figure 9-10 demonstrates this. In PROCEDURE SUM, the total of three numbers is assigned to variable X, which is then printed. After SUM has been executed, the values of A, B, and C are printed. The value of A is the same as it was before SUM was called. Although the value of the formal parameter X was changed in PROCEDURE SUM, this new value was not returned to the main program.

Value parameters protect variables from being changed accidentally. If the programmer needs to pass a parameter to a subprogram but does not want the value of that parameter to be changed in the calling program, a value parameter should be used.

171

```
PROGRAM TOTAL1;
(* THIS PROGRAM DEMONSTRATES THAT WHEN A VALUE PARAMETER IS CHANGED
IN A SUBPROGRAM THAT NEW VALUE IS NOT RETURNED TO THE CALLING
PROGRAM.   THIS PROGRAM READS THREE NUMBERS FROM THE  KEYBOARD AND CALLS
PROCEDURE SUM TO ADD THE THREE NUMBERS TOGETHER.   ALTHOUGH THE
VALUE OF VARIABLE X IS  CHANGED IN PROCEDURE SUM, THIS RESULT
IS NOT RETURNED TO THE CALLING PROGRAM. *)

VAR
   A, B, C : REAL;

(**********************************************************************)
PROCEDURE SUM (X, Y, Z : REAL);
(* THIS PROCEDURE ADDS X, Y, AND Z TOGETHER AND PUTS THE SUM IN
VARIABLE X *)

BEGIN    (* SUM *)

   X := X + Y + Z;
   WRITELN ('THE TOTAL IS ', X:7:2)

END;   (* SUM *)
(**********************************************************************)

BEGIN    (* TOTAL1 *)

   WRITELN ('TYPE IN THE 3 NUMBERS TO BE ADDED TOGETHER.');
   READ (A, B, C);
   SUM (A, B, C);
   WRITELN (' A= ',A:6:2, ' B= ',B:6:2, ' C= ',C:6:2)

END.   (* TOTAL1 *)




 Running. . .
TYPE IN THE 3 NUMBERS TO BE ADDED TOGETHER.
  45.88 719.03  19.66
THE TOTAL IS  784.57
 A=  45.88 B=  719.03 C=  19.66
```

Figure 9-10   PROGRAM TOTAL1

What if this new value of X calculated in PROCEDURE SUM needed to be returned to the main program? Then it would be necessary to make X a **variable parameter.** A variable parameter is a two-way parameter. Variable parameters return their values to the calling program. A variable parameter is always preceded by the word VAR in the formal parameter list. Figure 9-11 contains the same program as Figure 9-10, except that X is now a variable parameter. Notice that the new value of X is returned to the calling program.

If a parameter is a variable parameter, it must be listed as a variable name in the procedure call. It may not be an expression. This is because a value will be returned to this parameter. Suppose we had a procedure call like this:

```
PROGRAM TOTAL2;
(* THIS PROGRAM DEMONSTRATES THAT WHEN A VARIABLE PARAMETER IS CHANGED
IN A SUBPROGRAM THAT NEW VALUE IS RETURNED TO THE CALLING
PROGRAM.  THIS PROGRAM READS THREE NUMBERS FROM THE  MONITOR AND CALLS
PROCEDURE SUM TO ADD THE THREE NUMBERS TOGETHER.  THE VALUE OF THE
VARIABLE X IS CHANGED IN PROCEDURE SUM.  THIS NEW VALUE IS RETURNED
TO THE MAIN PROGRAM.  *)

VAR
   A, B, C : REAL;

(*******************************************************************)
PROCEDURE SUM (VAR X : REAL; Y, Z : REAL);
(* THIS PROCEDURE ADDS X, Y, AND Z TOGETHER AND PUTS THE SUM IN
VARIABLE X *)

BEGIN   (* SUM *)

   X := X + Y + Z;
   WRITELN ('THE TOTAL IS ', X:7:2)

END;   (* SUM *)
(*******************************************************************)

BEGIN   (* TOTAL2 *)

   WRITELN ('TYPE IN THE 3 NUMBERS TO BE ADDED TOGETHER.');
   READ (A, B, C);
   SUM (A, B, C);
   WRITELN (' A= ',A:6:2, ' B= ',B:6:2, ' C= ',C:6:2)

END.   (* TOTAL2 *)


Running. . .
TYPE IN THE 3 NUMBERS TO BE ADDED TOGETHER.
  45.88 719.03  19.66
THE TOTAL IS  784.57
 A=  784.57 B=  719.03 C=  19.66
```

Figure 9-11 PROGRAM TOTAL2

$$CHECK\ (X/2);$$

What if the procedure heading looked like this?

$$PROCEDURE\ CHECK\ (VAR\ TOT\ :\ REAL);$$

After PROCEDURE CHECK is executed, how would the value of TOT be returned to X/2? A value can be assigned to a variable name, but not to an expression. Because of this, only value parameters may be expressions.

It is not a good idea to use variable parameters in functions. Functions should be used to return a single value. That value will be assigned to the function name. If more than one value needs to be returned to the calling program, it is best to use a procedure.

PROGRAM ART

The program in Figure 9-12 determines what art supplies are needed for an art class. Each student is allowed to make one project: a ceramic vase, a watercolor, or a series of charcoal sketches. The name of the project and how many of that project will be made by the class are entered to the keyboard. After all the data are entered, the supplies needed are printed to the monitor.

Figure 9-12   PROGRAM ART

```
PROGRAM ART;
(* THIS PROGRAM DETERMINES THE QUANTITY OF SUPPLIES NEEDED FOR AN ART CLASS.
EACH STUDENT IS ALLOWED TO MAKE ONE PROJECT.  THE PROJECTS AND THE
SUPPLIES NEEDED FOR EACH ARE LISTED BELOW:

NAME OF PROJECT                 SUPPLIES NEEDED
1.  VASE                        0.5 POUNDS OF CLAY
                                5 OUNCES OF GLAZE
                                1 BRUSH


2.  WATER_COLOR                 1 BOX WATER COLORS
                                1 CANVAS
                                1 BRUSH


3.  SKETCHES                    4 PIECES OF CHARCOAL
                                8 PIECES OF NEWSPRINT

THE NAME AND QUANTITY OF EACH PROJECT TO BE MADE ARE ENTERED TO THE
KEYBOARD.  WHEN ALL THE DATA ARE ENTERED, THE AMOUNT OF SUPPLIES
NEEDED IS PRINTED TO THE MONITOR.  *)

VAR
    NUM, PAINTS, CANVAS, CHARCOAL, PAPER, BRUSH : INTEGER;
    CLAY, GLAZE : REAL;
    PROJECT : STRING;
    ANSWER : CHAR;

(***************************************************************)

PROCEDURE PROJECT1 (NUM:INTEGER; VAR CLAY, GLAZE:REAL; VAR BRUSH:INTEGER);
(* THIS PROCEDURE DETERMINES THE QUANTITY OF SUPPLIES NEEDED TO MAKE
CERAMIC VASES FOR AN ART CLASS *)

BEGIN    (* PROJECT1 *)

    CLAY := CLAY + NUM * 0.5;
    GLAZE := GLAZE + NUM * 5.0;
    BRUSH := BRUSH + NUM

END;    (* PROJECT1 *)

(***************************************************************)

PROCEDURE PROJECT2 (NUM : INTEGER; VAR PAINTS, CANVAS, BRUSH : INTEGER);
(* THIS PROCEDURE DETERMINES THE QUANTITY OF SUPPLIES NEEDED TO MAKE
WATER COLOR PAINTINGS FOR AN ART CLASS *)
```

Continued next page

Figure 9-12 (con't.)

```
BEGIN    (* PROJECT2 *)

   PAINTS := PAINTS + NUM;
   CANVAS := CANVAS + NUM;
   BRUSH :=  BRUSH + NUM

END;    (* PROJECT2 *)

(*********************************************************************)

PROCEDURE PROJECT3 (NUM : INTEGER; VAR CHARCOAL, PAPER : INTEGER);
(* THIS PROCEDURE DETERMINES THE QUANTITY OF SUPPLIES NEEDED TO MAKE
SKETCHES FOR AN ART CLASS *)

BEGIN    (* PROJECT3 *)

   CHARCOAL := CHARCOAL + 4 * NUM;
   PAPER := PAPER + 8 * NUM
END;    (* PROJECT3 *)

(*********************************************************************)

BEGIN    (* ART *)

   CLAY := 0.0;
   GLAZE := 0.0;
   PAINTS := 0;
   CANVAS := 0;
   CHARCOAL := 0;
   PAPER := 0;
   BRUSH := 0;

   (* LOOP TO ALLOW TYPE AND QUANTITY OF PROJECTS TO BE ENTERED *)
   REPEAT

      WRITELN ('WHICH OF THE THREE PROJECTS IS TO BE MADE?');
      WRITE ('THE CHOICES ARE A VASE, A WATER_COLOR, OR SEVERAL SKETCHES: ');
      READLN (PROJECT);
      WRITE ('HOW MANY OF THIS PROJECT ARE TO BE MADE? ');
      READLN (NUM);

      (* DETERMINE WHICH PROJECT IS TO BE MADE AND CALL APPROPRIATE
      SUBROUTINE *)
      IF PROJECT = 'VASE' THEN
         PROJECT1 (NUM, CLAY, GLAZE, BRUSH)
      ELSE IF PROJECT = 'WATER_COLOR' THEN
         PROJECT2 (NUM, PAINTS, CANVAS, BRUSH)
      ELSE IF PROJECT = 'SKETCHES' THEN
         PROJECT3 (NUM, CHARCOAL, PAPER);

      (* DETERMINE IF THERE ARE MORE PROJECTS TO BE ENTERED *)
      WRITELN ('ARE THERE MORE SUPPLIES TO BE ORDERED?');
      WRITELN ('IF THERE ARE, TYPE IN A Y AND HIT THE RETURN KEY.');
      WRITE ('IF YOU ARE DONE, JUST HIT THE RETURN KEY. ');
      READLN (ANSWER);

   UNTIL ANSWER <> 'Y';

   (* PRINT QUANTITIES OF ART SUPPLIES NEEDED TO THE TERMINAL *)
   WRITELN;
   WRITELN;
   WRITELN ('THE FOLLOWING ART SUPPLIES WILL BE NEEDED:');
   WRITELN ('_____');
   WRITELN;
   WRITELN (CLAY:7:2, ' POUNDS OF CLAY');
   WRITELN (GLAZE:7:2, ' OUNCES OF GLAZE');
   WRITELN (PAINTS:7, ' SETS OF WATERCOLORS');
   WRITELN (CANVAS:7, ' CANVASES');
```

Continued next page

```
     WRITELN (CHARCOAL:7, ' PIECES OF CHARCOAL');
     WRITELN (PAPER:7, ' SHEETS OF NEWPRINT');
     WRITELN (BRUSH:7, ' BRUSHES')

END.   (* ART *)
```

Running. . .
```
WHICH OF THE THREE PROJECTS IS TO BE MADE?
THE CHOICES ARE A VASE, A WATER_COLOR, OR SEVERAL SKETCHES: VASE
HOW MANY OF THIS PROJECT ARE TO BE MADE? 15
ARE THERE MORE SUPPLIES TO BE ORDERED?
IF THERE ARE, TYPE IN A Y AND HIT THE RETURN KEY.
IF YOU ARE DONE, JUST HIT THE RETURN KEY. Y
WHICH OF THE THREE PROJECTS IS TO BE MADE?
THE CHOICES ARE A VASE, A WATER_COLOR, OR SEVERAL SKETCHES: WATER_COLOR
HOW MANY OF THIS PROJECT ARE TO BE MADE? 8
ARE THERE MORE SUPPLIES TO BE ORDERED?
IF THERE ARE, TYPE IN A Y AND HIT THE RETURN KEY.
IF YOU ARE DONE, JUST HIT THE RETURN KEY. Y
WHICH OF THE THREE PROJECTS IS TO BE MADE?
THE CHOICES ARE A VASE, A WATER_COLOR, OR SEVERAL SKETCHES: SKETCHES
HOW MANY OF THIS PROJECT ARE TO BE MADE? 11
ARE THERE MORE SUPPLIES TO BE ORDERED?
IF THERE ARE, TYPE IN A Y AND HIT THE RETURN KEY.
IF YOU ARE DONE, JUST HIT THE RETURN KEY.


THE FOLLOWING ART SUPPLIES WILL BE NEEDED:
―――――――――――――――――――――――――――――――――――――

    7.50 POUNDS OF CLAY
   75.00 OUNCES OF GLAZE
       8 SETS OF WATERCOLORS
       8 CANVASES
      44 PIECES OF CHARCOAL
      88 SHEETS OF NEWPRINT
      23 BRUSHES
```

Figure 9-12   (con't.)

The program branches to one of three procedures, depending on which project has been chosen. The parameters passed depend on the materials needed for that project. The variable NUM is passed to let the procedure know how many of a particular project are to be made. NUM is a value parameter. Its value is to be unchanged. The art supplies are variable parameters. The new values of these supplies need to be passed back to the main program. Notice that the variable BRUSH is used by both PROCEDURE PROJECT1 and PROJECT2. Since in both cases BRUSH is a variable parameter, the main program is able to keep a running total of the number of brushes needed.

THE IMPORTANCE OF USING PARAMETERS

As has already been mentioned, variables that are declared in a main program may be referred to anywhere in that program. These global variables could be used in subprograms without being passed as parameters. This might seem easier than using parameters. But this approach can lead to many problems. For example, any changes made to the variables in the subprogram would be returned to the main program. It would not be possible to have value parameters. By listing the parameters used by a subprogram, it is easy to see which variables are used in that subprogram. Often a number of programmers will work together on a large program. Each may write certain subprograms. Parameters make such cooperation much easier. There is no problem if the variable names in the subprogram do not match those in the calling program. This also means that, if necessary, the same subprogram can be easily used in any number of different programs.

DOCUMENTING FUNCTIONS AND PROCEDURES

The functions and procedures written in this chapter have been short and easy to understand. In large programs, functions and procedures may become much more complex. There may be many parameters. Because of this, subprograms should be documented in the same way as a main program. There should be a general statement of the purpose of the subprogram after the heading. This should include a description of the parameters passed to the subprogram. The documentation should also describe any values that are returned to the calling program.

LEARNING CHECK 9-2

1. Explain the difference between a procedure and a function.
2. Give two reasons why subprograms are useful in Pascal programs.
3. Why must the actual parameter for a variable parameter be a variable name and not an expression?

Answers:

1. A procedure is a subprogram that is designed to perform a specific task. It has no value of its own. Any values that are to be returned from a procedure must be returned by using variable parameters. A function is a subroutine that determines a single value. This value is returned in the function's name. 2. a. Subprograms are useful to break programs down into logical units which are easier to handle and understand than one large program. b. Subprograms can be called any number of times in a program. 3. When you are using variable parameters, a value will be returned to the actual parameter. It is not possible to assign a value to an expression. Therefore the actual parameter must be a variable name.

SUMMARY POINTS

- Functions and procedures are the two types of Pascal subprograms. Subprograms are useful for two basic reasons:
  1. They may be called any number of times.
  2. They help to break programs down into smaller units.
- Functions are used to return a single value to the calling program. Procedures are used to perform a specific task.

177

- Global variables are variables that are declared in the declaration section of a main program. They may be referred to anywhere in that program. Local variables may only be referred to in the subprogram in which they are declared.
- Value parameters are not affected by changes made to them in subprograms. Their value remains unchanged in the calling program. Variable parameters return their value to the calling program.
- Subprograms should be documented thoroughly, just as though they were main programs.

VOCABULARY LIST

Actual parameter   The value that will replace the formal parameter when a subprogram is executed.

Formal parameter   A variable that represents a value to be passed to a function or procedure.

Function   A subprogram that can be used to determine a single value.

Function call   An expression that causes a function to be executed.

Global variable   A variable that is declared in the declaration section of a main program. It may be referred to anywhere in that program.

Local variable   A variable that is declared in a subprogram. It has no meaning outside that subprogram.

Parameter   A value that is passed from a calling program to a subprogram. The value may or may not be passed back to the main program.

Procedure   A subprogram that performs a specific task. Procedures allow a program to be broken down into smaller subprograms.

Procedure call   A statement that causes a procedure to be executed.

Value parameter   A parameter whose value is passed to a subprogram but for which changes in the value are not passed back to the calling program.

Variable parameter   A parameter whose value is passed to a subprogram and for which changes in the value are passed back to the calling program.

CHAPTER TEST

VOCABULARY

Match a term from the numbered column with the description from the lettered column that best fits the term.

1. Value parameter

2. Procedure call

3. Function call

4. Actual parameter

a. A statement that causes a procedure to be executed.

b. The value that will replace the formal parameter when a subprogram is executed.

c. A variable that is declared in a subprogram. It has no meaning outside that subprogram.

d. A variable that represents a value

to be passed to a function or procedure.

5. Procedure

e. A parameter whose value is
passed to a subprogram, but
changes in its value are not
passed back to the calling program.

6. Global variable

f. A subprogram that performs a
specific task.

7. Variable parameter

g. An expression that causes a function to be executed.

8. Local variable

h. A subprogram that can be used to
determine a single value.

9. Formal parameter

i. A variable that is declared in the
declaration section of a main program. It may be referred to anywhere in that program.

10. Function

j. A parameter whose value is
passed to a subprogram; changes
in its value are passed back to the
calling program.

QUESTIONS

1. What is the difference between a value parameter and a variable parameter? What are the advantages of each?
2. Look at Figure 9-4. What are the global variables in this program? What
are the local variables?
3. Look at the following function heading:

```
FUNCTION TOTAL (SUBTOT1, SUBTOT2, SUBTOT3, TAX : REAL) : REAL;
```

Tell what value will be substituted for each of the formal variables above,
given the function calls below:
a. `TOT_COST := TOTAL (105.06, 140.00, 1785.00, 0.05);`
b. `AMOUNT := TOTAL (1084.55, 77.66, 1054, 0.10);`
4. Write a function that has a letter of the alphabet passed to it. If the letter
is a vowel, the function returns the character "*". If the letter is a consonant, the letter is returned to the calling program unchanged.
5. Look at the program below. What will the values of the following variables
be after the program is run: NAME, BIRTH, AGE, GRADE, HEIGHT,
WEIGHT?

```
PROGRAM EXAMPLE;

VAR
    NAME, BIRTH : STRING;
    AGE, GRADE : INTEGER;
    HEIGHT, WEIGHT : REAL;

PROCEDURE CHANGE (VAR NEW_H : REAL; NEW_W : REAL; VAR NEW_BD : STRING;
NEW_AGE, NEW_GR : INTEGER);
```

```
BEGIN   (* CHANGE *)
   NEW_BD := '8/5/66';
   NEW_W := 108;
   NEW_GR := NEW_GR + 1;
   NEW_AGE := 18
END;   (* CHANGE *)

BEGIN   (* EXAMPLE *)

   NAME := 'KATHLEEN O''HARA';
   AGE := 17;
   HEIGHT := 62;
   GRADE := 10;
   CHANGE (HEIGHT, WEIGHT, BIRTH, AGE, GRADE);
   WRITELN('NAME':10,'BIRTH DATE':23,'AGE':6,'GRADE':8,'HEIGHT':8,'WEIGHT':8);
   WRITELN (NAME:18, BIRTH:15, AGE:6, GRADE:8, HEIGHT:8:2, WEIGHT:8:2)

END.   (* EXAMPLE *)
```

PROGRAMMING PROBLEMS

1. Write a program that reads a person's weight in pounds and then converts the weight to kilograms. This result is then printed to the monitor. Use a function to calculate the actual conversion. The main program should consist of the necessary READ and WRITE statements and the function call. There are approximately 2.2 pounds in a kilogram.

2. Write a program to determine whether or not a positive integer is prime. A prime number is a number that can be divided evenly (that is, with no remainder) only by itself and one. For example, 13 is a prime number. Call a BOOLEAN function to determine if the number is prime.

3. Write a program to calculate the gas mileage for a car. Read from the keyboard the number of city miles traveled and the number of highway miles traveled. Also read the number of gallons of gasoline used. Call a procedure to determine these three things:
   a. The miles per gallon in the city
   b. The miles per gallon on the highway
   c. The overall miles per gallon
   Use variable parameters for these three items. Print the results to the monitor from the main program.

4. Two bicyclists are racing. The first one can average 32 miles per hour. The second one can average 25 miles per hour. If the second one starts a half an hour before the first, how long will it take the first one to catch up? How far will they have traveled at this point? Use a procedure to determine these two figures. Print the results to the monitor.

CHAPTER 10

Predefined Functions and User-Defined Data Types

Handwritten note (margin):

```
function prime (num: int): Boolean;
var
    factor: integer;
Begin
    factor := 2;
    while
        (num MOD factor <> 0) and
        (factor < num) DO
            factor := factor + 1
            prime := (factor = num)
End;
```

LEARNING OBJECTIVES

After studying this chapter, you should be able to:

1. Use predefined functions in programs.
2. Explain how the ordering functions SUCC, PRED, ORD, and CHR work.
3. Use user-defined data types in programs.
4. List the advantages and disadvantages of user-defined data types.
5. Write programs using subrange data types.

INTRODUCTION

Chapter 9 covered functions written by the programmer. These are called user-defined functions. They are written by the user of the computer. Many tasks that need to be done by programmers are very common. An example of a common task would be finding the square root of a number. It is often necessary to find the square root of a number in programs that involve mathematical computations. Because of this, the people who wrote the UCSD Pascal compiler also wrote a number of functions that are included in UCSD Pascal. Since these functions are built-in, the programmer may call these functions whenever they are needed without having to write them. These functions are predefined functions. Sometimes they are referred to as library functions. Predefined functions will be studied in this chapter.

In Pascal it is possible to define original data types. The ability to define new data types is a useful feature of Pascal. It is also possible to define a subrange of an existing data type. How subranges and original data types are defined and used in programs will also be explained in this chapter.

PREDEFINED FUNCTIONS

There are many predefined functions available in UCSD Pascal. This chapter will discuss some that are commonly used. For a complete list of predefined functions refer to the documentation that came with your UCSD Pascal compiler.

The chart in Figure 10-1 shows some commonly used predefined functions. These functions are called in the same way as user-defined functions. This statement calls for the square root function:

```
ROOT := SQRT (18);
```

The actual parameter of this function is 18. The actual parameter of a function may also be called the function **argument.** This function call will return the square root of 18 to the variable ROOT. ROOT must

Function	Data type of X	Result
ABS (X)	INTEGER or REAL	Absolute value of X
TRUNC (X)	REAL	The integral part of X (X will be truncated at the decimal point)
ROUND (X)	REAL	X will be rounded to the closest integer value
ODD (X)	INTEGER	BOOLEAN value of true is returned if integer is odd
SQR (X)	INTEGER or REAL	The square of X
SQRT (X)	INTEGER or REAL	The square root of X
EXP (X)	INTEGER or REAL	The value of e (2.718282) raised to the power of X
SIN (X)	INTEGER or REAL (X must be in radians)	The sine of X
COS (X)	INTEGER or REAL (X must be in radians)	The cosine of X

Figure 10-1   COMMON PREDEFINED FUNCTIONS

be declared to be of data type REAL. Figure 10-2 is a short program that finds the absolute value of a number and then truncates this result. This number is then squared. This simple program demonstrates how easy it is to call predefined functions in programs.

Notice the ODD function. Remember the program in Chapter 9, Figure 9-6? It had a user-defined function named FIND to determine whether or not a number was even. The predefined function ODD could have been used in this program. It would have saved the effort of writing function FIND. ODD is a BOOLEAN function. It returns a result of true or false. After this statement is executed

$$FIND := ODD (235);$$

the value of FIND will be true.

Computers assign an order to everything. The computer knows that 2 + 5 is less than 10 and that the character N is alphabetically greater than A. It is this ordering that allows the computer to make comparisons. There are some predefined functions that use this ordering to find their results. These functions are SUCC, PRED, ORD, and CHR. These functions may only be used with the scalar data types: INTEGER, CHAR, BOOLEAN, and user-defined (user-defined data types will be explained later in this chapter.) A table of these functions is shown in Figure 10-3. SUCC returns the scalar value following the argument.

183

```
PROGRAM DEMO;
(* THIS PROGRAM DEMONSTRATES THE USE OF THREE PRE-DEFINED FUNCTIONS:
ABS, TRUNC, AND SQUARE *)

VAR
   NUM, ABSOLUTE, SQUARE : REAL;
   TRUNCATE : INTEGER;

BEGIN    (* DEMO *)

   WRITELN ('ENTER A NUMBER.');
   READLN (NUM);
   ABSOLUTE := ABS (NUM);
   WRITELN (ABSOLUTE:7:2);
   TRUNCATE := TRUNC (ABSOLUTE);
   WRITELN (TRUNCATE);
   SQUARE := SQR (TRUNCATE);
   WRITELN (SQUARE:7:2)

END.    (* DEMO *)
```

Running. . .
```
ENTER A NUMBER.
 44.57
  44.57
44
 1936.00
```

Figure 10-2   USING PREDEFINED FUNCTIONS

For the Apple User

When you are using the following functions (called transcendental functions) the statement
   USES TRANSCEND;
must be placed immediately after the program statement. The functions are:

SIN	ATAN	LOG
COS	LN	SQRT
EXP		

Figure 10-3   FUNCTIONS THAT DETERMINE ORDER

Function	Result
SUCC	Successor—The next scalar value
PRED	Predecessor—The previous scalar value
ORD	Ordinal—Integer corresponding to position of a scalar value
CHR	Character value corresponding to a given integer

For example:

```
AFTER := SUCC ('C');
```

will assign D to AFTER.
PRED returns the scalar value preceding the argument:

```
BEFORE := PRED ('C');
```

BEFORE will be assigned B.
The function ORD will return the position of a scalar value. This statement

```
PLACE := ORD ('C');
```

will assign 67 to the variable PLACE. This number represents the internal number code that the computer assigns to each character. A complete listing of this code is available in your compiler documentation. CHR will return the character value of a given integer.

```
VALUE := CHR (PLACE);
```

VALUE will be assigned the value C. When ORD and CHR are used with character data, they are opposites. Figure 10-4 demonstrates these four ordering functions.

Figure 10-4 ORDERING FUNCTIONS

```
PROGRAM ORDER;   (* THIS PROGRAM DEMONSTRATES FOUR ORDERING
FUNCTIONS:  SUCC, PRED, ORD, CHR *)

VAR
   LETTER, AFTER, BEFORE, VALUE : CHAR;
   PLACE : INTEGER;

BEGIN   (* ORDER *)

   WRITELN ('TYPE IN A LETTER.');
   READLN (LETTER);
   AFTER := SUCC (LETTER);
   WRITELN (AFTER);
   BEFORE := PRED (LETTER);
   WRITELN (BEFORE);
   PLACE := ORD (LETTER);
   WRITELN (PLACE);
   VALUE := CHR (PLACE);
   WRITELN (VALUE)

END.   (* ORDER *)
```

Continued next page

```
Running. . .
TYPE IN A LETTER.
S
T
R
83
S
```

Figure 10-4   (cont.)

LEARNING CHECK 10-1

1. What is a predefined function?
2. Write function calls to find the values below. Use predefined functions.
   a. Square X.
   b. Find the square root of 18.75.
   c. Truncate −168.753.
   d. Find the absolute value of variable TOTAL.
   e. Round 174.73.
3. Tell what the value of the following expressions will be:
   a. PRED('N')
   b. SUCC (1)
   c. SUCC ('X')
   d. PRED (2468)

Answers:

1. A predefined function is one that is already written for the programmer. All the programmer needs to do is call the function. 2. a. X := SQR (X); b. ROOT := SQRT (18.75); c. CUT := TRUNC (−168.753); d. ABSOLUTE := ABS (TOTAL); e. CLOSE := ROUND (174.73); 3. a. M, b. 2, c. Y, d. 2467

USER-DEFINED SCALAR DATA TYPES

One of the useful features of Pascal is that it allows the programmer to define new data types. These are called **user-defined scalar data types.** They are defined by using a TYPE definition. The format of the TYPE definition is shown in Figure 10-5. TYPE definitions come after any constant definitions but before the variable declarations.

These user-defined data types must always be scalar. This means that all possible values of the data type must be listed in the definition. Here is an example of a TYPE definition:

186

> **User-Defined Data Type**
>
> Type
>   type__name = (list of values);

Figure 10-5   THE TYPE DEFINITION

```
TYPE
    COLOR = (RED, YELLOW, GREEN, BLUE);
```

Now variables may be declared of type COLOR:

```
VAR
    TINT  : COLOR;
    SHADE : COLOR;
```

TINT and SHADE are now variables of type COLOR. They may have the value of RED, YELLOW, GREEN, or BLUE.

The computer assigns an order to these values. This is the same order in which the values were listed in the TYPE definition. In this case, RED will be assigned the ordinal value zero, YELLOW the number one, and so forth. Because these values have an order, the following expressions hold true:

> RED < GREEN
> BLUE <> YELLOW
> PRED (GREEN) = YELLOW
> SUCC (GREEN) = BLUE

The function ORD may also be used with user-defined data types. ORD will return the ordinal position of each value. If POS has been declared to be of data type INTEGER, the value of POS in this statement

```
POS := ORD (BLUE);
```

will be three.

Figure 10-6 shows how a user-defined data type MONTH could be useful in a program. This program prints the number of days in a given month. The name of the month is entered by using an integer representing that month. Using data type MONTH makes the logic of the program easier to follow and understand.

User-defined scalar data types are useful because they make programs more meaningful. The programmer can define data types specifically for a particular program. Unfortunately, these data types may not be read or written. For example, in program DAYS__MONTH, the statement

```
PROGRAM DAYS_MONTH;
(* THIS PROGRAM PRINTS THE NUMBER OF DAYS IN A GIVEN MONTH.   *)

TYPE
   MONTHS = (JAN, FEB, MARCH, APRIL, MAY, JUNE, JULY, AUG, SEPT,
   OCT, NOV, DEC);

VAR
   NUM_MONTH, LENGTH : INTEGER;
   LEAP_Y : CHAR;
   MONTH : MONTHS;

BEGIN   (* DAYS_MONTH *)

   WRITELN ('ENTER THE NUMBER CORRESPONDING TO THE MONTH.');
   READLN (NUM_MONTH);

   (* CASE STATEMENT TO ASSIGN CORRESPONDING NAME OF MONTH *)
   CASE NUM_MONTH OF
      1 : MONTH := JAN;
      2 : MONTH := FEB;
      3 : MONTH := MARCH;
      4 : MONTH := APRIL;
      5 : MONTH := MAY;
      6 : MONTH := JUNE;
      7 : MONTH := JULY;
      8 : MONTH := AUG;
      9 : MONTH := SEPT;
      10: MONTH := OCT;
      11: MONTH := NOV;
      12: MONTH := DEC
   END;    (* CASE *)

   (* ASSIGN CORRECT NUMBER OF DAYS *)
   IF MONTH = FEB THEN
      BEGIN
         WRITELN ('IF THIS IS A LEAP YEAR, ENTER A ''Y'' AND HIT THE ');
         WRITELN ('RETURN KEY.  OTHERWISE, JUST HIT THE RETURN KEY.');
         READLN (LEAP_Y);
         IF LEAP_Y = 'Y' THEN
            LENGTH := 29
         ELSE
            LENGTH := 28
      END
   ELSE IF (MONTH=SEPT) OR (MONTH=APRIL) OR (MONTH=JUNE) OR (MONTH=NOV) THEN
      LENGTH := 30
   ELSE
      LENGTH := 31;

   WRITELN ('THIS MONTH HAS ', LENGTH, ' DAYS. ')

END.   (* DAYS_MONTH *)
```

Running. . .

```
ENTER THE NUMBER CORRESPONDING TO THE MONTH.
11
THIS MONTH HAS 30 DAYS.
```

Figure 10-6   PROGRAM DAYS_MONTH

```
          WRITELN (MONTH);
```

would not be allowed. But other than this, they may be used just like
any other scalar data type.

SUBRANGE DATA TYPES

A **subrange data type** is a data type that contains a portion of a
predefined or user-defined scalar type. Subranges can be defined by
using a TYPE definition. The format for subrange definitions is shown
in Figure 10-7. Here is an example of a subrange definition:

```
        TYPE
            PASSING = 'A' .. 'D';
```

The variable PASSING is a subrange of type CHAR. CHAR is the **base
type** of subrange PASSING. Every subrange has a base type. The base
type is the data type from which the subrange is taken.

```
            TYPE
                AGE = 1 .. 20;
```

The base type of AGE is INTEGER. The base type of a subrange must
be a scalar data type. Here is an example of a subrange of a user-
defined data type:

```
TYPE
   MONTHS = (JAN, FEB, MARCH, APRIL, MAY, JUNE, JULY, AUG,
             SEPT, OCT, NOV, DEC);
   SUMMER = JULY .. SEPT;
```

SUMMER is a subrange of MONTHS. SUMMER may have the values
JULY, AUG, or SEPT.
    Subranges are useful in checking for incorrect data. If a program
asks for a person's age, AGE could be defined this way:

```
            TYPE
                AGE = 0 .. 110;
```

Any value entered for AGE would have to be an integer between 0

Figure 10-7 FORMAT FOR SUBRANGE DEFINITION

```
TYPE
   subrange_name = minvalue . . maxvalue;
```

and 110. Entering a value outside of this range will result in a run-time error.

Subranges are also important in declaring arrays, which will be discussed in Chapter 11.

◤LEARNING CHECK 10-2

1. What is meant by a user-defined scalar data type?
2. Name an advantage of user-defined scalar data types. Name two disadvantages.
3. Given the following TYPE definition, determine whether the expressions below evaluate as true or false.

```
TYPE
    JELLO = (STRAWBERRY, LIME, ORANGE, CHERRY, GRAPE);
```

   a. PRED (CHERRY) = ORANGE
   b. LIME <> SUCC (STRAWBERRY)
   c. CHERRY < STRAWBERRY
   d. ORD (LIME) = 1
   e. ORD (STRAWBERRY) + ORD (GRAPE) = 4
4. Define a subrange of data type JELLO (used in problem 3) that contains the values ORANGE, CHERRY, and GRAPE.

Answers:

SUMMARY POINTS

- Predefined functions are functions that are already written for the programmer. They may be called at any point in a program by using a function call. Predefined functions can save the programmer time.
- User-defined data types are original data types that can be defined to meet the needs of a specific program. All possible values of the data type must be listed in the definition. Variables of this data type may not be read or written in a program. Other than this, they may be used as any other scalar type. User-defined data types make programs more meaningful.
- Subranges are defined as being a portion of a particular scalar data type. Subranges are useful when a value should fall within a given range.

VOCABULARY LIST

Argument   The value on which a function is executed; the same as an actual parameter.

Base type   The data type from which a subrange is defined. The base type must be a scalar data type.

Subrange data type   A data type that contains a portion of a predefined or user-defined scalar data type.

User-defined scalar data type   A data type defined by the programmer in a TYPE definition. Every value of the data type must be listed in the definition.

CHAPTER TEST

VOCABULARY

Match a term from the numbered column with the description from the lettered column that best fits the term.

1. Argument

2. Subrange data type

3. User-defined scalar data type

4. Base type

a. A data type defined by the programmer in a TYPE definition. Every value of the data type must be listed in the definition.

b. The data type from which a subrange is defined.

c. A data type which contains a portion of a predefined or user-defined scalar data type.

d. Another name for the actual parameter of a function.

QUESTIONS

1. Explain the difference between a predefined function and a user-defined function.
2. How could PROGRAM SUMS in Figure 9-6 be changed to use the predefined function ODD? Would this make the program longer or shorter?
3. Explain what each of the ordering functions SUCC, PRED, ORD, and CHR do.
4. What is a subrange data type?
5. Use a TYPE definition to define a subrange of the characters J through O. List all the values this subrange includes.
6. Look at the program below. After execution, what will the values be of variables A, B, C, D, E, F, and G?

```
PROGRAM RESULT;

TYPE
    FLAVOR = (GRAPE, ORANGE, STRAWBERRY);
```

```
VAR
    I, A, C, D, E, F : INTEGER;
    LET1, B : CHAR;
    X     : REAL;
    POP, G  : FLAVOR;

BEGIN

    I := 5;
    LET1 := SUCC ('J');
    X := -173.55;
    POP := GRAPE;

    A := SUCC (SUCC(I+1));
    B := PRED(LET1);
    C := ABS (SQR(I));
    D := ABS (TRUNC(X));
    E := ABS (ROUND (X));
    F := ORD (POP);
    G := SUCC (POP)

END.
```

PROGRAMMING PROBLEMS

1. Write a program that will make the following calculations:
   a. Read two real numbers that have been entered to the keyboard.
   b. Add the numbers together.
   c. Find the absolute value of this sum.
   d. Find the square root of this result.
   e. Round off the result to two decimal places.
   f. Print this result to the monitor.
   Use as many predefined functions as possible.
2. Write a program that will decode a word. The following code is used:

Code: A B C D E F G H I J K L M N O P Q R S T U V W X Y Z
Actual
letter: B C D E F G H I J K L M N O P Q R S T U V W X Y Z A

Use the SUCC function to do the decoding. Print the decoded word to the monitor. The output should be formatted something like this:

Word to be Decoded:	Result:
Z	A
O	P
O	P
K	L
D	E

3. Write a program that will read a student's name and then a number representing the class of the student:
   - 1—Freshman
   - 2—Sophomore
   - 3—Junior
   - 4—Senior

Define a user-defined scalar data type called CLASS that looks like this:

```
TYPE
    CLASS = (FRESHMAN, SOPHOMORE, JUNIOR, SENIOR);
```

A CASE statement may be used to assign the appropriate class to its corresponding number. Then use this user-defined data type to:
a. Determine if the student is an underclassman or an upperclassman.
b. Determine what year the student will graduate. The output should be similar to this:

```
SARAH WILLIAMS IS AN UPPERCLASSMAN
AND WILL GRADUATE IN 1986.
```

4. In Montana there are four types of trout. For each type a different daily limit regulates how many may be caught.

TYPE	LIMIT
Brookie	8
Brown	4
Rainbow	6
Cutthroat	4

Use a case statement to read a code number representing the type of trout. Then use a user-defined scalar data type to assign a correct type of trout to the corresponding number.

Print a WRITE statement telling the user how many of a particular type of trout may be caught in a day.

For example, if 2 was typed to the keyboard (representing Brown) the following statement could be printed:

```
THE DAILY LIMIT ON THIS TYPE OF TROUT IS 4.
```

CHAPTER 11

Arrays

OUTLINE

LEARNING OBJECTIVES

After studying this chapter, you should be able to:

1. Explain what an array is.
2. Declare and use one-dimensional arrays in programs.
3. Explain what array subscripts are and what data types they may be.
4. Explain what is meant by a two-dimensional array.
5. Declare and use simple two-dimensional arrays in programs.
6. Explain how the bubble sort works.
7. Write programs using a bubble sort.

INTRODUCTION

In the programming problems done so far in this book, values have been read to a variable one at a time and any processing has been done before another value was read. If a number is read to the variable SCORE:

```
READLN (SCORE);
```

and then another number is read to score:

```
READLN (SCORE);
```

the value that was read the first time is lost. It is impossible to go back and do any processing with this first value. The second value read to SCORE has replaced the first. To avoid this problem, a variable could be declared for each of the scores:

```
VAR
    SCORE1, SCORE2 : REAL;

BEGIN

    READLN (SCORE1);
    READLN (SCORE2);
```

This way SCORE1 and SCORE2 can be referred to anywhere in the program. But suppose it was necessary to read and process 50 scores. It would be very time-consuming to declare 50 variables. You would need 50 READ statements to read them all.

A much easier way of doing this is to use an **array**. An array is an ordered set of related data items. This chapter will explain how to declare arrays and use them in programs. Also covered will be a way of putting the values in an array in a specific order, such as arranging a list of names alphabetically.

DECLARING ARRAYS

An array may be thought of as a table of values, all of the same data type. Figure 11-1 shows how arrays are declared. Arrays may be declared in two ways. First, array types may be declared under the TYPE definitions. Here is an example of an array type declaration:

```
TYPE
    CORRECT = ARRAY [1..10] OF REAL;
```

Then one or more variables may be declared of this type under the variable declarations:

```
VAR
    SCORE : CORRECT;
```

The second method of declaring an array is to declare it under the variable declarations with no TYPE declaration:

```
VAR
    SCORE : ARRAY [1..10] OF REAL;
```

The first method will be used in this book. This method makes it simple to declare as many variables of the same array type as are needed. For example, there could be a number of variables of type CORRECT:

```
VAR
    SCORE      : CORRECT;
    HI_SCORE   : CORRECT;
    LO_SCORE   : CORRECT;
```

Figure 11-1 FORMAT OF ARRAY DECLARATIONS

First Method

TYPE
    Array_type_name = ARRAY[subscript1 . . last_subscript] OF data_type;

VAR
    Array_name : Array_type_name;

Second Method

VAR
    Array_name : ARRAY[subscript1 . . last_subscript] OF data_type;

SCORE[1] SCORE[2] SCORE[3] SCORE[4] SCORE[5] SCORE[6] SCORE[7] SCORE[8] SCORE[9] SCORE[10]

Figure 11-2 TABLE REPRESENTING ARRAY SCORE

Arrays may be of any data type, including user-defined data types. The array SCORE shown above is of data type REAL. This is because each of the array's **elements** is of data type REAL. The individual values in an array are the array's elements. Figure 11-2 shows how SCORE could be represented in storage. There are ten storage locations, each of which may have a real number assigned to it.

ARRAY SUBSCRIPTS

Subscripts are used to refer to a particular array element. In an array declaration, the subscripts are always placed in brackets and establish the dimensions of the array. The first value is the smallest subscript for this array while the last value is the largest subscript.

In this example,

$$[1 .. 10]$$

determines that array SCORE may have up to ten elements. Array subscripts may be of the data types CHAR, BOOLEAN, user-defined, or a subrange of any scalar data type. The subscripts for the array SCORE are a subrange of INTEGER. The subrange is one to ten. This array could not be declared this way:

```
TYPE
     SCORE = ARRAY [INTEGER] OF REAL;
```

There are an infinite number of integers. The computer would not know how much storage to set aside for this array.

An individual array element may be referred to by using the array name with a subscript. For example, the third element of the array SCORE could be referred to this way:

```
SCORE[3] := 104.23;
```

This would assign 104.23 to the third element of array SCORE. Array subscripts may be any valid expression that evaluates as the data type of the subscript. For example:

SCORE[1+6] := 133.18;

		104.23				133.18	103.38		
SCORE[1]	SCORE[2]	SCORE[3]	SCORE[4]	SCORE[5]	SCORE[6]	SCORE[7]	SCORE[8]	SCORE[9]	SCORE[10]

Figure 11-3 ARRAY SCORE PARTIALLY FILLED WITH VALUES

would place 133.18 in the seventh array element.

```
SCORE[2*4] := 74.18 + 29.20;
```

would place 103.38 in the eighth array element. Figure 11-3 shows how these values could be represented in storage.

READING AND WRITING ARRAYS

Values may be read to an array by using a loop:

```
FOR I := 1 TO 10 DO
    READ (SCORE[I]);
```

This statement would read ten scores from the keyboard to array SCORE. The first number read would go to SCORE[1], the tenth number to SCORE[10]. The array does not have to be filled.

```
FOR I := 1 TO 8 DO
    READ (SCORE[I]);
```

would read values to array elements 1 through 8. The values of array elements SCORE[9] and SCORE[10] would be undefined.

Arrays may be written in the same way they are read:

```
COUNT := 1;
WHILE COUNT <= 10 DO
    BEGIN
        WRITELN (SCORE[COUNT]);
        COUNT := COUNT + 1
    END;
```

would print each value of the array on a separate line.

PROGRAM MAGAZINES

We will now write a program that prints a sales report for a band's magazine sale. The program prints each band member's name and the amount sold in a table. After the table, summary information is printed. This information includes total sales, average sales per student, and the name of the student selling the most magazines along with how much that student sold. Figure 11-4 presents program MAGAZINES. Notice that the number of salespeople is declared in a CONST declaration:

```
CONST
    NUM = 13;
```

Figure 11-4 PROGRAM MAGAZINES

```
PROGRAM MAGAZINES;
(* THIS PROGRAM READS MAGAZINE SALES FOR A HIGH SCHOOL BAND.
IT DETERMINES WHICH STUDENT MADE THE MOST MONEY IN SALES, THE
AVERAGE AMOUNT OF SALES BY EACH STUDENT, AND THE TOTAL AMOUNT
OF SALES.  A TABLE IS PRINTED TO THE   MONITOR GIVING EACH
STUDENT'S NAME AND SALES.  SUMMARY INFORMATION IS GIVEN AT THE
END OF THE PROGRAM.  *)

CONST
    NUM = 13;

TYPE
    STUDENT = ARRAY[1..NUM] OF STRING;
    AMOUNT = ARRAY[1..NUM] OF REAL;

VAR
    NAME : STUDENT;
    SALES : AMOUNT;
    TOT_SALES, AVE_SALES, HIGHEST : REAL;
    COUNT, I, HIGH : INTEGER;

BEGIN

    COUNT := 1;
    HIGHEST := 0.0;
    TOT_SALES := 0.0;

    (* LOOP TO READ EACH STUDENT'S NAME AND SALES.  DETERMINE STUDENT
    WITH HIGHEST SALES AND TOTAL SALES BY ALL STUDENTS. *)
    WHILE COUNT <= NUM DO
        BEGIN
            WRITELN ('ENTER NAME OF THE STUDENT.');
            READLN (NAME[COUNT]);
            WRITELN ('ENTER AMOUNT SOLD BY THE STUDENT IN DOLLARS.');
            READLN (SALES[COUNT]);
            TOT_SALES := TOT_SALES + SALES[COUNT];

            IF SALES[COUNT] > HIGHEST THEN
                BEGIN
                    HIGHEST := SALES[COUNT];
                    HIGH := COUNT
                END;

            COUNT := COUNT + 1
        END;    (* WHILE *)
```

Continued next page

```
       AVE_SALES := TOT_SALES / NUM;

       WRITELN ('SALES REPORT');
       WRITELN('_____');
       WRITELN;
       FOR I := 1 TO NUM DO
          WRITELN (NAME[I]:25, SALES[I]:8:2);
          WRITELN ('_____');
       WRITELN;
       WRITELN ('THE TOTAL SALES ARE: ', TOT_SALES:7:2);
       WRITELN ('THE AVERAGE SALES PER STUDENT ARE: ', AVE_SALES:7:2);
       WRITELN ('THE HIGHEST SALES WERE MADE BY: ', NAME[HIGH]);
       WRITELN ('THE HIGHEST AMOUNT SOLD WAS: ', SALES[HIGH]:7:2)

   END.  (* MAGAZINES *)
```

Running. . .
```
ENTER NAME OF THE STUDENT.
MAURICE
ENTER AMOUNT SOLD BY THE STUDENT IN DOLLARS.
  19.95
ENTER NAME OF THE STUDENT.
GEORGIA
ENTER AMOUNT SOLD BY THE STUDENT IN DOLLARS.
  56.60
ENTER NAME OF THE STUDENT.
PATRICK
ENTER AMOUNT SOLD BY THE STUDENT IN DOLLARS.
  40.00
ENTER NAME OF THE STUDENT.
MARY
ENTER AMOUNT SOLD BY THE STUDENT IN DOLLARS.
   0.00
ENTER NAME OF THE STUDENT.
BERNIC
ENTER AMOUNT SOLD BY THE STUDENT IN DOLLARS.
  89.90
ENTER NAME OF THE STUDENT.
PAUL
ENTER AMOUNT SOLD BY THE STUDENT IN DOLLARS.
 104.56
ENTER NAME OF THE STUDENT.
MATTHEW
ENTER AMOUNT SOLD BY THE STUDENT IN DOLLARS.
  10.75
ENTER NAME OF THE STUDENT.
JONATHAN
ENTER AMOUNT SOLD BY THE STUDENT IN DOLLARS.
  42.25
ENTER NAME OF THE STUDENT.
NAOMI
ENTER AMOUNT SOLD BY THE STUDENT IN DOLLARS.
  35.50
ENTER NAME OF THE STUDENT.
VAL
ENTER AMOUNT SOLD BY THE STUDENT IN DOLLARS.
  18.85
```

Continued next page

```
ENTER NAME OF THE STUDENT.
ERIC
ENTER AMOUNT SOLD BY THE STUDENT IN DOLLARS.
   0.00
ENTER NAME OF THE STUDENT.
PETER
ENTER AMOUNT SOLD BY THE STUDENT IN DOLLARS.
  25.99
ENTER NAME OF THE STUDENT.
MERIDITH
ENTER AMOUNT SOLD BY THE STUDENT IN DOLLARS.
  68.20

SALES REPORT
––––––––––––––––––––––––––––––––––––––––
                    MAURICE    19.95
                    GEORGIA    56.60
                    PATRICK    40.00
                       MARY     0.00
                     BERNIC    89.90
                       PAUL   104.56
                    MATTHEW    10.75
                   JONATHAN    42.25
                      NAOMI    35.50
                        VAL    18.85
                       ERIC     0.00
                      PETER    25.99
                   MERIDITH    68.20
––––––––––––––––––––––––––––––––––––––––

THE TOTAL SALES ARE:   512.55
THE AVERAGE SALES PER STUDENT ARE:    39.43
THE HIGHEST SALES WERE MADE BY: PAUL
THE HIGHEST AMOUNT SOLD WAS:   104.56
```

Figure 11-4 (con't.)

This program has two arrays, one containing the salesperson's name and the other the amount sold by each person. The values in these two arrays correspond to one another, that is, AMOUNT[3] contains the amount sold by NAME[3]. Notice that only the subscript of the array element containing the largest amount sold is saved. This makes it simple to print this person's name and sales at the end of the program.

LEARNING CHECK 11-1

1. What is an array?
2. Why are arrays useful in programming?
3. Fill in the table below using the following program segment:

```
PROGRAM COST;

TYPE
    ALL = ARRAY[1..5] OF REAL;

VAR
    TOTAL : ALL;
```

a. TOTAL[3] := 31.89;
b. TOTAL[5-4] := 21.85;
c. TOTAL[4] := 45 / 66;
d. TOTAL[2*1] := 14.67;

TOTAL[1] TOTAL[2] TOTAL[3] TOTAL[4] TOTAL[5]

4. Write a FOR loop that will read data from the keyboard to the array declared below. Write another FOR loop that will print the data to the monitor. Print each value on a separate line.

```
TYPE
    SIZE = ARRAY ['B'..'F'] OF CHAR;

VAR
    CODE : SIZE;
```

Answers:

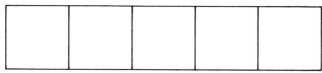

1. An array is an ordered set of related data items.   2. Arrays are useful because they allow related data items to be stored together. The individual values may be refered to simply by using a subscript with the array name.

3.

21.85	14.67	31.89	0.68 ✗	
TOTAL[1] TOTAL[2] TOTAL[3] TOTAL[4] TOTAL[5]

(TOTAL[5] is undefined.)

```
4. FOR LETTER := 'B' TO 'F' DO
     READ (CODE);

   FOR LETTER := 'B' TO 'F' DO
     WRITELN (CODE);
```

TWO-DIMENSIONAL ARRAYS

So far, the arrays discussed in this chapter have been one-dimensional arrays. One-dimensional arrays can be represented by a single row of values, as shown below:

This one-dimensional array could contain up to six values.

An array may have more than one dimension, however. A two-dimensional array may be thought of as a table with both rows and columns. Here is a table with five rows and four columns:

Columns

	1	2	3	4
A				
B				
C				
D				
E				

Rows

The subscripts in this array are subranges of data type CHAR and data type INTEGER. This two-dimensional array could be declared this way:

```
TYPE
    FEET = ARRAY['A'..'E', 1..4] OF REAL;

VAR
    SIZE : FEET;
```

The first dimension listed gives the number of rows. The subscripts for the rows will be A through E. The second dimension gives the columns. The subscripts for the columns will be 1 through 4. The statement below:

```
SIZE ['B',3] := 10.35;
```

will assign the value 10.35 to the second row, third column of array SIZE. Look at the assignment statements and the table in Figure 11-5. Make certain you understand how these assignment statements work.

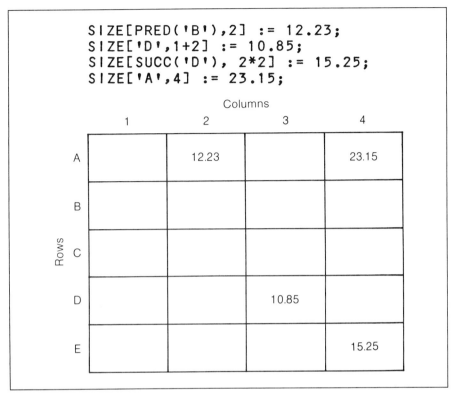

```
SIZE[PRED('B'),2] := 12.23;
SIZE['D',1+2] := 10.85;
SIZE[SUCC('D'), 2*2] := 15.25;
SIZE['A',4] := 23.15;
```

Columns

	1	2	3	4
A		12.23		23.15
B				
C				
D			10.85	
E				15.25

Rows

Figure 11-5   A TWO-DIMENSIONAL ARRAY

PROGRAM PRICE__TABLE

Program PRICE__TABLE is used to print a table of prices for items. The program is illustrated in Figure 11-6. Each item is assigned a number, 1 through 10. A price is entered to the monitor for each item. Discounts are given for buying items in quantity as follows:

- 1 to 4: no discount
- 5 to 9: 8.5% discount
- 10 to 19: 12.7% discount
- 20 or more: 15.0% discount

At the end of the program, a table is printed that gives the cost per item purchased, depending on the item and the quantity bought. Notice the use of nested FOR loops to print the table. The inside FOR loop prints each row of prices. The outside FOR loop prints the correct number of rows.

SORTING AN ARRAY

Sorting means organizing data items in a particular order. An example would be putting a list of names in alphabetical order or putting numbers in order from the smallest to the largest. There are many different

```
PROGRAM PRICE_TABLE;
(* THIS PROGRAM WILL PRINT A TABLE GIVING THE PRICE OF AN ITEM DEPENDING
ON THE QUANTITY BEING BOUGHT.  EACH ITEM IS ASSIGNED A NUMBER, 1-10.
THE PRICE FOR A PARTICULAR ITEM IS ENTERED TO THE  MONITOR .
QUANTITY DISCOUNTS ARE GIVEN AS FOLLOWS:
     1-4          - NO DISCOUNT
     5-9          - 8.5% DISCOUNT
     10-19        - 12.7% DISCOUNT
     20 OR MORE - 15% DISCOUNT    *)

CONST
   NUM = 10;

TYPE
   AMOUNT = ARRAY[1..NUM,1..4] OF REAL;

VAR
   PRICE : AMOUNT;
   I, J, K : INTEGER;
   COST : REAL;

BEGIN   (* PRICE_TABLE *)

   (*  LOOP TO READ IN PRICE AND CALCULATE COST PER ITEM DEPENDING
   ON THE QUANTITY *)
   FOR I := 1 TO NUM DO
      BEGIN
         WRITELN ('TYPE IN REGULAR PRICE OF ITEM NUMBER ', I);
         READLN (COST);
         PRICE[I,1] := COST;
         PRICE[I,2] := COST - (COST * 0.085);
         PRICE[I,3] := COST - (COST * 0.127);
         PRICE[I,4] := COST - (COST * 0.15);
      END;   (* FOR *)

   (* PRINT TABLE HEADINGS *)
   WRITELN ('PRICE TABLE':30);
   WRITELN ('_____');
   WRITELN;
   WRITELN ('1-4':16, '5-9':10,'10-19':12, '20 OR MORE':14);
   WRITELN ('_____');
   WRITELN ('ITEM NUMBER');

   (* PRINT TABLE *)
   FOR J := 1 TO NUM DO
      BEGIN
         WRITE (J:7);
         FOR K := 1 TO 4 DO
            WRITE (PRICE[J,K]:10:2);
         WRITELN
      END   (* FOR *)

   END.   (* PRICE_TABLE *)


 Running. . .

TYPE IN REGULAR PRICE OF ITEM NUMBER 1
   18.75
TYPE IN REGULAR PRICE OF ITEM NUMBER 2
   4.50
```

Figure 11-6   PROGRAM PRICE__TABLE

Continued next page

```
TYPE IN REGULAR PRICE OF ITEM NUMBER 3
  78.00
TYPE IN REGULAR PRICE OF ITEM NUMBER 4
  19.99
TYPE IN REGULAR PRICE OF ITEM NUMBER 5
  10.55
TYPE IN REGULAR PRICE OF ITEM NUMBER 6
  63.29
TYPE IN REGULAR PRICE OF ITEM NUMBER 7
  14.98
TYPE IN REGULAR PRICE OF ITEM NUMBER 8
   2.69
TYPE IN REGULAR PRICE OF ITEM NUMBER 9
  25.45
TYPE IN REGULAR PRICE OF ITEM NUMBER 10
  19.30
                      PRICE TABLE
         _____

              1-4        5-9       10-19      20 OR MORE
         _____

ITEM NUMBER
    1       18.75      17.16      16.37       15.94
    2        4.50       4.12       3.93        3.83
    3       78.00      71.37      68.09       66.30
    4       19.99      18.29      17.45       16.99
    5       10.55       9.65       9.21        8.97
    6       63.29      57.91      55.25       53.80
    7       14.98      13.71      13.08       12.73
    8        2.69       2.46       2.35        2.29
    9       25.45      23.29      22.22       21.63
   10       19.30      17.66      16.85       16.40
```

Figure 11-6 (con't.)

algorithms that have been developed for sorting. The one that will be explained here is the bubble sort. Bubble sorts are simple to write but use a great deal of computer time. For the small amount of data being sorted here, this is not important. But when you are dealing with large amounts of data, the time factor can be critical.

The bubble sort works by comparing two array items that are next to each other and interchanging them if they are out of order. The bubble sort works its way through the array, comparing items two at a time.

The steps used in sorting five integers will be shown. Here is the starting array containing five elements:

32	12	44	0	18

The first two array elements are compared and exchanged since they are out of order:

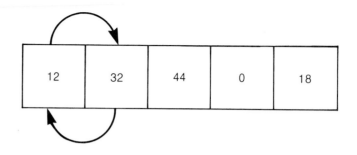

Next, the second and third elements are compared and not exchanged, since 32 is less than 44.

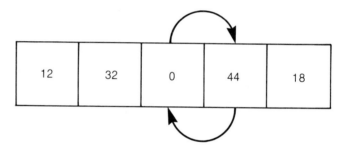

Elements 3 and 4 are compared and exchanged.

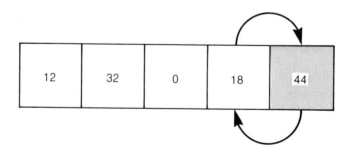

Lastly, the fourth and fifth elements are compared and exchanged.

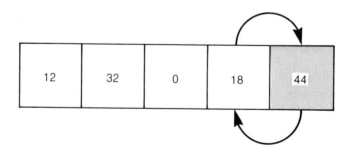

The array has been sorted through one time. The last array element is now in its correct place. This is why it is shaded.

Now the sort will go back to the beginning of the array. This time through the array, only elements 1 through 4 will be compared, since 5 is already in its correct place. At the end of the second time through the array, the elements will be in this order:

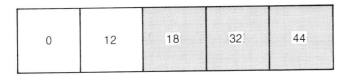

12	0	18	32	44

Notice that the last two elements are now in their correct positions. The third time through the array will look like this:

0	12	18	32	44

The last time through, elements 1 and 2 will be compared and no exchange will be made since they are already in order. The sorting is completed. Figure 11-7 shows a program that sorts an array of cities. Notice that the BOOLEAN variable SWITCH determines whether or not the loop will be repeated again. As long as changes have been made, the loop will be repeated. When the loop is executed and no changes are made, SWITCH will be false. Therefore, the sort will have been completed.

Figure 11-7 PROGRAM SORT__CITY

```
   PROGRAM SORT_CITY;
(* THIS PROGRAM SORTS A LIST OF 20 CITIES IN
ALPHABETICAL ORDER *)

CONST
   NUM = 20;

TYPE
   CITIES = ARRAY[1..20] OF STRING;

VAR
   I, J, NUMPASS : INTEGER;
   CITY   : CITIES;
   TEMP   : STRING;
   SWITCH : BOOLEAN;

BEGIN    (* SORT_CITY *)

   (* ENTER LIST TO BE SORTED *)
   WRITELN ('ENTER NAMES OF ',NUM,' CITIES, EACH ON A SEPARATE LINE');
   FOR I := 1 TO NUM DO
        READLN (CITY[I]);

   NUMPASS := NUM - 1;

   (* SORT UNTIL NO MORE CHANGES NEED TO BE MADE *)
   REPEAT
      SWITCH := FALSE;
```

Continued next page

```
        FOR J := 1 TO NUMPASS DO
            IF CITY[J] > CITY[J+1] THEN
                BEGIN
                    TEMP := CITY[J];
                    CITY[J] := CITY[J+1];
                    CITY[J+1] := TEMP;
                    SWITCH := TRUE
                END;    (* IF *)
            NUMPASS := NUMPASS -1
    UNTIL SWITCH = FALSE;

    (* PRINT SORTED LIST OF CITIES *)
    WRITELN;
    WRITELN ('SORTED LIST OF CITIES:');
    WRITELN ('_____');

    FOR I := 1 TO NUM DO
        WRITELN (CITY[I]:25)

END.  (* SORT_CITY *)
```

Running. . .

```
ENTER NAMES OF 20 CITIES, EACH ON A SEPARATE LINE
NEWARK
SANTA CLARA
SPOKANE
WHAT CHEER
EAST LANSING
CYGNET
ATLANTA
DENVER
BIG TIMBER
BOISE
PORTLAND
MOUNT PLEASANT
WAYNE
IOWA CITY
WESTON
DAYTON
ST. CLOUD
LAUREL
MIAMI
BOZEMAN


SORTED LIST OF CITIES:
_____
                ATLANTA
             BIG TIMBER
                  BOISE
                BOZEMAN
                 CYGNET
                 DAYTON
                 DENVER
           EAST LANSING
              IOWA CITY
                 LAUREL
                  MIAMI
         MOUNT PLEASANT
                 NEWARK
               PORTLAND
            SANTA CLARA
```

Continued next page

```
                    SPOKANE
               ST. CLOUD
                   WAYNE
                  WESTON
             WHAT CHEER
```

Figure 11-7   (con't.)

⬛LEARNING CHECK 11-2

1. What is the difference between a one-dimensional and a two-dimensional array?
2. How many elements do the following arrays have?
   a. POSITION = ARRAY['D'..'N'] OF INTEGER;
   b. CLASS = ARRAY[1..6, 5..10] OF CHAR;
   c. TAX = ARRAY['A'..'E', 1..9] OF REAL;
   d. MINUTES = ARRAY[1..5, 1..8] OF REAL;
3. Look at program SORT__CITY in Figure 11-7. Can you change it so that it will arrange the cities in reverse alphabetical order?

Answers:

1. A one-dimensional array has only one subscript. It can be thought of as a list of items. A two-dimensional array has subscripts for both the rows and the columns. It can be thought of as a table with both rows and columns.   2. a. 11 elements, b. 36 elements, c. 45 elements, d. 40 elements   3. IF CITY [J] < CITY [J + 1] THEN should be changed to IF CITY [J] > CITY [J + 1] THEN

SUMMARY POINTS

- This chapter has discussed declaring arrays and using them in programs. Arrays are useful when the programmer must deal with a number of related data items.
- All of the elements of an array must be of the same data type. Using arrays is an easy way to read and write these items.
- Individual array values are array elements. Array elements can be referred to by using an array subscript. The subscript makes it possible to locate a particular element in an array.
- Two-dimensional arrays contain two subscripts. The first subscript refers to the rows, the second to the columns.
- A simple way to put data in an array in order is to use a bubble sort. The bubble sort works by comparing each two adjacent elements of the array and exchanging them if they are out of order. The sort keeps going through the array until no more changes are needed.

VOCABULARY LIST

Array   An ordered set of related data items, all of the same data type.

Element   An individual value of an array. An array element must have a subscript.

Subscript A value enclosed in brackets that is used to refer to a particular array element. For example: NAME[3].

Sorting Organizing data items in a particular order.

CHAPTER TEST

VOCABULARY

Match a term from the numbered column with the description from the lettered column that best fits the term.

1. Subscript
2. Array

3. Sort
4. Element

a. An ordered set of related data items, all of the same data type.
b. A value enclosed in brackets that is used to refer to a particular array element.
c. An individual value of an array.
d. To arrange data items in a particular order, such as alphabetically.

QUESTIONS

1. Write type declarations and variable declarations for the arrays listed below.
   a. An array called PERCENT of type REAL that may contain up to 15 values.
   b. An array called WEEKDAYS of data type STRING that can contain up to seven values.
   c. An array called GRADE of data type CHAR that may contain up to three values.
2. Use the following program segment to fill in the table below.

```
PROGRAM ASSIGN;

    TYPE
        EMPLOYEE = ARRAY[1..5, 1..4] OF STRING;

    VAR
        I, J : INTEGER;
        WORKER : EMPLOYEE;

    BEGIN
        I := 2;
        J := 3;
        WORKER[I, J] := 'SAMPSON';
        WORKER[I*2, 4] := 'MOSES';
        WORKER[1, 1+1] := 'AARON';
        WORKER[I+3, J] := 'MICAH';
```

```
        WORKER[4, J-1] := 'JONATHAN';
        WORKER[3*1, 1] := 'SOLOMON'
   END.
```

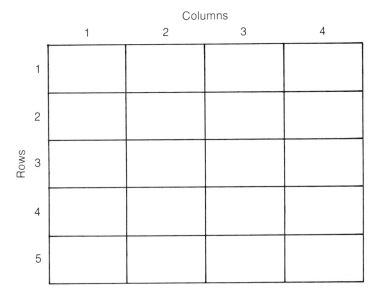

3. Write a bubble sort to sort five characters so they are in alphabetical order.

4. The program below contains several run-time errors. Type the program on your computer and run it once. Then use the program tracing techniques discussed in Chapter 8 to find and correct the run-time errors.

```
PROGRAM P_DIET;
(* THIS PROGRAM WILL READ IN THE MEALS FOR A 7 DAY DIET AND
   PRINT THE DAYS AND MEALS IN A TABLE FORMAT *)

   VAR
      DAY   : ARRAY[1..7] OF STRING[10];
      I     : INTEGER;
      J     : INTEGER;
      MEALS : ARRAY[1..7] OF STRING[15];

   BEGIN

      WRITELN ('YOU''VE BEEN CONTACTED BY A PUBLISHING COMPANY TO');
      WRITELN ('CREATE YOUR OWN DIET FOR A NEW BOOK. TYPE IN THE');
      WRITELN ('MAIN MEAL FOR EACH DAY OF YOUR DIET.');
      WRITELN;
      WHILE I <= 7 DO
         BEGIN
            I := I + 1;
            WRITE ('DAY ', I, ' OF THE DIET IS: ');
            READLN (DAY[I]);
            WRITE ('THE MEAL FOR ', DAY[I], ' IS: ');
            READLN (MEALS[I]);
            WRITELN
         END;
      WRITELN ('          YOUR DIET PLAN');
      WRITELN;
      WRITELN ('   DAY', '                    ', 'MEAL');
```

```
      REPEAT
         WRITELN (DAY[I], '                     ', MEALS[J]);
         WRITELN;
         J := J + 1
      UNTIL J = 8

   END.    (* OF PROGRAM P_DIET *)
```

5. The following program contains several logic errors. Type the program on your computer and run it once. Then use the program tracing and hand-simulation techniques discussed in Chapter 8 to find and correct the logic errors.

```
PROGRAM P_VACATION;
(* THIS PROGRAM READS IN THE NAMES OF CITIES OR VACATION SPOTS AND
   THE DISTANCES BETWEEN EACH CITY. A LIST OF THE VACATION PLAN IS
   PRINTED WITH NAME, DISTANCE, AND TRAVEL TIME LISTED *)
   VAR
      CITIES    : ARRAY[1..4] OF STRING[20];     (* ARRAY OF VACATION SPOTS *)
      CITY      : STRING[20];                     (* VACATION SPOT *)
      HOUR      : REAL;                           (* TRAVEL TIME *)
      HOURS     : ARRAY[1..4] OF REAL;            (* ARRAY OF TRAVEL TIMES *)
      I, J      : INTEGER;                        (* LOOP AND ARRAY COUNTERS *)
      MILES     : REAL;
      THOURS    : ARRAY[1..4] OF REAL;
      TMILES    : ARRAY[1..4] OF REAL;            (* ARRAY OF DISTANCES *)

   BEGIN

      WRITELN ('THIS PROGRAM WILL HELP YOU PLAN A TRIP TO 4 CITIES OR ');
      WRITELN ('VACATION SPOTS. THINK OF 4 PLACES YOU WOULD LIKE TO VISIT');
      WRITELN (', THE ORDER IN WHICH YOU WANT TO VISIT THEM, AND THE ');
      WRITELN ('DISTANCE BETWEEN EACH PLACE.');
      WRITELN;

      (* CITIES AND DISTANCES READ IN *)
      FOR I := 1 TO 4 DO
         BEGIN
            J := 1;
            WRITE ('CITY OR PLACE ', I, ' IS: ');
            READLN (CITY);
            CITIES[I] := CITY;
            IF I = 1 THEN                          (* FIRST CITY READ *)
               BEGIN
                  WRITE ('DISTANCE TO ', CITIES[I], ' :');
                  READLN (MILES);
                  TMILES[I] := MILES               (* DISTANCE CALCULATED *)
               END
            ELSE                                   (* OTHER CITIES READ *)
               BEGIN
                  WRITE ('DISTANCE TO ', CITIES[I], ' FROM ',
                         CITIES[J], ' : ');
                  READLN (MILES);
                  TMILES[J] := MILES               (* DISTANCE CALCULATED *)
               END;
            HOURS[I] := MILES * 55;                (* TRAVEL TIME CALCULATED = *)
            THOURS[I] := HOUR             (* MILES DIVIDED BY 55 MPH *)
         END;                            (* OF FOR *)

      (* VACATION PLAN PRINTED - PLACE, DISTANCE BTWN SPOTS, TIME *)
      WRITELN;
      WRITELN ('          YOUR VACATION PLAN');
      WRITELN ('   PLACE                  DISTANCE              TRAVEL TIME');
```

214

```
        FOR I := 1 TO 4 DO
            WRITELN (CITIES[I], '       ', MILES:6:2, '       ', HOURS[I]:5:2)
    END.    (* OF PROGRAM P_VACATION *)
```

PROGRAMMING PROBLEMS

1. Read 15 numbers to array A and 15 numbers to array B. Compute the product of these two numbers and place this result in Array PROD. Print a table similar to the one below at the end of your program.

A	B	PRODUCT
5	6	30
2	8	16
.	.	.
.	.	.

2. Write a program that will alphabetize the last names of the students in your class. Write it so that the names will be alphabetized in ascending order (A, B, C ...). Then change it so that the names are alphabetized in descending order (Z, Y, X ...).

3. Write a program that will read your last name and print it backwards to the monitor. Example:

INPUT

SCHWARTZ

OUTPUT

ZTRAWHCS

4. Ask 50 students the name of their favorite NFL team. Write a program that reads the name of each team and the number of students voting for that team. Sort the teams so that the most popular is first and the least popular is last. Print this list to the monitor. Here is an example of how the output might look:

NAME	NUMBER OF VOTES
STEELERS	12
COWBOYS	10
RAMS	7
.	.
.	.
.	.

5. Below is a list of schools and the number of wins each team had in four different sports. Write a program to read the name of the school and its wins in each of the four sports. Use a two-dimensional array. Put the results in a table. Set the table up as shown below:

SCHOOL	SPORT			
	BASEBALL	BASKETBALL	FOOTBALL	GOLF
LAKEVIEW	2	10	5	4
KIRKLAND	9	3	4	7
CAMBBRIDGE	14	7	5	3
JEFFERSON	7	9	8	5

Then print the name of the school with the most wins in each sport like this:

THE SCHOOL WHICH WON THE MOST BASEBALL GAMES IS:

CAMBRIDGE   14

.

.

.

CHAPTER 12

Records and Sets

OUTLINE

LEARNING OBJECTIVES

INTRODUCTION

RECORDS
Declaring Records • Referring to Individual Fields • Copying an
Entire Record • Arrays of Records • Program ODD_JOBS

LEARNING CHECK 12-1

SETS
Declaring sets • Assigning Values to Sets • Set Operators
Union
Intersection
Difference
Using Relational Operators with Sets • Program ACTIVITIES

LEARNING CHECK 12-2

SUMMARY POINTS

VOCABULARY LIST

CHAPTER TEST
Vocabulary • Questions

PROGRAMMING PROBLEMS

LEARNING OBJECTIVES

After studying this chapter, you should be able to:

1. Explain what is meant by a structured data type.
2. Declare and use records in programs.
3. Refer to the individual fields of a record.
4. Use the WITH statement in working with records.
5. Copy entire records.
6. Use sets in programs when appropriate.
7. Use the following set operators: $+$, $*$, $-$.
8. Use the following set relational operators: $=$, $>=$, $<=$, $<>$.

INTRODUCTION

Chapter 11 discussed one **structured data type:** arrays. In this chapter, two more structured data types will be covered: **records** and **sets.** These are called structured data types because they can be used to store many individual values. These individual values can then be referred to as a single unit. The format of each structured data type has strict rules that must be followed and each has situations in which it is useful.

The values in an array must all be of the same data type. An array cannot be declared that has some elements of data type STRING and others of data type INTEGER. There are many situations where it might be desirable to keep data of different types in a single unit. For example, think of the data an employer might want to keep on an employee. It might include the following information:

> name
> age
> sex
> social security number
> hourly pay rate

A record would be ideal for containing this information. A record is a group of related data items, not necessarily of the same data type, that are gathered together as a single unit.

Sets will also be covered in this chapter. A set consists of a collection of items that are classed together. All of the items in a set must be of the same base type.

RECORDS

Declaring Records

The format for declaring records is shown in Figure 12-1. A record for employees in a company could look like this:

```
TYPE
   record_name = RECORD
      field_name1 : data_type;
      field_name2 : data_type;
            .
            .
            .
      last_field_name : data_type
   END;
```

Figure 12-1   RECORD FORMAT

```
TYPE
   WORKER = RECORD
      NAME : STRING;
      AGE : INTEGER;
      SEX : CHAR;
      SS_NO : STRING;
      PAY_RATE : REAL
   END;
```

The name of this record is WORKER. All records are made up of **fields.** Each data item that is a part of the record is called a field. Record WORKER is made up of five fields. The fields may be of any data type. Notice that the first line of the record

```
   WORKER = RECORD
```

is not followed by a semicolon. The record is concluded with the reserved word END, even though there is no BEGIN.

To use this record in a program, one or more variables must be declared to be of type WORKER:

```
VAR
   EMPLOYEE : WORKER;
```

EMPLOYEE can now be used to refer to the record for each worker. Figure 12-2 shows how this record could be represented in storage.

Figure 12-2   A RECORD REPRESENTED IN STORAGE

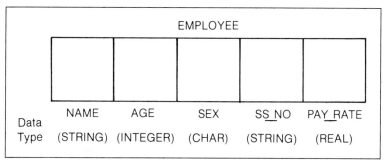

219

Referring to Individual Fields

There are two ways of referring to a field in a record. The first way is to place a period between the name of the record and the field name. The general format for this is:

record_name.field_name;

The NAME field of record EMPLOYEE could be assigned a value this way:

```
EMPLOYEE.NAME := 'JONES, VIOLA';
```

Even if there are other records with a NAME field, the compiler knows that the statement above refers to the NAME field of EMPLOYEE. The other fields in this record could also be assigned values in the same way:

```
EMPLOYEE.AGE := 47;
EMPLOYEE.SEX := 'F';
EMPLOYEE.SS_NO := '379-50-5244';
EMPLOYEE.PAY_RATE := 7.58;
```

Figure 12-3 demonstrates how this record could now be represented in storage. A simpler way of referring to the fields of a record is to use a WITH statement. The general format of the WITH statement is shown in Figure 12-4. The WITH statement could be used to assign values to record EMPLOYEE this way:

```
WITH EMPLOYEE DO
   BEGIN
      NAME := 'JONES, VIOLA';
      AGE := 47;
      SEX := 'F';
      SS_NO := '379-50-5244';
      PAY_RATE := 7.58
   END;
```

Figure 12-3 EMPLOYEE RECORD IN STORAGE

JONES, VIOLA	47	F	379-50-5244	7.58
NAME	AGE	SEX	SS_NO	PAY_RATE

```
WITH record__name do
   BEGIN
      .
      .
      .
   END;
```

In the body of the WITH statement, individual fields in a record may be referenced by simply using the name of the field.

Figure 12-4   WITH STATEMENT FORMAT

Notice that the word WITH is followed by the record name. The WITH statement starts with BEGIN and concludes with END.

Copying an Entire Record

A complete record may be copied to another record if both are of the same record type. In the previous example, EMPLOYEE is a record of type WORKER. Suppose two variables had been declared to be of this type:

```
VAR
     EMPLOYEE : WORKER;
     TEACHER  : WORKER;
```

In the previous section, the fields of EMPLOYEE have been assigned values individually. Suppose it was necessary to copy an entire record from EMPLOYEE to TEACHER. This could be done by using this statement:

```
TEACHER := EMPLOYEE;
```

Now every field of these two records will be the same. The general format for copying records is shown in Figure 12-5.

Arrays of Records

Records are most commonly used in groups. For example, an employer would want to be able to place all of the WORKER records in the previous section together. This could be done by declaring an array of records. An array of EMPLOYEES could be declared:

```
EMPLOYEES : ARRAY[1..10] OF WORKER;
```

Figure 12-6 illustrates how each array element contains a complete record. This declaration statement will set up an array that could hold

221

```
record_name1 := record_name2;
```

Record_name1 and record_name2 must be of the same record type.

Figure 12-5 FORMAT FOR COPYING RECORDS

Figure 12-6 ARRAY OF RECORDS

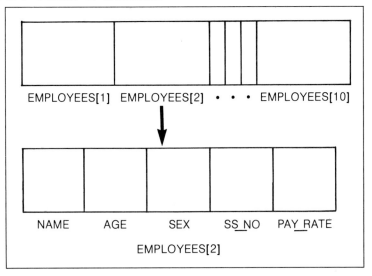

up to ten records. The fourth record in this array could be referred to by using a subscript:

`EMPLOYEES[4]`

Individual fields in this record can be referred to in the same way as fields in individual records. The only difference is an array subscript must be used to determine which array element is being referenced. The age field of the fourth record in the array EMPLOYEES could be assigned a value this way:

`EMPLOYEES[4].AGE := 47;`

This field could also be referred to by using a WITH statement:

```
WITH EMPLOYEES[4] DO
    BEGIN
        AGE := 47
    END;
```

Program ODD___JOBS

Eric needs a program to keep track of odd jobs he does in the neighborhood. He would like a record of each job done, containing the following information:

> name of person job was done for
> job (rake, mow, garden, and babysit)
> time spent on the job
> cost of the job

The program will be written so that Eric can enter the first three items at the keyboard. The amount to be charged for the job will be computed in the program. Look at the program in Figure 12-7. BILL is the name of the record. An array of these records is declared:

```
VAR
     CUSTOMER : ARRAY[1..20] OF BILL;
```

CUSTOMER may contain up to 20 records. After Eric is done entering information, the program prints a table containing the contents of each record. If Eric decides to change the amount he charges per hour for a particular job, he can easily change the program.

Figure 12-7   PROGRAM ODD____JOBS

```
PROGRAM ODD_JOBS;
(*  THIS PROGRAM READS A CUSTOMER'S NAME, THE TYPE OF JOB DONE
FOR THE CUSTOMER, AND THE NUMBER OF HOURS SPENT ON THIS JOB.
THE AMOUNT OWED BY THE CUSTOMER IS THEN COMPUTED.  UP TO
TWENTY JOBS MAY BE ENTERED AT A TIME.  THE FOLLOWING JOBS
MAY BE ENTERED:
    MOW
    RAKE
    GARDEN
    BABYSIT
AT THE END OF THE PROGRAM A TABLE IS PRINTED TO THE  MONITOR *)

TYPE
    BILL    = RECORD
      NAME : STRING[25];
      JOB  : STRING[10];
      TIME : REAL;
      COST : REAL
    END; (* BILL *)

VAR
    CUSTOMER : ARRAY[1..20] OF BILL;
    ANSWER : CHAR;
    I, COUNT : INTEGER;

BEGIN   (* ODD_JOBS *)
```

Continued next page

```
    COUNT := 0;

    (* SEE IF MORE DATA IS TO BE ENTERED *)
    WRITELN ('DO YOU WANT TO ENTER A JOB?');
    WRITELN ('IF YES, TYPE IN Y AND HIT RETURN KEY.');
    WRITELN ('IF NO, TYPE JUST HIT RETURN KEY.');
    READLN (ANSWER);

    WHILE ANSWER = 'Y' DO
        BEGIN
            COUNT := COUNT + 1;

            WITH CUSTOMER[COUNT] DO
                BEGIN
                    WRITELN ('ENTER CUSTOMER''S NAME');
                    READLN (NAME);
                    WRITELN ('ENTER THE JOB');
                    READLN (JOB);
                    WRITELN ('ENTER THE TIME SPENT ON THE JOB');
                    READLN (TIME);

                    (* COMPUTE AMOUNT OF BILL *)
                    IF JOB = 'MOW' THEN
                        COST := 3.50 * TIME
                    ELSE IF JOB = 'RAKE' THEN
                        COST := 3.00 * TIME
                    ELSE IF JOB = 'GARDEN' THEN
                        COST := 3.25 * TIME
                    ELSE IF JOB = 'BABYSIT' THEN
                        COST := 2.00 * TIME
            END;    (* WITH *)
            WRITELN ('DO YOU WANT TO ENTER A JOB?');
            WRITELN ('IF YES, TYPE IN Y AND HIT RETURN KEY');
            WRITELN ('IF NO, JUST HIT RETURN KEY');
            READLN (ANSWER)
        END;  (* WHILE *)

        (* PRINT TABLE TO MONITOR *)
        WRITELN ('NAME':20,'JOB':20,'TIME':10,'AMOUNT DUE':12);
        FOR I := 1 TO COUNT DO
                WITH CUSTOMER[I] DO
                        WRITELN (NAME:20, JOB :20, TIME:10:2, COST:10:2)
        END.    (* ODD_JOBS *)
```

Running. . .

```
DO YOU WANT TO ENTER A JOB?
IF YES, TYPE IN Y AND HIT RETURN KEY.
IF NO, TYPE JUST HIT RETURN KEY.
Y
ENTER CUSTOMER'S NAME
ALBERTSON
ENTER THE JOB
RAKE
ENTER THE TIME SPENT ON THE JOB
 2.50000
DO YOU WANT TO ENTER A JOB?
IF YES, TYPE IN Y AND HIT RETURN KEY
IF NO, JUST HIT RETURN KEY
Y
```

Continued next page

```
ENTER CUSTOMER'S NAME
JACKMAN
ENTER THE JOB
BABYSIT
ENTER THE TIME SPENT ON THE JOB
 4.00000
DO YOU WANT TO ENTER A JOB?
IF YES, TYPE IN Y AND HIT RETURN KEY
IF NO, JUST HIT RETURN KEY
Y
ENTER CUSTOMER'S NAME
HALL
ENTER THE JOB
MOW
ENTER THE TIME SPENT ON THE JOB
 3.75000
DO YOU WANT TO ENTER A JOB?
IF YES, TYPE IN Y AND HIT RETURN KEY
IF NO, JUST HIT RETURN KEY

              NAME              JOB      TIME    AMOUNT DUE
          ALBERTSON            RAKE      2.50       7.50
            JACKMAN         BABYSIT      4.00       8.00
               HALL             MOW      3.75      13.12
```

Figure 12-7   (con't.)

LEARNING CHECK 12-1

1. What is a record?
2. Declare a record named PLAYER. This record will be for baseball players on a team. The record should have the following fields:

          NAME   (name of the player)
          AGE   (age of the player)
          BAT_AVE   (batting average of the player)
          POS   (position played by the player)

Each field should be assigned an appropriate data type.
3. Study the program segment below.

```
PROGRAM GOLF;

TYPE
    PLAYER = RECORD
        NAME : STRING;
        AVERAGE : REAL
    END;
```

225

a. Declare an array of type PLAYER that can hold up to six records.

b. Write a loop to read six names and assign the names to the NAME field of each of the records in the array declared above. Be sure to write a prompt to tell the user when the name should be entered.

Answers:

SETS

Pascal is the first general-purpose programming language to include sets as a structured data type. A set is a collection of items that are classed together. Sets can be very useful in writing Pascal programs.

Declaring Sets

In mathematics a set containing the integers 1 through 7 would be written this way:

$$\{1, 2, 3, 4, 5, 6, 7\}$$

In Pascal, a SET is declared under the TYPE declarations:

```
TYPE
        SMALLNUM = SET OF 1..7;
```

A variable may then be declared of type SMALLNUM:

```
VAR
        LITTLE : SMALLNUM;
```

LITTLE could now be a set containing any of the integers between 1 and 7. Here are a few examples of how set LITTLE might look:

```
[2, 6, 7]
[5, 3, 1]     (Set elements do not have to be in order.)
[ ]
```

The last example above is called the empty set. It is useful when a set needs to be initialized to nothing. The following would not be sets of LITTLE:

```
[1, 8]          (No number may be larger than 7)
[-2, 3, 6]      (No number may be smaller than 1)
```

The elements of a set must all be of the same base type. In the set LITTLE above, the values are all of data type INTEGER. The base type of a set may be any scalar data type.

Assigning Values to Sets

Values may be assigned to a set using the assignment operator (:=) :

```
LITTLE := [1, 3, 4];
LITTLE := [6];
LITTLE := [ ];
```

All of the values assigned to a set must be separated by commas and enclosed in brackets.

Set Operators

There are three operators that may be used with sets. They are:

1. Union (+).
2. Intersection (*).
3. Difference (−).

Each will be discussed individually.

Union

The operator that is used to indicate the union of two sets is the plus sign (+). The union of two sets is a set of all of the elements that are in one or both of the sets. Here are two examples:

```
['A', 'B', 'Z'] + ['A', 'D', 'M'] = ['A', 'B', 'D', 'M', 'Z']
[2, 4, 12] + [6, 4, 8, 10, 12] = [2, 4, 6, 8, 10, 12]
```

Intersection

The intersection of two sets consists of a set containing only those values that are in both sets. The operator for set intersection is the asterisk (*). Below are two examples of set intersection:

```
['A', 'B', 'Z'] * ['A', 'D', 'M'] = ['A']
[2, 4, 12] * [6, 4, 8, 10, 12] = [4, 12]
```

Difference

The difference between two sets consists of all of the values that are in the first set but not the second. The minus sign (−) is used to represent set differences. These two examples would have the results shown:

$$['A', 'B', 'Z'] - ['A', 'B', 'M'] = ['Z']$$

$$[2, 4, 1] - [6, 4, 8, 10, 12] = [2, 1]$$

Notice that in determining the difference between two sets, the order of the sets affects the results. If the order of the first example above was changed, the result would be different:

$$['A', 'B', 'M'] - ['A', 'B', 'C'] = ['M']$$

However, in set union and intersection, the order of the sets does not make a difference. The table in Figure 12-8 gives some more examples of using set operators.

Using Relational Operators with Sets

The following relational operators may be used with sets:

$$= (\text{equal to})$$

A set is equal to a second set if both contain exactly the same elements. The order of the elements does not matter.

$$>= (\text{greater than or equal to})$$

A set is greater than or equal to a second set if the first set contains all of the elements in the second or all of the elements in the second plus additional elements.

$$<= (\text{less than or equal to})$$

A set is less than or equal to a second set if the first set contains all or some of the elements in the second set and no additional elements.

$$<> (\text{not equal to})$$

A set is not equal to a second set if the elements in the sets are not identical.

Given these two assignment statements:

Figure 12-8 EXAMPLES OF SET OPERATORS

Expression	Result
[2, 3, 8] + [1, 3]	[1, 2, 3, 8]
[2, 3, 8] * [1, 3]	[3]
[2, 3, 8] - [1, 3]	[2, 8]
['A', 'D'] - ['C']	['A', 'D']
['B', 'E', 'F'] + ['D']	['B', 'E', 'F', 'D']

Expression	Evaluates To
[7, 3, 4] = [4, 3, 7]	TRUE
[1, 2, 4] >= [1, 4]	TRUE
['D', 'F', 'H'] <= ['D', 'H']	FALSE
['A', 'G', 'I', 'M'] >= ['I']	TRUE

Figure 12-9   EXAMPLES OF SET RELATIONAL OPERATORS

```
VALUE1 := [2, 4, 8, 16, 32];
VALUE2 := [8, 32];
```

the following expressions would all evaluate as true:

```
VALUE1 >= VALUE2
VALUE1 <> [2, 4, 8, 16, 40]
VALUE2 <= [8, 12, 32]
[ ]     <= VALUE1
```

More examples of using relational operators with sets are shown in Figure 12-9.

Program ACTIVITIES

Sets are useful when a program needs to determine whether or not a given item is present. For example, program ACTIVITIES (Figure 12-10) reads an individual's name and three of that person's hobbies. The hobbies are entered by using an integer code. This list of hobbies is placed in a set. It is then easy to determine whether or not a particular person is interested in a given hobby. In the program this expression:

Figure 12-10   PROGRAM ACTIVITIES

```
PROGRAM ACTIVITIES;
(* THIS PROGRAM READS IN 10 INDIVIDUAL'S NAMES AND A LIST OF EACH
PERSON'S HOBBIES.  EACH PERSON SHOULD PICK THEIR THREE FAVORITE
HOBBIES FROM THE 8 LISTED BELOW.  THE HOBBIES ARE ENTERED USING
THE CORRESPONDING CODE NUMBER:
   1.  BASKETBALL
   2.  RACKETBALL
   3.  READING
   4.  TENNIS
   5.  BASEBALL
   6.  FOOTBALL
   7.  JOGGING
   8.  SEWING
AFTER ALL OF THE DATA ARE ENTERED, THE NAMES OF PEOPLE WHO ENJOY
BASKETBALL AND TENNIS ARE PRINTED TO THE  MONITOR .  ALSO
PRINTED ARE THE NAMES OF THE PEOPLE WHO DID NOT PICK JOGGING *)

TYPE
   ACTIVITY = SET OF 1..8;
```

Continued next page

```
    PERSON = RECORD
        NAME    : STRING[20];
        HOBBIES : ACTIVITY
    END;   (* PERSON *)

VAR
    PEOPLE : ARRAY[1..10] OF PERSON;
    I : INTEGER;
    A, B, C : INTEGER;

BEGIN

    (* ENTER THE DATA ON THE 10 PEOPLE *)
    FOR I := 1 TO 10 DO
        BEGIN
            WITH PEOPLE[I] DO
                BEGIN
                    WRITE ('ENTER NAME: ');
                    READLN (NAME);
                    WRITE ('ENTER HOBBIES USING THE INTEGER CODE: ');
                    READLN ( A, B, C);
                    HOBBIES := [A, B, C];
                END   (* WITH *)
        END;   (* FOR *)

    (* PRINT THE NAMES OF PEOPLE WHO ENJOY BASKETBALL AND TENNIS *)
    WRITELN ('THE FOLLOWING PEOPLE ENJOY BASKETBALL AND TENNIS');

    FOR I := 1 TO 10 DO
        WITH PEOPLE[I] DO
        IF HOBBIES >= [1, 4] THEN
            WRITELN (NAME);

    (* PRINT THE NAMES OF THE PEOPLE WHO DID NOT PICK JOGGING *)
    WRITELN;
    WRITELN ('THE FOLLOWING PEOPLE DID NOT PICK JOGGING:');
    FOR I := 1 TO 10 DO
        WITH PEOPLE[I] DO
        IF HOBBIES * [7] <> [7] THEN
            WRITELN (NAME)

END.   (* ACTIVITIES *)
```

Running. . .

```
ENTER NAME: JAMES
ENTER HOBBIES USING THE INTEGER CODE:    2   4   6
ENTER NAME: MARIA
ENTER HOBBIES USING THE INTEGER CODE:    1   4   8
ENTER NAME: SARAH
ENTER HOBBIES USING THE INTEGER CODE:    1   3   7
ENTER NAME: AGNES
ENTER HOBBIES USING THE INTEGER CODE:    5   6   8
ENTER NAME: SHARAD
ENTER HOBBIES USING THE INTEGER CODE:    2   6   7
ENTER NAME: JEANNE
ENTER HOBBIES USING THE INTEGER CODE:    1   5   7
```

Continued next page

```
ENTER NAME: DANNY
ENTER HOBBIES USING THE INTEGER CODE:    1   4   8
ENTER NAME: MARVIN
ENTER HOBBIES USING THE INTEGER CODE:    1   3   6
ENTER NAME: DEEDEE
ENTER HOBBIES USING THE INTEGER CODE:    2   3   6
ENTER NAME: ROBERTO
ENTER HOBBIES USING THE INTEGER CODE:    4   6   7

THE FOLLOWING PEOPLE ENJOY BASKETBALL AND TENNIS
MARIA
DANNY

THE FOLLOWING PEOPLE DID NOT PICK JOGGING:
JAMES
MARIA
AGNES
DANNY
MARVIN
DEEDEE
```

Figure 12-10 (con't.)

IF HOBBIES >= [1, 4] THEN

checks to see which people are interested in basketball and tennis.
Only those people who list both basketball and tennis as hobbies will
have their names printed. The expression:

IF HOBBIES * [7] <> [7] THEN

will evaluate as true only if jogging is not listed as a hobby. It would
be easy to add more statements to this program to check for other
hobbies.

LEARNING CHECK 12-2

1. What is a set?
2. What are the three operations that may be performed with sets? Explain what each one does.
3. Answer the questions below using the following TYPE declarations:

```
TYPE
    DAYS = SET OF 1..7;
    WHOLE = SET OF 1..20;
```

a. Declare a variable WEEKDAYS to be of type DAYS. Assign the values 1, 2, 3, 4, and 5 to
   WEEKDAYS.
b. Declare a variable ODD of type WHOLE and assign all of the odd values in WHOLE to this
   variable.

c. Declare a variable MULTTWO of type WHOLE. Assign to it all the multiples of two up to 20 (2, 4, 6, 8, . . .)

Answers:

1. A set is a structured data type consisting of a collection of values that are classed together. All of these values must be of the same base type. 2. The operators are: a. Union (+)—results in a set containing all of the elements that are in one or both of the sets., b. Intersection (*)—results in a set containing those values that are in both sets., c. Difference (−)—results in a set consisting of all the values that are in the first set but not present in the second.

SUMMARY POINTS

- This chapter discussed two structured data types: records and sets. A record is a group of related data items that are gathered together as a single unit. These items do not have to be of the same data type. Records are very useful in business, where a number of facts need to be kept together. An example would be a record containing information about a student in a school. The record could contain a variety of information about the student. Each item is contained in a field of the record. Records can have any number of fields. Records are often placed in arrays. An array can contain a large number of records.
- A set is a collection of items that are classed together. All of the values in a set must be of the same base type. Three set operators may be used in Pascal:

$$\text{union} \ (+)$$
$$\text{intersection} \ (*)$$
$$\text{difference} \ (-)$$

The following relational operators may be used with sets:

$$=$$
$$> =$$
$$< =$$
$$<>$$

Records and sets can both be useful in handling data in Pascal programs.

VOCABULARY LIST

Field A data item that is part of a record.

Record A structured data type that contains a group of related data items, not necessarily of the same data type, that are gathered together in a single unit.

Set A structured data type consisting of a collection of values that are classed together. All of the values must be of the same base type.

Structured data type   A data type that can store many individual values, which may then be referred to as a single unit. Each structured data type has strict rules concerning how it is to be declared and used in programs. The structured data types in Pascal are arrays, records, sets, and files.

CHAPTER TEST

VOCABULARY

Match each term from the numbered column with the description from the lettered column that best fits the term.

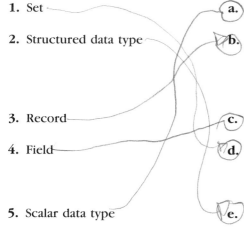

1. Set

2. Structured data type

3. Record

4. Field

5. Scalar data type

a. A data type whose values may all be listed.

b. A structured data type that contains a group of related data items, not necessarily of the same data type, that are gathered together in a single unit.

c. A data item that is part of a record.

d. A structured data type consisting of a collection of values that are classed together. All of the values must be of the same base type.

e. A data type that can store many individual values which may then be referred to as a single unit. Records and sets are examples of this data type.

QUESTIONS

1. What are the two ways of referring to an individual field in a record? Give an example of each. *script / with statement*
2. Use the following program segment to answer the questions below.

```
TYPE
    AUTO = RECORD
        MAKE : STRING;
        YEAR : INTEGER;
        COLOR : STRING
    END;

VAR
    CAR : AUTO;
    CLUNKER : AUTO;
```

a. Use the WITH statement to assign these values to the following fields of record CAR:

$$MAKE = CHEVROLET$$
$$YEAR = 1982$$
$$COLOR = BLUE$$

b. Assign the values listed in part *a* to record CAR, using this format:

record-name.field

c. Copy record CAR into record CLUNKER.

3. Given the following program segment, answer the questions below.

```
TYPE
    ALPHA = SET OF 'A'..'Z';

VAR
    VOWELS : ALPHA;
    SMALPHA : ALPHA;

BEGIN

    VOWELS := ['A', 'E', 'I', 'O', 'U'];
    SMALPHA := ['A', 'B', 'C', 'D', 'E'];
```

a. What is the value of COMBINE?

```
COMBINE := VOWELS + ['Y', 'W'];
```

b. What is the value of TOG?

```
TOG := VOWELS * SMALPHA;
```

c. What is the value of DIFF?

```
DIFF := ['B', 'C', 'F', 'G'] - SMALPHA;
```

d. What is the value of FINAL?

```
FINAL := ['B', 'C', 'F', 'G'] * SMALPHA;
```

4. Look at the program segment below. Determine if the expressions that follow evaluate as true or false.

```
TYPE
    NUM = SET OF 1..20;

VAR
    POINTS1 : NUM;
    POINTS2 : NUM;
```

```
        POINTS1 := [2, 4, 10, 18];
        POINTS2 := [4, 8, 11, 20];
```

a. POINTS1 >= POINTS2;
b. [ ] <= POINTS1;
c. POINTS2 >= [4, 8, 11, 19, 20];
d. POINTS2 <> [4, 8, 11, 19, 20];
e. [4, 10, 18] >= POINTS1;

PROGRAMMING PROBLEMS

1. Survey your class to see which of the following toppings people like on their hamburgers. Have each student pick three favorite toppings. Use the following code list:

> cheese: 1
> catsup: 2
> mustard: 3
> onions: 4
> pickles: 5
> tomatoes: 6
> lettuce: 7
> bananas: 8

Use a set to hold the code numbers of the toppings. Enter each student's name and the set of toppings to a record. After all the data are entered, print the following headings along with the names of the students who fit into each category:

a. THE FOLLOWING STUDENTS DIDN'T CHOOSE CATSUP AS A FAVOR-ITE TOPPING:
b. THE FOLLOWING STUDENTS LIKE ONIONS AND TOMATOES:
c. THE FOLLOWING STUDENTS CHOSE CHEESE AS ONE OF THEIR FA-VORITE TOPPINGS:

2. Write a program that will print a list of the students who are eligible for driver's education. In order to be eligible for driver's education at City High a student must be at least 15 years old and have at least a 2.5 grade point average. Each student's record looks like this:

```
STUD_REC = RECORD
    NAME : STRING[20];
    AGE : INTEGER;
    GPA : REAL
END;
```

Use the following data to test this program:

NAME	AGE	GPA
MORRISON, SAM	17	2.0
JEFFERSON, JANE	15	3.6
ADAMS, SARAH	14	3.2
ROSS, BETSY	16	3.0
PAINE, TOM	15	2.5

3. Mrs. Walsh needs a program to calculate the average score on two physics tests. An array of records should be used to hold the information. Each student's record should hold the following information:

NAME	(student's name)
TEST1	(score on the first test)
TEST2	(score on the second test)
AVE	(student's average on the two tests)
DIFF	(student's difference from the class average)

The first three items will be entered by the user. The student's average can then be figured at this point. After all the records have been entered, the class average can then be calculated. The program should then go back to the beginning of the array and calculate the difference between each student's average and the class average. Output should be similar to that below:

NAME	TEST1	TEST2	AVERAGE	DIFFERENCE FROM THE CLASS AVERAGE
MORRIS	77.0	83.0	80.0	3.5
STEPHENS	72.0	70.0	71.0	−5.5

The class size will not be greater than 20. You may write your own input data to test this program.

4. Charlie's Used Cars would like a program to print a table that contains all the cars the firm currently is offering for sale. The program should use an array of records. There will never be more than 40 cars for sale at one time. Each record should contain the following information:

MAKE
YEAR
CONDITION (excellent, good, fair, poor)
COST
TOT__COST

TOT__COST includes the sales tax, which is 6 percent. After all the data are entered and TOT__COST is calculated for each car, print the information in table form. Make up your own data to test the program.

CHAPTER 13

Files

OUTLINE

LEARNING OBJECTIVES

After reading this chapter, you should be able to:

1. Define the terms *file, sequential file,* and *random-access file.*
2. Describe why files are important.
3. Describe what is meant by text and interactive files.
4. Declare sequential files.
5. Describe and use the REWRITE and RESET procedures.
6. Describe and use a file pointer and a buffer variable.
7. Describe and use the PUT and GET procedures.
8. Describe and use the end-of-file and end-of-line markers and functions.
9. Describe and use the CLOSE and LOCK procedures.
10. Read and write data to and from sequential files.
11. Describe the primary difference between text and interactive files.

INTRODUCTION

Disk files are commonly used to store program output. Up to this point, program output could only be saved by printing either to the screen or to a printer. By using a disk file, data can be stored and reused by a program. Data stored on a diskette is not lost when the computer is turned off.

A Pascal disk file is an ordered collection of data items, of the same data type, that is stored on a disk. Disk files can contain data of type ARRAY, CHARACTER, INTEGER, REAL, RECORD, or STRING. Disk files must be declared in the VAR section of a program. The format for declaring a file is:

Filename : FILE OF type;

Figure 13-1 illustrates a few examples of file declaration. Example A shows the declaration of file COUNT in the VAR section. Example B shows the declaration of the files CLIENT and SALESPERSON in the VAR section. Notice that CLIENT and SALESPERSON are files of type PEOPLE. PEOPLE is declared in the TYPE section. If several files of the same type are used in a program, this type of format should be used. Example C in Figure 13-1 shows the declaration of the file CLASS. CLASS is a file of records. Because CLASS has been declared as a file of records, it can store data of many types. Notice that CLASS contains characters, integers, and strings. Many businesses, schools, and organizations use files of records. These files might contain names, social security numbers, addresses, and other related information. Though the data are of different types, one file can store all these data if they are organized into records.

```
A. VAR
       COUNT : FILE OF REAL;

B. TYPE
       PEOPLE = FILE OF STRING[10];

   VAR
       CLIENT        : PEOPLE;
       SALESPERSON   : PEOPLE;

C. TYPE
       STUDENT = RECORD
           NAME : STRING[20];
           YEAR : INTEGER;
           GRADE : CHAR
       END;

   VAR
       CLASS : FILE OF STUDENT;
```

Figure 13-1 FILE DECLARATIONS

TYPES OF PASCAL FILES

Sequential and **random-access files** are the two main types of files in UCSD Pascal. In a sequential file, data items are stored one right after another. Data items must be accessed in sequence. For example, to access the tenth item in a sequential file, a program must read through the first nine items. This process can be very slow if a file is large. Sequential files are most often used to store data that are rarely changed.

Random-access files allow data items to be stored anywhere within a file. Data items can be directly accessed. For example, a program could directly access the tenth item in a random-access file. Random-access files require the computer to keep track of the locations of all the data within a file. This often makes a program using a random-access file more complex than a program using a sequential file.

Text and interactive files are special types of sequential files. They are found in most versions of UCSD Pascal. Text files are used when data are in the form of lines or strings. Interactive files allow the computer to communicate with other devices besides the disk drive. Two frequently used interactive files are INPUT and OUTPUT. These files are automatically opened when any UCSD Pascal program first executes. The INPUT file allows the keyboard to send commands to the computer. The OUTPUT file allows the computer to send data to the monitor screen. Files are an important part of the Pascal language.

239

1. What do disk files allow programs to do?
2. Describe the following terms:
    disk file
    sequential file
    random-access file
    text file
    interactive file
3. Where are Pascal files normally declared?

Answers:

1. Disk files allow programs to store program output on a diskette. The data will not be lost when the computer is turned off. Also, the data can be retrieved and reused. 2. Disk file: An ordered collection of data items of the same data type. Sequential file: A file that stores data items one right after another. Data items must also be accessed in sequence. Random-access file: A file that allows data items to be stored anywhere in a file. Data items can then be directly accessed. Text file: A sequential file used with string data or data in the form of lines. Interactive file: A sequential file used when a programmer wants to read or store data from devices other than the disk drive. 3. Files are normally declared in the VAR section.

CREATING AND WRITING TO A FILE

Disk files are used in two ways. Data can be written to a file or data can be read from a file. Pascal requires a program to specify how a disk file will be used. First, creating and writing to a file will be discussed.

To use a disk file, it must first be created. Creating a file is a two-step process. First, a file must be declared in the VAR section of a program. Second, a disk file must be opened and assigned space on a diskette. The REWRITE procedure opens a disk file and allows data to be written to the file. The format of the REWRITE statement is:

REWRITE (program filename, 'directory name');

The program filename is the name of the disk file declared in the program. The directory name is the name of the disk file in the directory of the diskette. Figure 13-2 illustrates the program name and directory name of a file in a REWRITE statement. In this example, the program file CUSTOMER will be stored in diskette APPLE0: under the name CUSTFILE.

Once a file is created, data can be written to the disk file. Data are written to a file by using a file pointer, a buffer variable, and the PUT procedure. When a file is opened by REWRITE, the computer automatically creates a file pointer and a buffer variable. Imagine the file pointer as an arrow in the computer's memory that points to data items in a file. The file pointer points to the beginning of a file when the file is first opened. The buffer variable is a window through which

```
CUSTOMER : FILE OF STRING[20];

Program filename


                    REWRITE (CUSTOMER, 'APPLE0: CUSTFILE');
```

Figure 13-2   USING THE REWRITE STATEMENT

a program can write to and read data from a file. The buffer variable is referenced by typing the program filename and a caret $\wedge$. Some computers use the up arrow ($\uparrow$) symbol instead of the caret ($\wedge$) to represent the buffer variable. For example, the buffer variable for the file STUDENT is STUDENT $\wedge$, or on some computers STUDENT $\uparrow$. Buffer variables can be used like any variable. Data are assigned to the buffer variable by using an assignment statement in the following format:

program filename$\wedge$:= variable;

The PUT procedure actually writes the data to the file. The PUT statement will first make a copy of the current contents of the buffer variable. It will then insert the copy into the file location marked by the file pointer. The format of the PUT statement is:

PUT (program filename);

Figure 13-3 illustrates the relationship among the file pointer, buffer variable, and program.

Let's try writing some data to the file STUDENT. First, the file STUDENT must be opened by using REWRITE. Second, the data to be sent to the file are assigned to the buffer variable. Figure 13-4 illustrates a program segment that writes names to the file STUDENT. Notice that the variable NAME is of the same type (STRING) as the file STUDENT. Any data that are assigned to the buffer variable must be of the same type as the file. The third step in writing data to a file is the PUT statement. The PUT statement inserts a copy of the contents of the buffer variable into the file.

CLOSING A FILE: 1

A file must be closed to save its contents. The data in the file can then be used again. Any file that is opened in a UCSD Pascal program must be closed before the end of the program. A **program error** will occur if a file is not closed. UCSD Pascal files are closed with the CLOSE and LOCK statements. The format of the CLOSE and LOCK statements are:

CLOSE (program filename, LOCK);   **241**

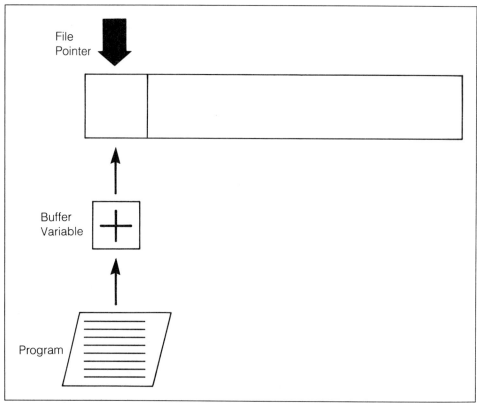

Figure 13-3 WRITING TO A FILE

Figure 13-4 WRITING DATA TO A FILE WITH A PUT STATEMENT

```
PROGRAM FILE_WRITE;

   VAR
      NAME : STRING[20];
      STUDENT : FILE OF NAME;

   BEGIN

      REWRITE (STUDENT, 'APPLEO: STUDFILE');
      WRITELN ('ENTER STUDENT NAME:');
      READLN (NAME);
      STUDENT^ := NAME;
      PUT (STUDENT);
```

The CLOSE command alone will satisfy the compiler. However, if the LOCK statement is not used, the file will be lost after it is closed. The LOCK statement tells the compiler to make the file permanent. The file's directory name will then be placed in the diskette's directory.

Now you can create, write to, and save a disk file. Learning to use disk files is not always easy. But with a little practice, you can learn to use disk files in useful ways. Once you understand the ideas in this chapter, you can learn even more complex, interesting ways to use disk files.

LEARNING CHECK 13-2

1. What are the two steps necessary to create a disk file?
2. Describe the file pointer and buffer variable. How do they work together?
3. Use a buffer variable and a PUT statement to write:
   a. The contents of variable TEAM to the file TEAMS.
   b. The contents of variable FRIEND to the file FRIENDS.
   c. The contents of variable HOURS to the file WORK.
4. Close and save the contents of the files TEAMS, FRIENDS, and WORK.

Answers:

1. The two steps necessary to create a disk file are (a) declaring the disk file and (b) opening the disk file. 2. The file pointer points to a file location. The buffer variable is a window that can send data to a file location. The buffer variable is used to send data from the program to the file location marked by the file pointer. 3. a. TEAMS^ := TEAM; PUT (TEAMS); b. FRIENDS^ := FRIEND; c. WORK^ := HOURS; 4. CLOSE (TEAMS, LOCK); PUT (FRIENDS); CLOSE (FRIENDS, LOCK); PUT (WORK); CLOSE (WORK, LOCK);

READING A FILE

Disk files are often used to store data that are used at a later time. To use data in a disk file, the disk file is read. Then, the data can be used or changed in a program.

In order to access a saved file, the file must be opened. First, the file must be declared in the VAR section of the program. Second, the computer must be told how the file is to be used. The RESET procedure opens a file so that it can be read. The format of the RESET statement is:

RESET (program filename, 'directory name');

The RESET statement must appear before the program tries to use data from the file. The RESET command will cause the compiler to look for a file in a diskette's directory that matches the declared directory name. If the file is found, a file pointer is assigned to the first data item of the file. Then, the first data item is read to the file's buffer variable and the file pointer is moved to the second data item.

Data are read from a file with the buffer variable and GET procedure. The GET procedure copies the file contents marked by the file pointer, moves the copy to the buffer variable, and moves the file

243

pointer to the next data item. The RESET procedure performs an automatic GET after it has located a file. The format of the GET statement is:

GET (program filename);

The buffer variable acts as a window to read or write data. Once a GET procedure is executed, the contents of the buffer variable can be assigned to a program variable. Then, the data can be used within a program. Figure 13-5 illustrates the relationship among the file pointer, buffer variable, and the GET procedure.

Files must be read in a specific way since the RESET statement automatically performs a GET procedure. Figure 13-6 illustrates a program that reads all the data in the file HOURS. Notice that the file is declared in the VAR section and opened with a RESET statement. Next, a WHILE loop is used to read all the data out of the file HOURS. Notice that the tested condition of the WHILE loop is NOT EOF (HOURS). EOF is a function that returns the BOOLEAN value true when the file pointer has reached the end of file. The end-of-file marker is automatically assigned to a file when it is closed. The WHILE loop in Figure 13-6 repeats until the end-of-file marker in the file HOURS is reached.

Figure 13-5 READING FROM A FILE

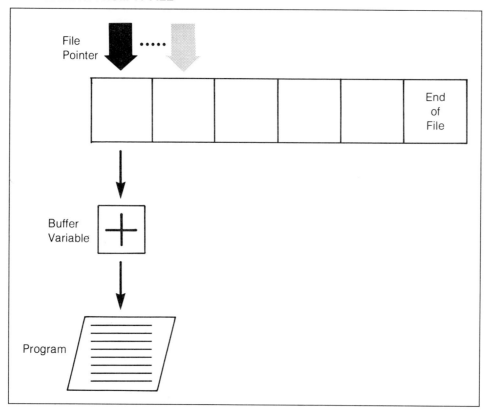

```
PROGRAM P_HOURS;

    VAR
        HOUR   : REAL;
        HOURS  : FILE OF REAL;
        I      : INTEGER;

    BEGIN

        RESET (HOURS, 'APPLEO: HOURSFILE');
        WHILE NOT EOF (HOURS) DO
            BEGIN
                HOUR := HOURS^;
                GET (HOURS)
            END;
        CLOSE (HOURS)

    END.
```

Figure 13-6 USING EOF TO READ A FILE

Next, notice the position of the GET and buffer variable within the WHILE loop. The contents of the buffer variable are first assigned to the program variable HOUR. Then, a GET statement is executed. The first data item would be lost if a GET statement was executed first. Since the RESET statement automatically performs a GET, the buffer variable automatically holds the value of the first data item in the file HOUR. Thus, the GET would erase the first data item and re-place it with the second data item. A WHILE loop is the easiest and safest way to read the contents of a file.

One of the advantages of UCSD Pascal is the way records can be handled. Reading a file of records is the same as reading any other file. Figure 13-7 illustrates a program that reads all the records in the file CLASS. Notice that the variable STUDENT is assigned the value of the buffer variable CLASS. The variable STUDENT is a record that contains the name and address of students. Once a record is read, the record's information can be used in the program. In Figure 13-7, the names and addresses of the students are printed on the monitor screen.

CLOSING A FILE: 2

All disk files opened in a program must be closed before the end of a program. Reading a file does not change the contents or organization of a disk file. The rules, or syntax, of Pascal still require opened disk files to be closed. Disk files that are opened by a RESET statement can be closed by a CLOSE statement. The LOCK statement is not neces-

```
PROGRAM CLASS_READ;

TYPE
    STUD_REC = RECORD
        NAME    : STRING[20];
        ADDRESS : STRING[30]
    END;

VAR
    CLASS   : FILE OF STUD_REC;
    STUDENT : STUD_REC;

BEGIN

    RESET (CLASS, 'APPLE1: CLASSFILE');
    WHILE NOT EOF (CLASS) DO
        BEGIN
            STUDENT := CLASS^;
            WRITELN ('NAME OF STUDENT: ', STUDENT.NAME);
            WRITELN ('ADDRESS OF STUDENT:', STUDENT.ADDRESS);
            GET (CLASS)
        END;
    CLOSE (CLASS)

END.
```

Figure 13-7 READING A FILE OF RECORDS

sary. For example, the file STUDENT would be closed by the statement CLOSE (STUDENT);.

LEARNING CHECK 13-3

1. Open the following disk files so that they can be read. Use your own program filenames.
   a. JOG
   b. BASEBALL
   c. PHONEBOOK
2. Read one data item from the files below. You can assume that the files have been opened and no GET statements have been executed.

   JOG, a file of real numbers
   BASEBALL, a file of records
   PHONEBOOK, a file of records

3. Why must a file be closed if it is opened within a program?

TEXT AND INTERACTIVE FILES

Up to this point, disk files were only used to store data on a diskette and to write data to a diskette. Text and interactive files allow programs to output to the printer and to use the keyboard for input. On some systems, only interactive files may be used to transfer output to the printer. Text and interactive files are an easy way to add to the variety of UCSD Pascal programs.

Text files are very useful when a program reads or writes strings. The structure of text files makes them useful. Text files are made up of lines terminated with end-of-line (EOLN) markers. Figure 13-8 illustrates the structure of a typical text file.

Like the end-of-file marker, the end-of-line marker can be used to test for the end of a section of data. The EOLN function returns the BOOLEAN value true when the file pointer reaches the end of a line. The BOOLEAN value false is returned if the file pointer is not positioned at the end of a line.

Text files must be declared in the VAR section of a program. The format for declaring a text file is:

filename: TEXT;

Text files must also be opened for reading or writing with either the RESET or REWRITE statements. So far, text files are very similar to the sequential files already discussed. Reading and writing text files, though, is much easier than reading or writing normal sequential files. Text files may be read with a modified version of the READLN statement. The format of the modified READLN statement is:

READLN (program filename, program variable);

Do you remember how the buffer variable and GET statement were used to read data? The modified READLN statement performs the entire reading process in one statement. Figure 13-9 compares the two file reading methods. Remember, both methods do the same thing!

Figure 13-8 STRUCTURE OF A TEXT FILE

String	EOLN	String	EOLN	String	EOLN	String	EOLN	EOF

```
READLN (CONCERTS, SHOW);                                    SHOW := CONCERTS^;
                                                            GET (CONCERTS);


READLN (CAR, GAS);                                          GAS := CAR^;
                                                            GET (CAR);
```

Figure 13-9 COMPARISON OF THE TWO METHODS OF READING A FILE

Text files are written with a modified version of the WRITELN statement. The format of the WRITELN statement is:

WRITELN (program filename, program variable);

The modified WRITELN statement performs the functions of the buffer variable and PUT statement. Figure 13-10 compares the two methods of file writing.

A common use for text files is to print the contents of a file. Text files can be sent to the printer. The program in Figure 13-11 reads data from the disk file PAPERFILE and writes it to the file PRINTER:. Notice that the REWRITE statement opens communication to the line printer by opening the file PRINTER:. Instead of data being sent to a diskette, they are sent to a printer.

Next, look at the READLN and WRITELN statements. The READLN statement copies the current file's contents into the variable LINE and moves the file pointer past the EOLN marker to the next line. The WRITELN statement copies data from the variable LINE, sends the data to the printer, and adds an EOLN marker. When the printer receives the EOLN marker, it performs a carriage return and moves the printer paper up a line. The WHILE loop that encloses the READLN and WRITELN statements uses the EOF function. The EOF function stops the execution of the WHILE loop when the end-of-file marker is reached. Finally, the program uses CLOSE statements to close both files.

Interactive files are used when devices other than the disk drive are used to input or output data. The **predefined files** INPUT and

Figure 13-10 COMPARISON OF THE TWO METHODS OF WRITING A FILE

```
WRITELN (CONCERTS, SHOW);                                   CONCERTS^ := SHOW;
                                                            PUT (CONCERTS);


WRITELN (CAR, GAS);                                         CAR^ := GAS;
                                                            PUT (CAR);
```

```
PROGRAM PRINT_OUT;

    VAR
        LINE    : STRING[80];
        PAPER   : TEXT;
        PRINT   : TEXT;

    BEGIN

        RESET (PAPER, 'PAPERFILE');
        REWRITE (PRINT, 'PRINTER:');
        WHILE NOT EOF (PAPER) DO
            BEGIN
                READLN (PAPER, LINE);
                WRITELN (PRINT, LINE)
            END;
        CLOSE (PAPER);
        CLOSE (PRINT)

    END.
```

Figure 13-11   USING A TEXT FILE TO PRINT A FILE

OUTPUT are interactive files. Also, the predefined file KEYBOARD is an interactive file. KEYBOARD represents data sent from the keyboard.

Interactive files can use all the file commands described for text files. Interactive files must be declared in the VAR section, except for INPUT, OUTPUT, and KEYBOARD. The format for declaring an interactive file is:

filename: INTERACTIVE;

The biggest difference between interactive files and other sequential files lies in how the file is read. Remember that the RESET statement automatically performs a GET procedure. The buffer variable then contains a copy of the contents of the first file location. The RESET statement, however, does not perform an automatic GET on interactive files. Since interactive files often represent the monitor keyboard, the file has no contents until a key is pressed. If an automatic GET is performed before a key is pressed, the program would find nothing in the file. Figure 13-12 illustrates the difference between the interactive READLN and the text READLN. Notice that the individual statements look identical. In fact, the interactive and text READLN statements can be used in the same way. Be aware, though, that they perform the GET and the buffer variable assignment statements in reverse order.

Disk files are useful and often necessary in many programs. To use disk files well, you must practice using disk files in different programs. The problems at the end of this chapter should only be a be-

Interactive READLN	Text READLN
GET (KEY);	GRADE := KEY^;
GRADE := KEY^;	GET (KEY);

Figure 13-12 COMPARISON OF THE INTERACTIVE AND TEXT READLN STATEMENTS

ginning. Think of how you could use disk files to store information and try to write your own programs. You will soon realize the usefulness of disk files.

 LEARNING CHECK 13-4

1. Describe the structure of a text file.
2. When does the EOLN function return the BOOLEAN value true?
3. Open the files below. Include the variable declarations and RESET or REWRITE statements.
   a. SENTENCES, a disk file, to read text.
   b. WORK, a file to write text to the printer.
   c. WROTE, a disk file, to write text.

Answers: 1. Text files are made up of lines or strings of text terminated by end-of-line markers. The entire file ends with an end-of-file marker. 2. The EOLN function returns the BOOLEAN value true when the file pointer is located at an end-of-line marker. 3. a. SENTENCES : TEXT; b. WORK : TEXT; c. WROTE : TEXT; RESET (SENTENCES,'SENTENFILE:'); REWRITE (WORK,'PRINTER:'); REWRITE (WROTE,'WROTEFILE:');

SUMMARY POINTS

- UCSD Pascal can handle sequential and random-access files. With sequential files, data must be accessed one item after another. With random-access files, data can be accessed directly.
- To create a sequential file, the file must be declared in the VAR section and it must be opened with a REWRITE statement. Data are written to a sequential file with a buffer variable and a PUT statement. Any files opened within a program must be closed before the end of the program. New files are usually closed with the CLOSE and LOCK statements. The LOCK statement permanently adds a file to a diskette.
- To read a sequential file, the file must be declared in the VAR section of a program and the file must be opened with a RESET statement. Data are read from a sequential file with a buffer variable and a GET statement.
- Text and interactive files are special forms of the sequential file. Text files are made up of lines of strings which end with end-of-line markers. Text files are often used to write a file on a printer. Interactive files are used to access devices other than the disk drive or printer. Data are read from and written to text and interactive files by using modified versions of the READLN and WRITELN statements.

VOCABULARY LIST

Predefined file A file that is declared and opened automatically by the UCSD Pascal system.

Program error A flaw or error in a program that causes the program not to run properly. Program errors can cause a program to stop executing or compiling or produce incorrect program output.

Random-access file A file that allows data items to be stored anywhere in a file. Data items can then be directly accessed.

Sequential file A file that stores data items one after another. Data items must be accessed in sequence.

CHAPTER TEST

VOCABULARY

Match a term from the numbered column with the description from the lettered column that best fits the term.

1. Predefined file

2. Sequential file

3. Program error

4. Random-access file

a. A flaw or error in a program that causes the program not to run properly.

b. Stores data items one right after another. Data items must also be accessed in sequence.

c. A file that is declared and opened automatically by the UCSD Pascal system.

d. Allows data items to be stored anywhere in a file. Data items can then be directly accessed.

QUESTIONS

1. Declare the following files in the VAR section of a program.
   a. ORDERS, a file of real numbers.
   b. DELIVERIES, a file of records that contains the variables DRIVER: string[20], CASES: integer, TIME: real, and NEXT_DEL: string [8].
   c. CUSTOMERS, a file of string[20].
2. What is the difference between sequential and random-access files?
3. Create the files listed below. Write a VAR section and REWRITE statement. Use your own directory names.
   a. TEAMS, a file of string[20].
   b. FRIENDS, a file of records that contains the variables NAME: string[200], ADDRESS: string[30], CITY: string[15], and ZIP: integer.
   c. WORK, a file of real numbers.
4. Why must a file that is opened in a program be closed and locked before the end of the program?

251

5. Write a program segment that opens the file PHONEBOOK, reads all of the records it contains (that is, reaches the end of file), and stores the contents of the file in an array of records. The layout of the file is described below. Include your variable declarations. Use your own directory name.

   PHONEBOOK: a file of records
           NAME: STRING[20];
      ADDRESS: STRING[30];
      NUMBER: INTEGER[10];

6. Describe how the file pointer, buffer variable, and GET statement work to read a file.

7. Explain the difference between reading text files and reading interactive files.

PROGRAMMING PROBLEMS

1. Write a program that stores the following strings in a text file:
   - UCSD Pascal is a structured
   - programming language that allows
   - you to write clear, organized
   - programs

2. Write two programs, one that writes the contents of the above text file to the screen and one that writes to a printer.

3. Write a program that stores the miles jogged by a user Sunday through Saturday. The program should prompt the user to enter the number of miles jogged each day. For example, the program could prompt, "Miles Jogged on Saturday:," and the user would enter the number of miles jogged that day.

4. Write a program that creates an electronic phonebook. The program should prompt a user to enter the name, address, and phone number of at least two people. Treat each person's name, address, and number as a record.

5. Write a program that writes to the screen or printer the contents of the electronic phonebook created above.

CHAPTER 14

Program Testing

OUTLINE

LEARNING OBJECTIVES

After reading this chapter, you should be able to:

1. Describe the different interests of users and programmers.
2. Describe how good programming style helps the development and maintenance of a program.
3. Describe why program testing is necessary.

4. Describe some program testing methods.
5. Describe why programs should be user friendly.
6. Describe some methods of writing user-friendly programs.

INTRODUCTION

Computer programs are usually written to accomplish a particular task. Programs are used at home and at work. They can be used for entertainment, education, record maintenance, word processing, and many other jobs. The purpose of many computer programs is to help people, or **users,** perform a job.

Two basic groups of people are involved with computer programs. Programmers develop, maintain, and update programs; they are interested in the logic and inner workings of a computer program. Users want a computer program to help complete a task. They are usually interested not in how a program works, but in its applications. Users are interested in what data must be entered to a program and what results the program obtains. Computer programs need to be written and tested so that both programmers and users are able to work with them.

PROGRAMMING STYLE

In Chapter 8, the concept of programming style was described. Structured programming and program documentation help the programmer to debug program errors. Programming style is the organization and documentation of a program. Good programming style helps programmers follow the logic and purpose of a program.

In the workplace, different programmers develop, maintain, and debug a program. **Maintenance programmers** often must fix a program that has **crashed** (stopped executing). Without clear program structure and documentation, the job of debugging a program that you did not write is very difficult. Programming in industry is usually done by teams of programmers. Programmers must write parts of a very large program (up to 25,000 lines!) or write a program that must interact with others. Good program structure and documentation are essential to help other programmers understand programs that they did not write. Good programming style makes the job of combining programs or program segments easier by making it easier for programmers to communicate.

PROGRAM TESTING

The user of a computer program rarely understands or wants to understand the inner workings of a program. The user usually inputs data to a computer and expects to receive some type of output. Problems can arise at two points. First, how will the program react if the user inputs unexpected data? Second, will the user be able to use the program easily? This section will discuss the problem of anticipating user input and will describe how to protect a program from unexpected input.

Program users can and will input data that the program does not expect. **Program testing** means checking a program for flaws or errors. Good program testing methods will ensure that a program reacts well to most input. The worst program reaction occurs when a program crashes or returns incorrect output. Such reactions might be caused by run-time and logic errors.

Most programs should execute under any given input. How does the programmer ensure that a program will execute? A basic rule is to insert conditional statements after any READ or READLN of user input. All user input should be tested to ensure that it is within the correct range of values. If an incorrect value is entered, the program should print an error message and loop back to the READ or READLN statement. Figure 14-1 illustrates a program segment where the user is prompted to enter the amount of a deposit. If the input value is less than 0 or greater than 999.99, an error message is printed. The user is then prompted to reenter the deposit amount.

Run-time errors will often result if variables, arrays, functions, or procedures are not protected by conditional statements. A second basic rule of program testing is to test the common problem areas of a program. For example, if a program contains an IF/THEN/ELSE statement, data should be entered to the program so that all possible paths of the statement are tested.

It is often difficult to see errors or flaws in your own program. In general, people are not objective when testing their own programs. Several methods exist for testing a program. First, a group of users can be asked to use the program. Watching users can produce good information about possible input errors and input that a program is not protected against. Second, other programmers are able to give feedback about problems within a program. **System testers** are programmers who test other people's programs. When errors are found within a program or the program is found not to be protected against some

Figure 14-1 SAMPLE ERROR MESSAGE

```
READLN (DEPOSIT);
WHILE (DEPOSIT < 0) OR (DEPOSIT > 999.99) DO
   BEGIN
       WRITELN ('DEPOSIT AMOUNT IS INCORRECT');
       WRITE ('PLEASE REENTER DEPOSIT: ');
       READLN (DEPOSIT)
   END;
```

types of input, the systems tester usually returns the program to the developing programmer. A program may be returned to the developing programmer several times before the program is finally passed by the systems tester. Even in organizations that employ systems testers, programs with problems make their way to the user. All possible user responses cannot be anticipated. Program testing will, though, reduce the number of program errors caused by unexpected user input.

WRITING USER-FRIENDLY PROGRAMS

Most computer programs interact with humans in some way. The purpose of many programs is to help a user perform some task. Programs should thus be designed to be as easy as possible to use. Users typically deal with the input and output of a computer program. **User-friendly programs** are written so that users can easily understand what information must be entered. The programmer should determine what the user needs to know to operate the program. A set of program instructions should accompany the program to provide the user with the necessary information to use the program. The programmer should also examine the ease of entering data. Are clear prompts included? Are the error messages clear? Finally, a user-friendly program should output information so that it is easily understood. Is the output clearly labeled? The programmer needs to do more than just think about these areas. Typical users should try the program. Then the programmer can test the user-friendliness of the program and collect information to improve the program.

The concepts of programming style, program testing, and user-friendly programs are important. How a programmer develops these concepts will largely determine how useful the resulting program will be to other programmers and users. When you write programs in the future, try to keep in mind some of the ideas presented in this chapter. They should help you to write clear, well-organized programs that are easy to follow for programmers and users.

 LEARNING CHECK 14-1

1. What is program testing?
2. List three rules of program testing.
3. What is a systems tester?

Answers: 1. Program testing means checking a program for flaws or errors. Good program testing ensures that programs react correctly to most input. Also, program testing involves checking for correct program output under most conditions. 2. Protect READ and READLN statements of user input with conditional statements; test all possible paths of data; protect variables and arrays from run-time errors; let other programmers test your program; let users test your program. 3. A systems tester is a programmer who tests other programmer's programs for possible flaws or errors.

SUMMARY POINTS

- Computer programs are used by programmers and users. Programmers are interested in how a program works; users are interested in how to work a program.
- Programming style is the organization and documentation of a computer program. Good programming style helps programmers communicate with each other about a program's purpose and logic.
- Program testing is the set of methods used to test a program for flaws or errors. Good program testing will ensure that a program will react correctly to any possible input.
- Programs are usually written to help a user do a job. User-friendly programs communicate clearly to the user and are easy to use.
- By using the concepts of programming style, program testing, and user-friendly programs, programmers can write easy-to-understand and easy-to-use computer programs.

VOCABULARY LIST

Crash An unplanned halt in the execution of a program before its end. Data are usually lost when a program crashes.

Maintenance programmer A programmer who updates and debugs programs. Maintenance programmers usually maintain other programmers' programs.

Program testing Checking a program for flaws or errors. Program testing usually seeks to catch program errors caused by either the program itself or user input.

Systems tester A programmer who tests other programmers' programs. The tester's job is to find any possible flaws in programs and to find areas of a program that are not protected against unexpected input.

Users The people who use a computer program.

User-friendly programs Programs that communicate clearly to the user. User-friendly programs should be easy to use.

CHAPTER TEST

VOCABULARY

Match a term from the numbered column with the description from the lettered column that best fits the term.

1. Maintenance programmer

2. User-friendly programs

3. Systems testers

4. Users

a. Programs that communicate clearly to the user.

b. The people who use a computer program.

c. A programmer who updates and debugs programs.

d. Programmers who tests other

programmers' programs. Their job is to find any possible flaws in programs and to find areas of a program that are not protected against unexpected input.

5. Crash

    e. When a program stops running or executing before it is supposed to.

6. Program testing

    f. Checking a program for flaws or errors; usually directed at catching program errors caused by the program or user input.

QUESTIONS

1. Describe the two basic groups who interact with computer programs, noting their different interests.
2. What is programming style?
3. Why is programming style important to maintenance programmers?
4. What are three important areas to consider in writing user-friendly programs?

Turtlegraphics

OUTLINE

LEARNING OBJECTIVES

After reading this chapter, you should be able to:

1. Describe the monitor screen.
2. Name the two types of screen images.
3. Describe and use the USES and INITTURTLE statements to invoke Turtlegraphics.
4. Describe and use the VIEWPORT, FILLSCREEN, and PENCOLOR procedures.
5. Describe and use the TURNTO, TURN, MOVE, and MOVETO procedures.
6. Describe and use the TURTLEX, TURTLEY, TURTLEANG, and SCREENBIT functions.
7. Describe the use of keyboard characters as program input.
8. Understand the idea of a random number.
9. Describe and use the RANDOM function.
10. Write simple graphics programs that create a variety of graphic images.

INTRODUCTION

The creation and use of graphics are a popular application of computers and computer programs. Video games, at home and in arcades, are complex graphics programs. Also, many of the special visual effects in movies, television, and magazines are created by graphics programs. With Pascal, graphics programs can be written to draw figures or words or even create simple video games.

SCREEN MODES AND TURTLEGRAPHICS

The monitor screen of the computer is an essential tool for writing graphics programs. It allows you to see the results of a program. The monitor screen is a grid of small blocks, or pixels (picture elements). From left to right, the X direction, the screen is 280 pixels wide; from bottom to top, the Y direction, it is 192 pixels high. Figure 15-1 illustrates the design of the screen.

The monitor screen accepts two types of images in its blocks: text or graphic images. You are probably most familiar with text images, such as letters and numbers. Most computers and monitor screens are set to accept text images when they are turned on. The monitor screen is in the text mode when it accepts text images. In this chapter, you will learn how to switch the screen and computer to graphics mode and how to program graphic images on an Apple II computer.

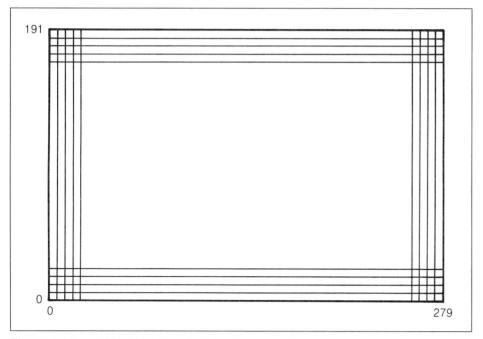

191

0

0

279

Figure 15-1 DESIGN OF THE TERMINAL SCREEN

The APPLE II version of UCSD Pascal includes the **Turtlegraphics** package. Turtlegraphics is a set of programs and procedures created by a group of programmers at the Massachusetts Institute of Technology. Turtlegraphics uses a small figure on the screen, a **turtle,** to draw figures on the terminal screen. Since Turtlegraphics is a set of system-defined procedures, the computer must be told a program uses Turtlegraphics. The USES TURTLEGRAPHICS and INITTURTLE statements are used to invoke the Turtlegraphics package. The USES statement should appear immediately after the program heading. The INITTURTLE statement should appear immediately after the BEGIN statement of the program. Figure 15-2 illustrates the format of these statements.

The USES statement tells the computer that the program uses Turtlegraphics. The INITTURTLE procedure then clears the monitor screen, sets the screen to graphics mode, and places the turtle in the

Figure 15-2 FORMAT OF USES AND INITTURTLE STATEMENTS

```
PROGRAM GRAPHICS;

    USES TURTLEGRAPHICS;
    BEGIN

        INITTURTLE;
```

middle of the screen facing right. Now that Turtlegraphics has been invoked, you can start using the turtle.

THE TURTLE AND TURTLEGRAPHICS PROGRAMS

The idea behind the turtle is simple. The turtle moves across the screen dragging a pen. So, as the turtle moves in different directions for different distances, lines will appear on the screen. Turtlegraphics programs have three parts. The first part describes the type of screen where the turtle travels. The second part tells the turtle in what direction and how far to travel. The third part uses conditional statements, keys on the keyboard, and random functions to create special features in the program.

Changing the Screen

You are able to change three aspects of the screen on which the turtle travels. First, the area of the screen that you can see the turtle travel across can be changed. The INITTURTLE procedure allows the entire screen to be seen. The VIEWPORT procedure allows the size of the viewing area to be decreased or increased.

The VIEWPORT procedure is like a set of blinds on a window. You can lower the blinds and decrease the viewing area of a window. But things still happen outside the window, even though you cannot see all of them. The VIEWPORT procedure works in a similar way. You can reduce or increase the viewing area of the screen with VIEWPORT. The turtle can move outside the viewing area. You, however, won't be able to see the turtle move.

The format of the VIEWPORT procedure statement is:

VIEWPORT (left, right, bottom, top)

Remember that the monitor screen is 280 pixels wide by 192 pixels high. Figure 15-3 illustrates the effect of invoking the procedure VIEWPORT (0, 140, 0, 150). You can only see the turtle move in the shaded area. Remember, the turtle can move outside the marked part of the screen—you just won't see it.

The second characteristic of the screen that can be changed is the background color. The FILLSCREEN procedure allows the background color of the monitor screen to be changed. The format for the FILLSCREEN procedure statement is:

FILLSCREEN (color)

Only the colors black and white are used in this chapter. If you have a color monitor, refer to your Pascal manual for instructions on obtaining a colored background. A REVERSE command can also be in-

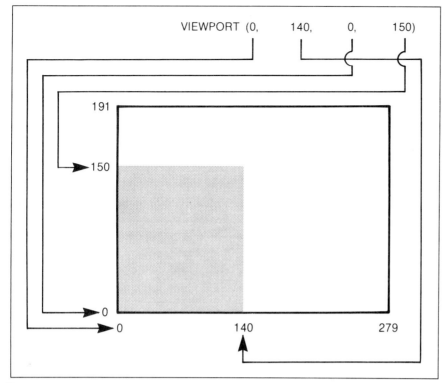

Figure 15-3 SAMPLE VIEWPORT STATEMENT

cluded in the color part of the FILLSCREEN statement. The REVERSE command reverses the present background color of the screen.

The third feature of the screen that can be changed is the color of the pen that the turtle drags. The PENCOLOR procedure will change the color of the line created by the turtle. The format of the PENCOLOR procedure statement is:

PENCOLOR (color)

Again, only BLACK, WHITE, and REVERSE are used here. You can use other colors if you have a color monitor. With the VIEWPORT, FILL-SCREEN, and PENCOLOR procedures, several different screens can be created for turtle movement.

Controlling the Turtle's Movement and Location

Turning the Turtle

The next step in creating a Turtlegraphics program is to learn how to turn and move the turtle. The INITTURTLE procedure places the turtle in the middle of the screen (140 blocks left, 96 blocks up = 139, 95), facing right. An important step in moving the turtle is knowing how to change its direction. The turtle can turn in any direction (except into or out of the screen!). Two procedures can be used to turn the turtle. The TURNTO procedure turns the turtle from 0° to 360°, left or right. The format of the TURNTO procedure statement is:

TURNTO (degrees)

The number of degrees should be an integer between −359 and 359. Think of the turtle as sitting in the middle of a clock. The TURNTO procedure turns the turtle like a hand on a clock. Zero degrees is three o'clock; the degrees increase up to 359 as we go counterclockwise. Using a negative number of degrees in the TURNTO procedure will turn the turtle clockwise. Figure 15-4 illustrates the difference between positive and negative degrees.

The second way to turn the turtle to a new direction is to use the TURN procedure. The format of the TURN procedure is:

TURN (degrees)

The degrees again range from −359 to 359. When a TURN procedure is invoked, the turtle will turn the specified number of degrees counterclockwise (positive degrees) or clockwise (negative degrees). The TURN procedure is not the same as the TURNTO procedure. Regardless of where the turtle is pointed, a TURNTO (180) turns the turtle to 180° (nine o'clock). A TURN (180) turns the turtle 180° counterclockwise from wherever it presently points. Look at Figure 15-5. If a turtle pointed straight up (12 o'clock) and a TURNTO (180) statement was used, the turtle would turn to point at 180° (9 o'clock). If instead a TURN (180) statement was used, the turtle would be turned 180° and point to 270° (six o'clock). If you wanted to use the TURN procedure to point the turtle at 180°, you would use the TURN (90) statement, as illustrated in Figure 15-6. TURN (−270) would achieve the same result.

Figure 15-4 POSITIVE AND NEGATIVE DEGREES

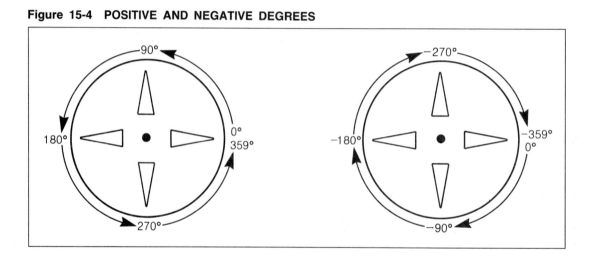

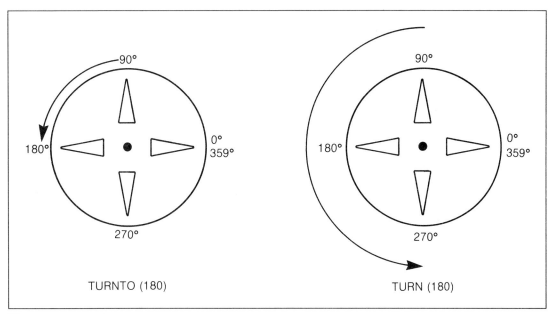

Figure 15-5 TURN AND TURNTO PROCEDURES

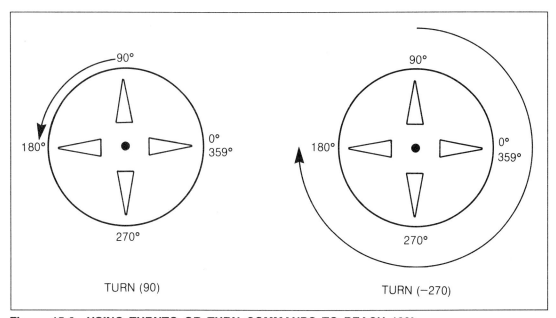

Figure 15-6 USING TURNTO OR TURN COMMANDS TO REACH 180°

LEARNING CHECK 15-1

1. What type of screen images are accepted on a monitor screen?
2. Where was the Turtlegraphics package developed?
3. What two statements must be included in a program that uses Turtlegraphics?
4. Write the statement that would only allow you to see the turtle in the shaded area.

265

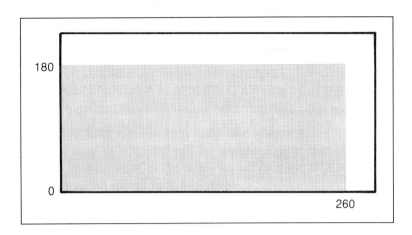

Moving the Turtle

The MOVE and MOVETO procedures move the turtle across the monitor screen. Once you understand the turning and moving commands of Turtlegraphics, you can begin to write some graphics programs. The MOVE procedure tells the turtle how far to move in its current direction. The format of the MOVE statement is:

MOVE (distance)

The distance is an integer that represents the number of pixels to be crossed. As the turtle moves, it leaves a trail in the current pen color.

The MOVETO procedure will move the turtle to any pixel without turning it. The format of the MOVETO procedure statement is

```
MOVETO (X, Y);
```

X and Y are screen coordinates. Remember that the monitor screen is actually a two-dimensional grid. Each pixel is numbered by a X and a Y coordinate. Look at Figure 15-7. Block A's screen coordinates are (200, 140). This means that Block A is the 201st pixel from the left side of the screen and the 141st pixel from the bottom of the screen (since the first block in each direction is numbered 0).

To use the MOVETO procedure, remember that the monitor screen is 280 pixels wide (0 to 279) in the X direction and 192 pixels high (0 to 191) in the Y direction. Then you just have to decide how far to the right (X) and how far up (Y) you want to move the turtle. By using the MOVETO procedure, a line can be drawn between any two points on the screen without changing the direction of the turtle. Have you seen the Hyperspace button on many video games work? You press the button and your ship disappears and reappears in a new

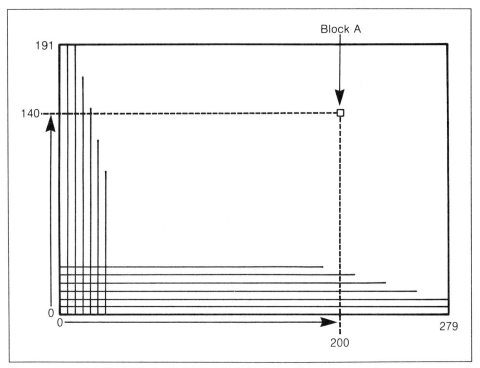

Figure 15-7 LOCATING A BLOCK ON THE SCREEN

location, facing the same direction. The Turtlegraphics commands PENCOLOR (NONE), MOVETO (X, Y), and PENCOLOR (WHITE) correspond to a press of the Hyperspace button.

You can now write a graphics program to draw almost any shape. The next set of exercises ask you to write parts of programs that draw various shapes. Draw out the figures before you write your program. Graphics programming is much easier if you can see what you want to create.

LEARNING CHECK 15-2

1. What are the screen coordinates of the four corners of the monitor screen?
2. Use a set of MOVETO statements to put the turtle in each of the four corners of the screen. Start with the lower left-hand corner and move clockwise.
3. Use MOVE and TURNTO statements to do problem 2.

Answers:

1. (0, 0) LOWER LEFT 2. MOVETO (0, 0); 3. TURNTO (90);
   (0, 191) UPPER LEFT MOVETO (0, 191); MOVE (191);
   (279, 191) TOP RIGHT MOVETO (279, 191); TURNTO (0);
   (279, 0) BOTTOM RIGHT MOVETO (279, 0); MOVE (279);
                                            TURNTO (270);
                                            MOVE (191);
                                            TURNTO (180);
                                            MOVE (279);

Locating the Turtle

To write a graphics program that does more than just draw figures, you need to be able to ask the computer for the location of the turtle. Action-oriented graphics programs are often based on the idea that if a figure collides with an object, some action occurs. The use of conditional statements (IF/THEN/ELSE, WHILE/DO, REPEAT/UNTIL) is an important part of video game graphics programs.

Turtlegraphics provides three functions that will return the present location of the turtle. The TURTLEX function will return the present X location of the turtle. The TURTLEY function will return the

Figure 15-8 PROGRAM SWITCH

```
PROGRAM SWITCH;
   USES TURTLEGRAPHICS;

   VAR
      DIRECTION : INTEGER;
      I : INTEGER;

   BEGIN

      INITTURTLE;
      PENCOLOR (NONE);
      FILLSCREEN (BLACK);
      MOVETO (0,0);
      MOVE (1);
      PENCOLOR (WHITE);
      WHILE (TURTLEY < 191) DO
         BEGIN
            WHILE (TURTLEX > 0) AND (TURTLEX < 279) DO
               BEGIN
                  MOVE (1);
                  FOR I := 1 TO 10 DO
               END;
            DIRECTION := TURTLEANG;
            TURNTO (90);
            MOVE (10);
            IF (DIRECTION = 0) THEN
               TURNTO (180)
               ELSE
                  TURNTO (0);
            MOVE (1);
            FOR I := 1 TO 10 DO
         END

   END.
```

present Y location of the turtle. The program in Figure 15-8 causes the turtle to move across the screen from left to right and from bottom to top. The TURTLEX function is used to determine whether the turtle has reached the edge of the screen. A TURNTO statement is then invoked to turn the turtle upward. A TURTLEY function is used to test if the turtle has reached the top of the screen. A MOVETO statement is included to return the turtle to the bottom right of the screen if the turtle reaches the top of the screen. Notice the FOR loop; this delays the turtle long enough for you to see it. Figure 15-9 illustrates the pattern that the turtle travels in. The TURTLEANG function returns the present direction, in positive degrees, of the turtle. Notice that in Figure 15-10 TURTLEANG returns 90 when the turtle faces 12 o'clock, not −270. The SCREENBIT function returns a Boolean value (true or false) based on the color of a specified pixel. If the specified pixel is white (on), SCREENBIT returns true. If the specified pixel is black (off), SCREENBIT returns false. This function is normally used to test if the turtle is at a specific screen position. The format of the SCREENBIT function statement is:

$$SCREENBIT \ (X, \ Y);$$

X and Y are the screen coordinates of the screen block being tested. For example, if the object of a program is for the turtle to intercept a plane moving across the top of the screen, a SCREENBIT function would be inserted into an IF statement to test whether the turtle was

Figure 15-9 GRAPHIC PATTERN CREATED BY PROGRAM REVERSE

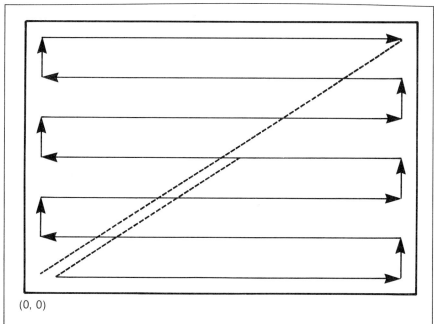

(0, 0)

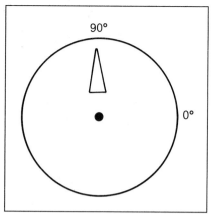

Figure 15-10 TURTLEANG RETURNS POSITIVE VALUES: 90, NOT −270, IN THIS EXAMPLE

in the current location of the plane. This function can also be used to test for a turtle collision with screen edges, lines, or laser blasts.

Special Features of Apple Turtlegraphics

Action-oriented graphics programs usually allow the user to manipulate figures on the screen. In this section, the KEYPRESS and RANDOM functions are described. These functions are helpful in designing action-oriented graphics. A USES statement must be placed at the beginning of any UCSD Pascal program that uses either of these functions. If you are using an Apple microcomputer, the word APPLESTUFF should be added to the USES statement. The format of the USES statement for an Apple microcomputer is illustrated in Figure 15-11.

The keyboard can be used for user input. The keys on the keyboard can be used to manipulate action on the screen. Input obtained from the keyboard is of the data type INTERACTIVE. To read a character from the keyboard, the KEYPRESS function and the KEYBOARD file are used. The KEYPRESS function returns the BOOLEAN value true if a key is pressed and the value false if a key has not been pressed. The value of KEYPRESS is false until a key is pressed. Once a key has been pressed, KEYPRESS' value remains true until the keyboard is read. The KEYBOARD file represents the computer keyboard. To use input from the keyboard, you must read the KEYBOARD file when KEYPRESS is true. Figure 15-12 illustrates a typical program segment using the KEYBOARD file, the KEYPRESS function, and a READ statement. Key-

Figure 15-11 THE USES STATEMENT FOR TURTLEGRAPHICS

```
USES TURTLEGRAPHICS, APPLESTUFF;
```

```
IF KEYPRESS THEN
    BEGIN
        READ (KEYBOARD, REV);
        IF REV = 'R' THEN TURN (180)
    END;
```

Figure 15-12 TYPICAL PROGRAM SEGMENT FOR READING KEYBOARD CHARACTERS

board input in this example is used to reverse the direction of the turtle.

The complexity of a graphics program can also be increased by using the RANDOM function. The RANDOM function randomly returns an integer from 9 to 32767, when invoked. A **random number** means that any number within a certain range, in this case 9 to 32767, has an equal chance of being returned. Most microcomputers have a version of the RANDOM function, so consult your user's manual for the statement format for your microcomputer.

The RANDOM function can be used in a program by typing the word RANDOM in a program. Figure 15-13 illustrates several uses of the RANDOM function. The MOD function is used to convert the generated random number, which may be from 9 to 32767, to a value between 0 and the number inserted after MOD. Remember that the MOD function returns the remainder of a division operation.

With Turtlegraphics, you can create a variety of different graphics programs. You should try to use Turtlegraphics to create your own graphic images and games. The problems at the end of this chapter provide a starting point for creating different types of graphics. Although many computers may not have Turtlegraphics, the concepts introduced in this chapter are common to many graphics programs.

Figure 15-13 SOME USES OF THE RANDOM FUNCTION

```
X := RANDOM MOD 280;       Moves turtle to a randomly selected block
Y := RANDOM MOD 192;       on the screen.
MOVETO (X, Y);



DEG := RANDOM MOD 360;     Turns turtle to a randomly selected
TURNTO (DEG);              direction, from 0° to 360°.



DIST := RANDOM MOD 100;    Moves turtle a random number of blocks,
MOVE (DIST);               from 0 to 100.
```

1. What three Turtlegraphics functions return the present location of the turtle?
2. In what type of statements do these functions usually appear?
3. What are some typical uses of the location functions?
4. What angle would the TURTLEANG function return if the turtle faced the following directions?

   A. △ B. ▷ C. ◁
5. If the turtle sat in the middle of the screen and a SCREENBIT (139, 95) statement was used, what value would be returned?

Answers:

1. The TURTLEX, TURTLEY, and TURTLEANG functions return the present location of the turtle. 2. The location functions are usually used within conditional statements. 3. The location functions can indicate when the turtle has collided or reached a specified area of the screen and if a specified action should be carried out. 4. a. 90, b. 0, c. 270 5. The BOOLEAN value true would be returned.

SUMMARY POINTS

- Graphics programming is used in many ways to create different types of graphic images.
- Turtlegraphics is a set of system-defined procedures in UCSD Pascal that can be used to write graphics programs.
- The monitor screen is an important tool in writing Turtlegraphics programs. The monitor screen is actually a grid of small blocks, 280 blocks wide and 192 blocks high.
- The USES and INITTURTLE statements are necessary to invoke Turtlegraphics and to set the screen to accept graphics images.
- The VIEWPORT, FILLSCREEN, and PENCOLOR procedures are used to change the color and size of the monitor screen. The MOVE, MOVETO, TURN, and TURNTO procedures move the turtle, a figure that drags a colored pen across the screen, to any point on the screen. The TURTLEX, TURTLEY, TURTLEANG, and SCREENBIT functions can be used with conditional statements to locate the turtle. With Apple special features, the keyboard and the RANDOM function can add arcade effects to Turtlegraphics programs.

VOCABULARY LIST

Random number A number, within a certain range, that has an equal chance of being chosen as any other number in the specified range.

Turtle A small figure that can be moved on the screen; used in graphic programs.

Turtlegraphics A set of graphics programs and procedures created by programmers at the Massachusetts Institute of Technology.

CHAPTER TEST

VOCABULARY

*Match a term from the numbered column with the description from the lettered column that fits it best.**

1. Element

a. When a program stops running before the planned end of the program.

2. Predefined file

b. A data type that contains a portion of a predefined or user-defined scalar data type.

3. Users

c. An individual value in an array.

4. Parameter

d. An ordered set of related data items, all of the same data type.

5. Debugging

e. A data item that is part of a record.

6. Random-access file

f. A value that is passed from a program to a subprogram. The value may or may not be passed back to the calling program.

7. Array

g. A file that is declared and opened automatically by the UCSD Pascal system.

8. Subrange data type

h. A data type that can store many individual values which may be referred to as a single unit.

9. Function

i. A file in which data items may be accessed directly.

10. Field

j. A subprogram that can be used to determine a single value.

11. Structured data type

k. The process of finding and correcting program errors.

12. Crashing

l. The people who use a computer program.

QUESTIONS

1. Draw the screen and the viewing area produced by this statement: VIEWPORT (0, 5, 10, 100).

2. What are the differences between the MOVE and MOVETO procedures?

3. Assuming that the turtle is in its starting position (after INITTURTLE), use MOVE and TURN statements to draw a line to the very top left-hand corner of the screen.

---

*This vocabulary test contains a review of terms introduced in the last half of this book.

273

4. What data type are keyboard characters? What is the format for reading keyboard characters?
5. What range of integers can be returned by the RANDOM function?
6. What does the word *random* mean when used in Turtlegraphics?
7. What statement must be changed to use the RANDOM function? How is it changed?
8. Write a program segment that invokes Turtlegraphics and creates a black screen with the turtle able to draw white lines in the illustrated area.

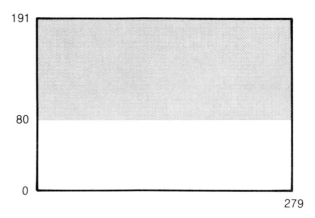

9. How many degrees can the turtle be turned? In what directions?
10. What is the primary difference between the TURN and TURNTO statements?
11. Using a TURNTO and TURN statement in each case, turn the turtle to the indicated directions.

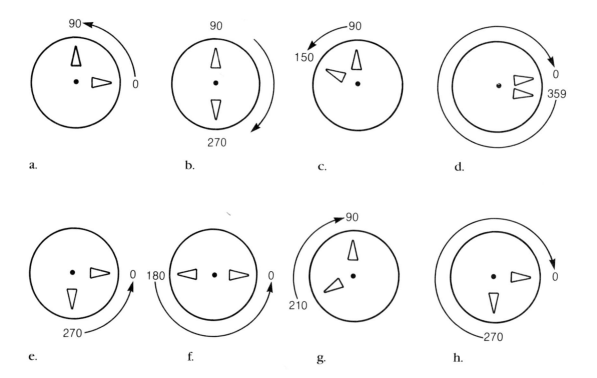

a.

b.

c.

d.

e.

f.

g.

h.

PROGRAMMING PROBLEMS

1. Write a Turtlegraphics program that draws the following figure.

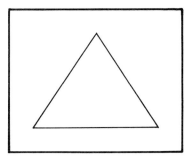

2. Write a Turtlegraphics program that writes your initials.
3. Write a Turtlegraphics program to draw a figure you have created.
4. Write a Turtlegraphics program, using location functions and conditional statements, that causes the turtle to bounce across the screen. The turtle should return to its starting place after it reaches the right side of the screen. The figure below illustrates the screen and the pattern that the turtle should move in.

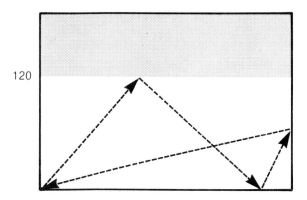

5. Write a Turtlegraphics program that uses keyboard characters to move the turtle up, down, left, and right.

APPENDIX A

Identifiers

UCSD Pascal identifiers must follow these rules:

- They begin with a letter.
- They contain only letters or numbers or the underscore character (_).
- Upper-case and lower-case characters are seen by the compiler as being the same.
- The underscore character is ignored by the compiler.
- The compiler considers only the first eight characters of an identifier.

Syntax Diagrams

SYNTAX FIGURES

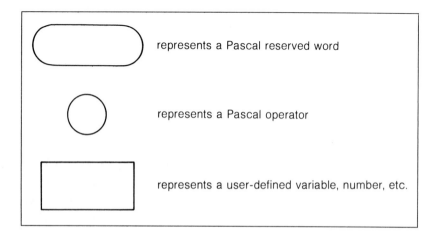

represents a Pascal reserved word

represents a Pascal operator

represents a user-defined variable, number, etc.

PROGRAM

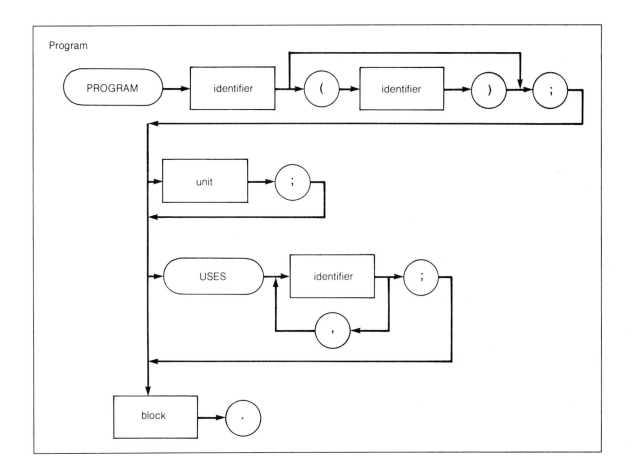

DECLARATIONS

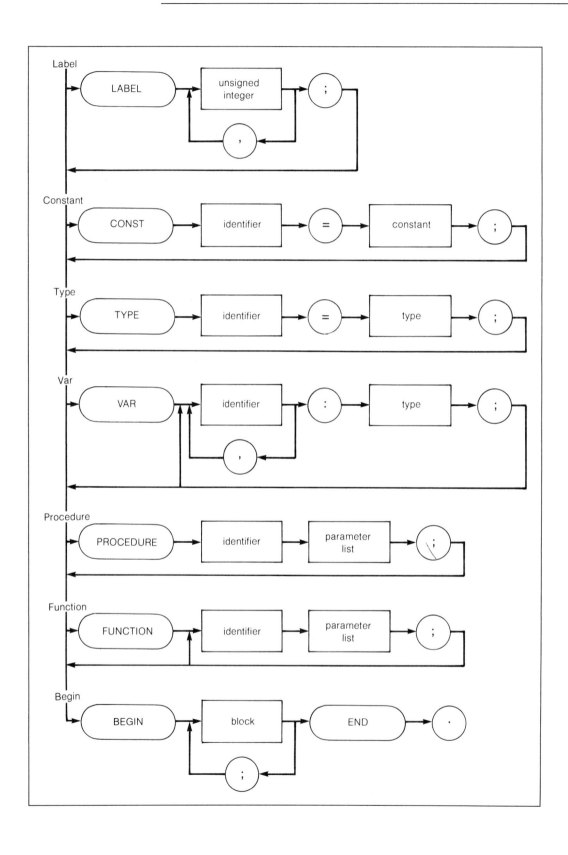

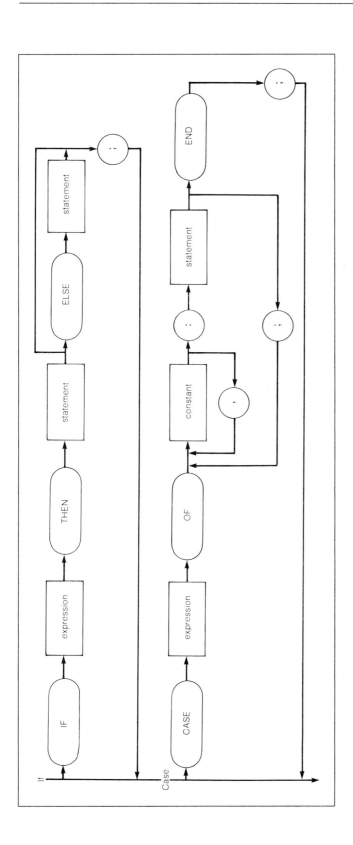

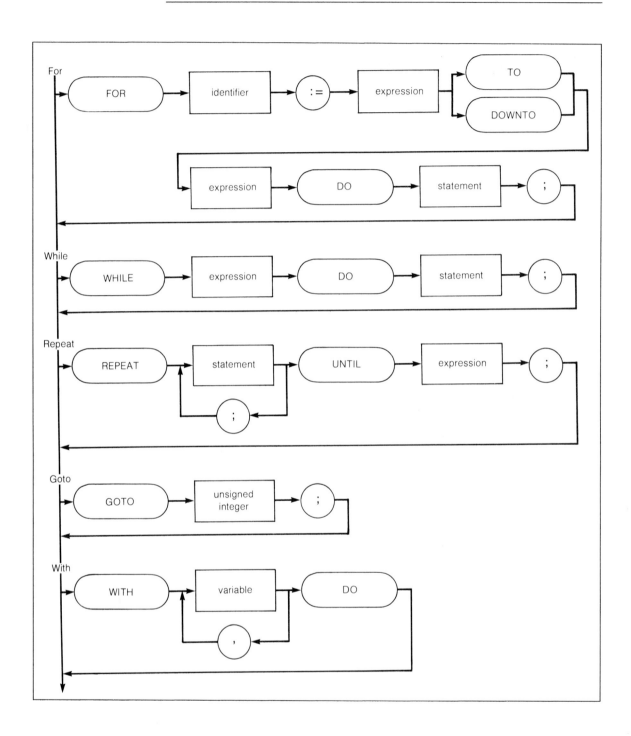

Pascal Reserved Words

AND	FILE	NOT	TO
ARRAY	FOR	OF	TYPE
BEGIN	FORWARD*	OR	UNITE
CASE	FUNCTION	PACKED†	UNPACKED†
CONST	GOTO	PROCEDURE	UNTIL
DIV	IF	PROGRAM	USES*
DO	IN	RECORD	VAR
DOWNTO	IMPLEMENTATION*	REPEAT	WHILE
ELSE	INTERFACE*	SEGMENT	WITH
END	LABEL	SET	
EXTERNAL*	MOD	THEN	

*UCSD Pascal only.
†Standard Pascal only.

Pascal Standard Identifiers

ABS	GOTOXY*	PENCOLOR*	SUCC
APPLESTUFF*	INITTURTLE*	POS	TEXT
BOOLEAN	INPUT	PRED	TRUE
BUTTON*	INTEGER	PUT	TRUNC
CHAR	INTERACTIVE*	RANDOM*	TURN
CLOSE*	KEYBOARD	READ	TURNTO
CONCAT*	KEYPRESS	READLN	TURTLEANG
COPY*	LENGTH	REAL	TURTLEGRAPHICS
COS	LOG	RESET	TURTLEX
DELETE*	MAXINT	REWRITE	TURTLEY
EOF*	MOVE	ROUND	UNPACK
EDLN	MOVETO	SCREENBIT*	VIEWPORT
EXIT	ODD	SEEK*	WRITE
EXP*	ORD	SIN	WRITELN
FALSE	OUTPUT	SQR	
FILLSCREEN*	PACK	SQRT	
GET	PADDLE*	STRING	

*UCSD Pascal only.

Pascal Operators

RELATIONAL

=	equal to
<>	not equal to
>	greater than
>=	greater than or equal to
<	less than
<=	less than or equal to

ARITHMETIC

( )	parentheses
DIV MOD	integer division, remainder of integer
/ *	division, multiplication,
+ −	addition, subtraction

BOOLEAN

NOT	evaluates to the opposite (or the negation) of the operand
AND	evaluates to true only if both operands are true
OR	evaluates to true if one or both operands are true

Filer and Editor Basics

The filer and editor of the P-system are frequently used in the creation, editing, and storage of UCSD Pascal programs. To program in the UCSD Pascal system, the programmer must learn at least a few basics about the filer and editor. This section will outline a few simple ways to use the filer and editor to create, edit, save, and run UCSD Pascal programs. For a detailed explanation of the capabilities of the filer and editor, take a look at the User's Manual for your version of UCSD Pascal.

CREATING A PROGRAM

To create a UCSD Pascal program, you must first boot the P-system on a microcomputer. The main menu of UCSD Pascal (see Figure F-1) should now be on the monitor screen. If you are in another menu, type Q. This should bring up the main menu.

Follow these steps to enter the editor:

1. Type E.
2. a. If the next message says NO WORKFILE PRESENT, press the RETURN key.
   b. If a program appears, you must delete it from the P-system's workfile. To do this type Q. Then type E. You should now be at the main menu again. Now, you must enter the filer. To do this, type F. Then, type N for the new command. When the message THROW AWAY CURRENT WORKFILE? appears, type Y. Now, return to the main menu by typing Q. Follow steps 1 and 2a to reenter the editor.

You should now be in the P-system editor. Figure F-2 illustrates the editor screen. To begin entering a program, simply press I and begin typing your program. Press the RETURN key at the end of each line.

Figure F-1   THE MAIN MENU OF UCSD PASCAL

```
Command: E(dit, R(un, F(ile, C(omp, L(ink, X(ecute, A(ssem
```

```
>Edit: A(djst C(py D(let F(ind I(nsrt J(mp K(ol R(plc Q(uit X(ch Z(ap
```

Figure F-2 THE EDITOR SCREEN

At the end of your program, press the CTRL and C keys. Notice that you can now move the cursor across the editor screen. If you are satisfied with your program, type Q. Then, type U to store the current version of your program in the P-system's workfile. You should now see the main menu. If you need to make corrections to your program, see the section on editing a program.

SAVING A PROGRAM

To save the workfile, first enter the P-system's main menu. Next, enter the filer by typing F. Then, type S for the SAVE command. The message

SAVE AS volume name: file name ?

may appear. At this point, you must make a decision. On what diskette do you want to store your program? You should insert that diskette into drive number 5 (for two-drive users) or drive #4 (for one-drive users). In most cases, you will type N to the above message. Another message will appear that asks SAVE AS? or SAVE AS WHAT FILE? Type in the volume name of your diskette (or #4 for one-drive users, #5 for two-drive users), a colon (:), and a file name. Then press the RETURN key. Your program should now be saved.

- Example
- Prompt: SAVE AS SYSTEM.WORK.TEXT?
- Response: N
- Prompt: SAVE AS WHAT FILE?
- Response: MYDISK:PROGRAM1
                   Press RETURN.

RUNNING A PROGRAM

In order to run a program, the program should be in the workfile. If the program is not in the P-system's workfile, read the section on editing a program now. It will show you how to move a program into the P-system's workfile. If the program is in the workfile, enter the P-system's main menu. Next, if you have a two-drive system, insert the APPLE2: or PASCAL: diskette into the second drive (#5). Finally, type R. The P-system will then compile the program in the workfile. Program errors will be noted by the P-system's compiler. If the program does not have any syntax errors, the program will be executed.

287

EDITING A PROGRAM

Program errors are part of the programming process. Everyone makes errors at some time. The USCD P-system allows you to edit program files easily. This section will show you how to edit files that are already in the P-system's workfile and how to edit files that are stored on a diskette.

To edit a program file, you must move the program file into the P-system's editor. If your program is currently in the P-system's workfile, follow the following steps to enter the editor:

1. Enter the P-system's main menu. In most cases, pressing Q will move you to the main menu.
2. Type E. You should now be in the editor. You should see your program.

If your program is currently not in the P-system's workfile and is on a diskette, follow the following steps:

1. If you have a program in the P-system's workfile and you want to keep that program, save the program. Follow the instructions in the section on saving a program. Then, go to step 4 in these instructions.
2. Enter the P-system's main menu.
3. Type F to enter the filer.
4. Type N to clear the P-system's workfile.
5. When the message "THROW AWAY CURRENT WORKFILE?" appears, type Y.
6. If you have a one-drive system,
    a. Type T.
    b. Remove the system diskette (APPLE1:) and insert the diskette with the program.
    c. When the message "TRANSFER?" appears, type the name of the diskette, a colon, and the name of the program file. Then, press the RETURN key.
    d. When the message "TO WHERE?" appears, type: APPLE1:SYSTEM.WRK.TEXT and press the RETURN key.
    e. Insert the APPLE1: diskette and press the space bar.
7. If you have a two-drive system,
    a. Insert the diskette with the program in drive 5.
    b. Type G.
    c. When the message "GET?" appears, type #5: and the name of the program file. Then, press the RETURN key.
8. Type Q to exit the filer.
9. Type E to enter the editor. You should now be in the editor; you should see your program.

Now that you have the program in the editor, you can edit the program. The P-system's editor is very powerful. This section will cover how to insert and delete lines and characters. The editor can do much more. Refer to your User's Manual for more information on the editor.

To insert or delete part of a program, you must move the cursor. The four basic keys that move the cursor in Apple's version of USCD Pascal are → to move right one character; ← to move left one character; ↑ or CTRL-O to move up one line; ↓ or CTRL-L to move down one line. Try moving the cursor with these keys. You can move the cursor quickly to most parts of a program.

To delete characters, move the cursor directly on top of the first character to be deleted. Then type D. Notice that the line

DELETE: < > <MOVING COMMANDS> [<ETX> TO DELETE, <ESC> TO ABORT]

appears at the top of the screen. If you press the → key, the character under the cursor is deleted. If you press the ← key, the character to the left of the cursor disappears. Press CTRL and C when you are done deleting characters on a line to make the deletions permanent. Press the <ESC> key to cancel the deletions. To delete lines, move the cursor to the beginning of a line. Type D. Press the <RETURN> key. Press CTRL and C to permanently delete the line. Press the <ESC> key to cancel the deletion.

To insert characters, move the cursor to the character left of the position where you want to add characters. For example, if you had this line in a program:

WRITE ('THIS IS AN EXAMPLE');

and you wanted to add LN to the WRITE, you would move the cursor on top of the E. Then, you must type I. Notice that the line

INSERT: TEXT [<BS> A CHAR, <DEL> A LINE] [<EXT> ACCEPTS, <ESC> ABORTS]

appears at the top of the screen. Now just type the necessary characters onto the line. To make an insertion permanent, press the CTRL and C keys. To cancel an insertion, press the <ESC> key. To insert a line, move the cursor to the end of the line above the position you want to insert the new line. For example, if you had the program segment below:

```
FOR I := 1 TO 10 DO
    BEGIN
        WRITELN ('THIS IS AN EXAMPLE');
        WRITELN ('FOR INSERTING LINES')
```

and wanted to insert an END statement, you would move the cursor to the end of the WRITELN ('FOR INSERTING LINES') line. Then,

289

press the I and <RETURN> keys. You can then type in the new line and, if necessary, add more lines. Do not forget to press the CTRL and C keys to make the insertions permanent or to press the <ESC> key to cancel the insertions.

Now your program is corrected or changed. To exit the editor, type Q. You have a number of options at this point. The most commonly used option is to update the workfile. This tells the editor to save your corrections and to erase the old version of the program in the workfile.

This section has only covered the basics of the P-system's editor and filer. As you use the P-system more often, you may need to use more of UCSD's abilities. The User's Manuals are good sources of information. With a little effort, you can find the editor and filer functions best suited to your needs.

Glossary

Acronym A word whose letters each stand for another word.

Actual parameter The value that will replace the formal parameter when a subprogram is executed; also known as an **argument**.

Algorithm A sequence of steps used to solve a problem.

Argument See **Actual parameter**.

Arithmetic operator A symbol that stands for an arithmetic process, such as addition or subtraction.

Arithmetic/logic unit (ALU) The part of the CPU that performs arithmetic and logical operations.

Array An ordered set of related data items, all of the same data type.

Assignment statement A statement that allows a value to be stored in a variable.

Base type The data type from which a subrange is defined. The base type must be a scalar data type.

Central processing unit (CPU) The part of a computer that does the work. The CPU also directs the order in which operations are done and has a memory.

Comments Statements in a computer program that explain to people what is being done in the program. They are ignored by the computer.

Compiler A program that translates an entire source program into machine language. The resulting program is the object program.

Compile-time errors See **Syntax errors**.

Compound statement A series of statements that starts with BEGIN and concludes with END.

Computer programmer A person who writes instructions for the computer to solve a problem.

Constant An identifier whose value cannot change during program execution.

Constant declaration statement The statement that tells the compiler the specified value to be associated with a constant.

Control statement A statement that allows the programmer to determine whether or not a statement (or a group of statements) will be executed and how many times the statements will be executed.

Control unit The part of the CPU that determines the order in which computer operations will be performed.

Crashing When a program stops running or executing before the planned end of the program. Data are usually lost when a program crashes.

Cursor A box that indicates where information entered to the monitor will appear on the screen.

Data Facts that the computer uses as input.

Debugging The process of finding and correcting program errors.

Decision step A step in solving a problem where a comparison is made. The action that will be taken next depends on the results of that comparison.

Defensive programming The anticipation of potential program errors and the inclusion of program statements that keep track of the variable values and flag program errors.

Descriptive variable name A variable name that explains what the variable represents. For example, the variable AVE could be used to represent the average of a group of numbers.

Double-alternative decision step A decision step in which a subsequent step is executed only if the comparison made in the decision step is true. A different subsequent step is executed if the comparison is false.

Element An individual value of an array. An array element must have a subscript.

Execute To read and carry out the instructions in a program.

Exponential notation The representation of a real number with only one digit to the left of the decimal point, multiplied by the given power of ten. For example, in Pascal 153.25 would be represented in exponential notation as 1.53250E2, which is equivalent to 1.53250×10^2.

Expression Any valid combination of variables, constants, operators, and/or parentheses.

Field A data item that is part of a record.

Flowchart A method of visually representing the steps in solving a problem.

Formal parameter A variable that represents a value to be passed to a function or procedure.

Format To control the way in which output will be printed.

Function A subprogram that can be used to determine a single value.

Function call An expression that causes a function to be executed.

Global variable A variable that is declared in the declaration section of a main program. It may be referred to anywhere in that program.

Hand simulation A debugging technique where the programmer pretends to be the computer. The programmer performs by hand all the operations normally done by the computer in a program.

Hard copy Output that is printed on paper.

Identifier A name chosen by the programmer to represent a storage location.

Infinite loop A loop in which the condition controlling loop repetition will never contain the value needed to stop the loop.

Initialize To set a variable to a starting value.

Input Data that are entered into a computer to be processed.

Input devices Equipment such as a monitor, disk drive, or cassette recorder used to enter data into a computer.

Input variable A value that is entered into the computer to obtain a needed result.

Integer A whole number, and its opposite.

Interpreter A program that translates a source program into machine language a line at a time.

Local variable A variable that is declared in a subprogram. It is undefined outside of that subprogram.

Logic errors Flaws in a program's algorithms, formulas, or logic that cause incorrect program output.

Loop A structure that allows a section of a program to be repeated as many times as is needed; a control statement that allows a series of instructions to be executed repeatedly as long as specified conditions are constant.

Loop control statement A control statement that allows a series of instructions to be executed repeatedly, as long as specified conditions are constant.

Loop control variable A variable whose value is used to control the repetition of a loop.

Machine language The language a program must be in for a computer to be able to execute it.

Main memory The storage area where the computer keeps information.

Maintenance programmer A programmer who updates and debugs programs. Maintenance programmers usually maintain other programmers' programs.

Microcomputer A digital computer with most of the capabilities of larger computers; the center of the computer is the microprocessor.

Microprocessor A single silicon chip in a microcomputer, on which the CPU is located.

Modules See **Subprograms.**

Nested statement A statement that is contained within another statement.

Object program The program that results when a compiler translates a source program into machine language.

Operand A value on which an arithmetic operation is performed.

Operator A symbol that stands for a process.

Order of operations The sequence in which expressions are evaluated.

Ordinal data type See **Scalar data type.**

Output Results the computer obtains after processing input.

Output devices Equipment such as a monitor, disk drive, cassette recorder, or printer used to store or print out information.

Output variable Information the computer gives as the result of processing input.

Parameter A value that is passed from a program to a subprogram. The value may or may not be passed back to the main program.

Personal computer See **Microcomputer.**

Predefined file A file that is declared and opened automatically by the UCSD Pascal system.

Predefined identifiers Words that have a specific meaning to the Pascal compiler. They should not be redefined by the programmer.

Procedure A subprogram that performs a specific task. Procedures allow a program to be broken down into smaller subprograms.

Procedure call A statement that causes a procedure to be executed.

Program List of instructions for a computer to use to solve a specific problem.

Program documentation A written description of a program and what it accomplishes.

Program error A flaw or error in a program that causes the program not to run properly. Program errors can cause a program to stop executing or compiling or to produce incorrect output.

Program statement The first statement in a Pascal program. It contains the reserved word PROGRAM followed by the name of the program.

Program testing Checking a program for flaws or errors. Program testing is usually directed at catching program errors caused by the program itself or user input.

Program tracing A debugging technique that can be used to find run-time and logic errors. WRITE and WRITELN statements are inserted into a program to allow the programmer to examine the variable values and follow the program logic.

Programmer See **Computer programmer.**

Programming languages Languages that can be used to give instructions to a computer.

Programming style Writing a program in a way that will make it easier for people to read and understand the program.

Prompt A sentence printed on the monitor that tells the user that data should be entered at this point.

Pseudocode Program statements written briefly in English, not in a programming language; a narrative description of the programming logic.

Random number A number, within a certain range, that has an equal chance of being chosen as any other number in the specified range.

Random-access file A file that allows data items to be stored anywhere in a file. Data items can then be directly accessed.

Record A structured data type that contains a group of related data items, not necessarily of the same data type, that are gathered together in a single unit.

Relational operators Operators that compare one operand with another.

Reserved words Words that have a specific meaning to the Pascal compiler. They may not be redefined by the programmer.

Right-justified Used of information that is lined up on the right side of the field. Any blank spaces will be on the left side of the field.

Run-time errors Flaws in a program that often cause the program to stop running early.

Scalar data type A data type where all of the values of that data type may be listed. INTEGER, CHAR, BOOLEAN, and USER-DEFINED are all scalar data types.

Scientific notation See **Exponential notation.**

Sequential file A file that stores data items one after another. The data items must be accessed in sequence.

Set A structured data type consisting of a collection of values that are classed together. All of the values must be of the same base type.

Single-alternative decision step A decision step in which a subsequent step is executed only if the comparison made in the decision step is true. If the comparison is false, nothing is done.

Soft copy Output displayed on the monitor.

Sorting Organizing data items in a particular order.

Source program A program that must be translated into machine code before it can be executed.

Standard identifier See **Predefined identifier.**

Storage locations The part of the computer where information can be kept; the memory.

Structured data type A data type that can store many individual values that may then be referred to as a single unit. Each structured data type has strict rules concerning how it may be declared and used in programs. The structured data types in Pascal are arrays, records, sets, and files.

Structured programming language A programming language that allows a large problem to be broken down methodically into smaller units. It also allows the programmer to control the order in which a program will be executed in a simple, efficient way. This leads to programs that are logical and easy to understand.

Subprogram A part of a larger program that performs a specific job.

Subrange data type A data type that contains a portion of a predefined or user-defined scalar data type.

Subscript A value enclosed in brackets that is used to refer to a particular array element. For example: NAME[3].

Syntax errors Violations of the grammatical rules of a programming language that make it impossible for a program to be compiled.

Syntax rules Rules that explain how the parts of a language should be put together.

Systems tester A programmer who tests other programmers' programs. The tester's job is to find any possible flaws in programs and to find areas of a program that are not protected against unexpected input.

Top-down programming A method of writing computer programs where a large problem is broken down into smaller and smaller problems.

Truncate To cut off a part of a value. For example, if 17.23 was truncated at the decimal point the result would be 17.

Turtle A small figure that can be moved on the screen; used in graphics programs.

Turtlegraphics A set of graphics programs and procedures created by programmers at the Massachusetts Institute of Technology.

USCD Pascal Compiler The compiler most widely used for Pascal on microcomputers.

Unary minus sign A symbol (−) used alone with a number which gives the opposite of the number.

Unary plus sign A symbol (+) used alone with a number which leaves the number unchanged.

User-defined scalar data type A data type defined by the programmer in a TYPE definition. Every value of the data type must be listed in the definition.

User-friendly programs Programs that communicate clearly to the user. User-friendly programs should be easy to use.

Users The people who use a computer program.

Valid Used of an expression that is correct; follows the rules.

Value parameter A parameter whose value is passed to a subprogram, but whose value is not passed back to the calling program.

Variable A name chosen by the programmer to represent a storage location. The value of the storage location may change during program execution.

Variable declaration statement The statement that tells the compiler the variable names that will be used to represent storage locations and what their types will be.

Variable name See **Variable.**

Variable parameter A parameter whose value is passed to a subprogram and whose value is also passed back to the calling program.

Index

295